SOUTHERN SLAVERY

IN ITS

PRESENT ASPECTS:

CONTAINING

A REPLY

TO A LATE WORK OF THE

BISHOP OF VERMONT ON SLAVERY.

BY

DANIEL R. GOODWIN.

NEGRO UNIVERSITIES PRESS
NEW YORK

Originally published in 1864
by J. B. Lippincott & Co.

Reprinted from a copy in the collections
of the Brooklyn Public Library

Reprinted 1969 by
Negro Universities Press
A DIVISION OF GREENWOOD PUBLISHING CORP.
NEW YORK

SBN 8371-2687-8

PRINTED IN UNITED STATES OF AMERICA

ADVERTISEMENT.

WHEN the late work of the Bishop of Vermont on Slavery first appeared, it seemed to me, in common with many of my clerical brethren, from what I could learn indirectly of its character and contents, that it was not worth while to trouble the public with an answer. Until the latter part of April I had never read the book. But the late lamented BENJAMIN GERHARD, ESQ, of this city, in a conversation with me, about that time, took an entirely different view from that which I entertained and expressed; and earnestly insisted that it ought to be answered, and that I should answer it. At his urgent and repeated solicitations, the work was at length undertaken; and, after his death, I felt bound to complete it, as an act of obedience to his dying commands. If the performance has any merit, I desire it to stand as a tribute to the memory of one who was a kind and faithful friend, as well as an unflinching and devoted patriot. Its defects will of course belong exclusively to myself.

D. R. GOODWIN.

PHILADELPHIA, September, 1864.

CONTENTS.

CHAPTER I.

CHAPTER II.

CHAPTER III.

CHAPTER IV.

CHAPTER V.

CHAPTER VI.

CHAPTER VII.

CHAPTER VIII.

CHAPTER IX.

CHAPTER X.

SOUTHERN SLAVERY.

CHAPTER I.

THE "PROTEST" AND ITS DEFENCE.

Protest of the Bishop and Clergy of the Diocese of Pennsylvania against Bishop Hopkins's Letter on African Slavery.

ON the 15th day of April, 1863, certain gentlemen of Philadelphia, Messrs. George M. Wharton, A. Browning, John Stockton Littell, Samuel Jackson, M.D., Charles J. Biddle and Peter McCall, addressed a note to the Right Rev. John Henry Hopkins, D.D., Bishop of the Diocese of Vermont, requesting him to favor them with his "views on the Scriptural aspect of Slavery."

"We believe," they said, "that false teachings on this subject have had a great deal to do with bringing on the unhappy strife between two sections of our common country, and that a lamentable degree of ignorance prevails in regard to it;" and they concluded by expressing the belief, "that the communication of his views as a Christian Bishop on the Scriptural aspect of Slavery, may contribute" to the formation of a "sound public opinion on this topic."

On the 2d day of May, 1863, Bishop Hopkins replied to this note by saying, that in January, 1861, he had published a pamphlet on the subject referred to, which was at their service; that the views then and there set forth were not only unchanged, but that the numerous replies had "strengthened his conviction as to the sanction which the Scriptures give to the principle of Negro Slavery, so long as it is administered in accordance with the precepts laid down by the Apostles," and that " such was the universal doctrine of Christian ministers, Christian lawyers and Christian statesmen one hundred years ago, with a few exceptions."

"With this brief introduction," the Bishop said, " I proceed to the very serious question which your friendly application has submitted for discussion"— thus endorsing and re-issuing the original document.

In the letter in which Bishop Hopkins discusses this question of Negro Slavery, he maintains that the Holy Scriptures established the principle of perpetual bondage, " *servitude for life descending to the offspring.*"

He also asserts that the truths which lie at the foundation of the Declaration of Independence, "that all men are created equal, and that they are endowed by their Creator with certain unalienable rights, that among these are life, liberty and the pursuit of happiness," are "no truths at all," that these rights are only "imaginary," that he "utterly discards" them, and " doubts whether the annals of civilized mankind can furnish a stronger instance of unmitigated perversity" than that of " our orators, our preachers, and our politicians" in their appeals to this famous document to justify the doctrine of universal liberty.

The Bishop also justifies the "presumed cruelty" of the system of Slavery by the facts that "Northern law allows the same in the case of children and apprentices," and that the "Saviour himself used a scourge of small cords when he drove the money-changers from the temple." "Are our modern philanthropists," he asks, "more merciful than Christ and wiser than the Almighty?"

The separation of husband and wife, of parents and children, he extenuates by the fact that the laboring man places his children out to service and as apprentices, that many leave "their homes to seek their fortunes in the gold regions," and that "many in Europe have abandoned their families for Australia, or the United States, or the Canadas."

The conclusion which the Bishop arrives at is this: "The Slavery of the Negro Race as maintained in the Southern States appears to me fully authorized both in the Old and New Testament."—"That very slavery, in my humble judgment, has raised the negro incomparably higher in the scale of humanity, and seems in fact to be the only instrumentality through which the heathen posterity of Ham have been raised at all."

Such are some of the views of Bishop Hopkins on the subject of African Slavery, as set forth in his letter to these gentlemen of Philadelphia — but the document itself should be read to appreciate its character. This letter was scattered broadcast over the State of Pennsylvania. As coming from a Bishop who is widely known throughout the Diocese, the Bishop and Clergy of Pennsylvania felt constrained to enter against it the following Protest:

The subscribers deeply regret that the fact of the extensive circulation throughout this Diocese of a letter by "John Henry Hopkins, Bishop of the Diocese of Vermont," in defence of Southern Slavery, compels them to make this public protest. It is not their province to mix in any political canvass. But as ministers of Christ, in the Protestant Episcopal Church, it becomes them to deny any complicity or sympathy with such a defence.

This attempt not only to apologize for slavery in the abstract, but to advocate it as it exists in the cotton States, and in States which sell men and women in the open market as their staple product, is, in their judgment, unworthy of any servant of Jesus Christ. As an effort to sustain, on Bible principles, the States in rebellion against the government, in the wicked attempt to establish by force of arms a tyranny under the name of a Republic, whose "corner-stone" shall be the perpetual bondage of the African, it challenges their indignant reprobation.

PHILADELPHIA, September, 1863.

Alonzo Potter,	Thomas S. Yocum,
John Rodney,	Benjamin Dorr,
E. A. Washburne,	Jehu C. Clay,
Peter Van Pelt,	William Suddards,
H. W. Ducachet,	D. R. Goodwin,
John S. Stone,	M. A. DeW. Howe,
George Leeds,	Henry S. Spackman,
Richard D. Hall,	James May,
Joseph D. Newlin,	John A. Childs,
B. Wistar Morris,	Thomas C. Yarnall,
Daniel S. Miller,	Edward Loundsbery,
Kingston Goddard,	Henry M. Stuart,

Phillips Brooks,
Addison B. Atkins,
Herman Hooker,
Benjamin Watson,
Edward I. Lycett,
Lewis W. Gibson,
R. W. Oliver,
Henry Brown,
W. R. Stockton,
Edward A. Foggo,
J. Isador Mombert,
Joel Rudderow,
Archibald Beatty,
C. A. L. Richards,
George A. Strong,
Gustavus M. Murray,
George W. Shinn,
Samuel Hall,
George G. Field,
Reese C. Evans,
Robert G. Chase,
Samuel Hazlehurst,
Edwin N. Lightner,
David C. Page,
John Cromlish,
William Preston,
George Slattery,
Francis J. Clerc,
Robert J. Parvin,
Richard Newton,
G. Emlen Hare,
W. W. Spear,
H. J. Morton,
Jacob M. Douglass,
R. A. Carden,

J. Gordon Maxwell,
John A. Vaughan,
Charles D. Cooper,
Wilbur F. Paddock,
Thomas Crumpton,
George D. Miles,
B. B. Killikelly,
Alexander McLeod,
Leighton Coleman,
Richard Smith,
Thomas H. Cullen,
J. McAlpin Harding,
William Ely,
Marison Byllesby,
J. Livingston Reese,
Augustus A. Marple,
B. T. Noakes,
D. Otis Kellogg,
Daniel Washburn,
Samuel E. Smith,
Treadwell Walden,
Herman L. Duhring,
Charles M. Dupuy,
John H. Babcock,
Anson B. Hard,
George A. Latimer,
R. Heber Newton,
John C. Furey,
Charles A. Maison,
Charles W. Quick,
H. T. Wells,
D. C. Millett,
J. W. Leadenham,
Frederick W. Beasley,
John P. Lundy,

R. C. Matlack,
L. Ward Smith,
Samuel E. Appleton,
William J. Alston,
John Adams Jerome,
Joseph A. Stone,
Albra Wadleigh,
W. S. Perkins,
Francis E. Arnold,
George H. Jenks,
William S. Heaton,
Robert B. Peet,
John Reynolds,
William Hilton,
Washington B. Erben,
John Ireland,
Benjamin J. Douglass,
D. C. James,
E. N. Potter,
W. H. D. Hatton,
Thomas W. Martin,
Alfred Elwyn,
James W. Robins,
George Bringhurst,
Charles W. Duane,
George B. Allinson,
Joseph N. Mulford,
James DeW. Perry,
Thomas G. Clemson,
Francis D. Hoskins,
William P. Lewis,
J. L. Heysinger,
John Long,
Ormes B. Keith,
William N. Diehl,

George A. Crooke,
Richardson Graham,
E. S. Watson,
Samuel Edwards,
George A. Durborow,
Joseph R. Moore,
Thomas B. Barker,
S. Tweedale,
Marcus A. Tolman,
John H. Drumm,
S. Newton Spear,
Louis C. Newman,
Edward C. Jones,
E. W. Hening,
Samuel Durborow,
C. C. Parker,
Henry Purdon,
Benjamin H. Abbott,
John H. Marsden,
Samuel B. Dalrymple,
William V. Feltwell,
John Leithead,
George C. Drake,
Peter Russell,
Roberts Paul,
George Kirke,
Henry B. Bartow,
John K. Murphy,
J. F. Ohl,
John Tetlow,
J. C. Laverty,
Charles Higbee,
William Wright,
S. T. Lord.
Charles R. Hall.

Such is the much-abused Protest of the Clergy
of Pennsylvania against the pro-slavery letter of
the Bishop of Vermont. The gentlemen who asked
for the letter are not obscure men in Church or
State, but prominent politicians of notorious parti-
zan affinities. The letter itself began to be circulated in Pennsylvania (so far as I have been able
to ascertain) in the month of August, 1863, just on
the eve of a sharply-contested political campaign.
Under these circumstances the Protest was issued.
It called forth a retort from Bishop Hopkins, followed by a book entitled "A View of Slavery,"
containing an elaborate defence of the institution,
"Scriptural, Ecclesiastical and Historical." To this
book and the letter I propose, in the sequel, to make
a brief reply. But first of all the Protest, and the
manner in which it has been treated, demand some
further passing remark.

The circumstances under which the Protest was
issued, its substance, style and spirit, are before the
reader. What, now, are the style and spirit of the
Bishop's retort? "A gross insult," "a false accusation," "a bitter and unjust assault," "vituperation,"
"reviling," "vilifying," "grossly insulting," "brand-
ing and calumniating," "personal defamation,"
"endorsing a calumny," "slander," "gross libel,"
"insulting aggression," "false and violent accusation," "bitter and groundless accusation," "gross
and scandalous libel," "public and libellous denunciation," "false and libellous Protest," "demented:"
such are some of the terms and epithets poured
forth by the meek and charitable and pious Bishop,
so strictly Apostolical, so exceeding Christ-like, who
"trusts that he has learned, when he is reviled, not
2

to revile again." One is tempted to ask whether he really supposes that scripture to imply, conversely, that when a Christian is not reviled at all, then he may revile as much as he will? For, what reviling, vilifying, calumny, vituperation, slander, insult, or libel, with or without the epithets false, bitter, gross, groundless, scandalous, &c., can be found in the Protest?

"The subscribers deeply regret that the fact of the extensive circulation through this Diocese of a letter by 'John Henry Hopkins, Bishop of the Diocese of Vermont,' in defence of Southern Slavery, compels them to make this public protest. It is not their province to mix in any political canvass. But as ministers of Christ, in the Protestant Episcopal Church, it becomes them to deny any complicity or sympathy with such a defence." Is there any reviling, vilifying, calumny, vituperation, slander, insult, or libel in that? "This attempt not only to apologize for slavery in the abstract, but to advocate it as it exists in the cotton States, and in States which sell men and women in the open market as their staple product, is, in their judgment, unworthy of any servant of Jesus Christ." Can Bishop Hopkins say that he did not attempt to apologize for slavery? If so, it must be because he will maintain that defending it as in itself right and good, as an unspeakable blessing to master and slave, as scriptural and Christian, and denouncing its opponents as impious, infidels, and rebels against the divine government, cannot be called an attempted apology, but a bold and defiant vindication. But this would only strengthen the ground of the Protest. Will he say that his letter, so circulated, was not an attempt to advocate

slavery as it exists in the cotton States, and in States
which sell men and women in the open market as
their staple product? But, in his letter, he says expressly : " The slavery of the negro race, *as maintained in the Southern States,* appears to me fully authorized both in the Old and the New Testament."
I suppose he will not deny that some of the slave
States are familiarly called Cotton States, or that in
others men and women are sold in the open market,
and are bred with a view to such a sale. So much
for the facts; then follows the judgment that such
an attempt is " unworthy of any servant of Jesus
Christ."

The facts being admitted, is this judgment to be
charged as reviling, vilifying, calumny, vituperation,
slander, insult, libel? It was undoubtedly the sincere and conscientious judgment of those who uttered
it. It was uttered with deep regret. It is not personal. It characterizes the act and not the man; or
rather if it does by implication characterize the man,
it characterizes him as contradistinguished from the
act; for if the act were unworthy of any servant
of Jesus Christ, still more was it unworthy of any
Christian Bishop, and especially unworthy of the
venerable and learned Bishop of Vermont.

There remains only the final sentence of the Protest : "As an effort to sustain, on Bible principles,
the States in rebellion against the government, in
the wicked attempt to establish by force of arms a
tyranny under the name of a Republic, whose ' corner-stone' shall be the perpetual bondage of the
African, it challenges their indignant reprobation."

Here it is to be observed that the letter of Bishop
Hopkins is not expressly declared to be such an

"effort" as is described; but it is declared that, regarded as such, it challenges indignant reprobation.
The signers of the Protest undoubtedly thought it
might and would be so regarded. Originating as it
did, and being circulated as it was, had they not a
right so to think? For myself, I cannot doubt that
the leaders of the so-called Peace-democracy are
now, and were then, the most venomous and dangerous enemies of their country, and the most insidious
and efficient supporters of the wicked rebellion that
is raging against its existence and integrity, that are
anywhere to be found. They may be too cautious
or too cowardly to incur the legal criminality of
aiding and abetting that rebellion; but while they
desire its success, sympathize with its perpetrators,
and give it their moral countenance and support,
they take upon themselves the full burden of its
moral guilt. This sentiment I desire to place on
record as my calm deliberate judgment.

How far all the signers of the Protest may agree
in the sentiment I know not. One thing is plain—
the letter in question was sought and circulated as
an electioneering document. As such, and as tending
to commit them and their Church to the defence of
negro slavery and the support of the Southern rebellion, it fell under the notice of the clergy of Pennsylvania. They attacked no person or persons. They
accused no individual of treason, rebellion, or sedi-
tion. They uttered no crimination. They pronounced
a moral judgment. And, in so doing, they avoided
personality as far as possible, for they simply disclaimed and denounced the document itself. That
that document actually tended to strengthen the
hands of the rebellion, and weaken the hands of the

government in the pending struggle, who can deny? Who of all the rebels would not rejoice in its circulation and influence? So far as it went it would manifestly operate on their side. And, under the circumstances, was there not good reason to presume that it was intended so to operate. No mere act can be condemned, without assuming a motive. *That* motive is to be assumed of course which stands printed and patent on the face of the act, unless the contrary is shown. The burden of proof is on the other side. Bishop Hopkins has since, indeed, "utterly denied that he either wrote his pamphlet for the service of any political party, or gave his consent to the publication of *the Bible View of Slavery*, under an expectation at the time that it would be used by any such party." It is hard enough to believe this, now that the Bishop expressly gives his word for it. But before this disclaimer, and looking at the facts as they were, I contend that the signers of the Protest were justified in presuming the document to have been issued with an intelligent knowledge of the circumstances of the case, of the purposes for which it was to be used, and of the results which it was fitted to accomplish. The letter was asked for with the professed view of correcting "the false teachings which have had a great deal to do with bringing on the unhappy strife between two sections of our common country." Observe here that the war waged by the Southern insurgents is not recognized as a rebellion against our common country, but as an unhappy sectional strife, engendered in great measure by the anti-slavery doctrines of the North. Could a man of common sense and common intelligence be supposed to doubt of the

2 *

political character and aims of the men who in such
terms asked for that "letter?" In his answer the
Bishop offers them the pamphlet of January, 1861,
to which they had referred, "in its original form;"
and declares that since its issue "he has seen no
cause to change his opinion." That pamphlet contained a formal defence of secession. "First," says
he, "it may be asked, whether the Southern States
have a right to secede for any cause? Secondly, if
they have the right, is the cause sufficient to justify
its exercise? *In my humble judgment they have a right
to secede.*" These passages were omitted in the letter
as re-published and circulated in Pennsylvania, whether by the prudence of the astute politicians who
asked for it, or by the Bishop himself, does not certainly appear. The latter would, on some accounts,
seem the more probable; for the personal response
to those politicians is closed thus: "With this brief
introduction, *I proceed* to the very serious question
which your friendly application has submitted for
discussion. Your faithful servant in Christ, John H.
Hopkins, Bishop of the Diocese of Vermont;" and
then the whole letter, without any marks of erasure
or omission, is closed anew with the signature, "I
remain, with great regard, your faithful servant in
Christ, John H. Hopkins, Bishop of the Diocese of
Vermont."

From this the natural inference would seem to be,
that the letter was expurgated and prepared by the
Bishop himself for its re-issue; although it would
seem, also, from his previous statement, that he left
his political friends the option of taking it either
"in its *original*" or in its amended form. At all

events, *whatever the re-issue contains must be regarded as dating in* 1863, *and not in* 1861.

It will not do for the Bishop to maintain that, being published before the formation of the Southern Confederacy, it cannot be intended " to support the wicked attempt to establish by force of arms a tyranny under the name of a Republic, whose ' corner-stone' shall be the perpetual bondage of the African." So far as such a defence is a quasi confession that, if issued in 1863, the letter might fairly be considered as having such an intent ; the Bishop has admitted his own guilt. For it *was* issued by his own authority, and probably with his special revision, in 1863. Its present date is 1863. In 1863 it was to do its work. To 1863 it had its proper application. And though the direct defence of secession is not re-issued in 1863, the document which is issued contains the following among other statements : " Who are we that are ready to trample on the doctrine of the Bible, and tear to shreds the Constitution of our country, and even plunge the land into the untold horrors of civil war, and yet boldly pray to the God of Israel to bless our very acts of rebellion against his own sovereign authority ?"

Now, when the Bishop says " we," he certainly does not mean exclusively himself and his political friends. It is manifest he means the people, the free and freedom-loving people, the loyal people, of the North. And he charges them with trampling on the doctrine of the Bible, tearing in shreds the Constitution of their country, *and even plunging the land into the untold horrors of civil war,* and yet boldly praying to the God of Israel to bless their very acts of rebellion against his own sovereign authority; and this, revised and published in 1863 ! Is not this open encouragement and justification to the Southern insurgents? Is not this " an effort to sustain the States in rebellion against the government?" The signers of the Protest thought it might naturally be so regarded. I submit to the intelligent reader that they were justified in so thinking, and in saying what they thought. And so thinking, they declared that it challenged their " indignant reprobation." Now here, if anywhere, must be found the " reviling, vilifying, calumny, vituperation, slander, insult and libel—false, bitter, gross, groundless, scandalous, and demented." Let the reader quietly set against all these terms and epithets, the simple expression, uttered with deep regret, of "indignant reprobation." Is, then, John Henry Hopkins, Bishop of the Diocese of Vermont, entirely above the reproof of his brethren? Is their reproof, their "indignant reprobation," and that too not of him, but of one of his acts, to be met with such language as he has poured forth upon it ? Are the claims of the Bishop of Vermont higher than those of the Pope of Rome ? Is the Bishop of Vermont superior to St. Peter himself? The Apostle Paul once " withstood Peter to the face, because he was to be blamed," and severely reproved him, and that publicly,—" before them all." We do not read that St. Peter retorted with charges of " reviling, vilifying, calumny, vituperation, slander, insult, and libel, false, bitter, gross, groundless, scandalous and demented." If we may suppose he had attained to the " ornament of a meek and quiet spirit" so conspicuously displayed by the Bishop of

Vermont, he certainly had not learned the dialect in which that spirit has found its utterance.

One thing more. The signers of the Protest had reason to denounce Bishop Hopkins's letter when sent by him into the Diocese of Pennsylvania for circulation, not only as calculated to encourage the rebellion and to bring into contempt our common Christianity, but especially as tending to place the Episcopal Church in a false position before the world, and as being virtually the obtrusion of one Bishop into the Diocese of another. Of course I do not here use the word obtrusion in any technical, legal sense, but in its moral and practical signification. The Bishop could not be ecclesiastically tried and convicted for the act he committed. But it does not follow from that, that its commission was any the more consistent with the principles of manliness, or with the rules of courtesy and fraternal intercourse. The Bishop forthwith raises himself to his full height, and challenges ecclesiastical prosecution. But is his standard of moral duty graduated to the level of legal obligation? What would he think of the honesty of a man who, upon being asked to pay a debt, should reply, "the term of the statute of limitions is past, I owe you nothing, no legal debt, sue me if you dare?"

But the Bishop insists that the issuing of the "letter" was not an "official act." Of course it was not an "official act," in the sense of being an act specifically authorized and appointed by the law of the Church as pertaining to his Episcopal office. Indeed it is rather as an *officious* than as an *official* act that it is complained of. And yet there are several things which tend to show that it assumed to be of, at least, a semi-official character. The writer was expressly requested to give his "views as a Christian Bishop." To the views which he gave in response he affixed his signature as "*Bishop of the Diocese of Vermont.*" Whether, therefore, it were an "official act" or not, it was, on the face of it, an act performed as a Bishop, and would have, and was intended to have, the weight and moral influence of a Bishop's authority. At least so the signers of the Protest, it would seem, had a right to presume. But Bishop Hopkins denies their right to make this inference; because, says he, the Archbishop of Canterbury might publish a book, on whose title-page he should be described as "Archbishop of Canterbury," and yet such a publication would not thereby be made official; and because, even in private correspondence, his Grace always retains his official designation, thus, Joh. Cantuar; and in like manner the English Bishops generally. I will not call these suggestions a subterfuge. I will leave it to the reader to characterize them appropriately. Suppose the Archbishop should affix such a signature to his "views," when they had been expressly desired, and were accompanied by the statement that they had been expressly desired, *as the views of a Christian Archbishop?* What then? Besides, is Bishop Hopkins accustomed to translate the style of their Anglican Lordships, and affix his signature to his every-day private correspondence as "Bishop of the Diocese of Vermont." This certainly is not the custom of the American Bishops generally; and the signers of the Protest had no reason to suppose it was the custom of his lordship of Vermont. The Bishop suggests that he published his letter or

pamphlet in fulfilment of his ordination vows—" so
to minister the DOCTRINE and sacraments and discipline of Christ as the Lord hath commanded, and as
this Church hath received the same," and " with all
faithful diligence to banish and drive away from the
Church all erroneous and strange doctrines, contrary
to God's word."

Being then in fulfilment of his ordination vows,
was the publication, or was it not, " an official act ?"
And did those vows require him to exercise the
functions referred to, in his own diocese, or in the
diocese of a brother Bishop ? If his brother Bishop
were faithfully performing his ordination vows, such
interference would seem quite unnecessary; and if he
were violating them, why not present him for trial ?
Indeed it might not have been amiss, for one so scru-
pulous in the exact observance of duty, to have
noted what is added to each of the " ordination
vows" which he has cited; — to the first, " so that
you teach *the people committed to your care and charge*
with all diligence to keep and observe the same;"
and to the second, " and to use both public and private monitions, as well to the sick as to the whole,
within your cure, as need shall require and occasion
shall be given."

It is curious to observe that, further on in his book,
(p. 215,) the Bishop having made a long citation
" from a late work of the Rev. Chr. Wordsworth,
D.D., Canon of Westminster," adds, " with these excellent comments of the Rev. Canon Wordsworth, I
concur most heartily : in fervent thankfulness to
God, that up to the year 1859, our venerated mother
Church of England has proclaimed none other but
the pure doctrine of the Apostles, and that her latest

utterance is in harmony with the only divine standard of wisdom, truth, and peace." Thus the Church
of England is represented as speaking, as making
" her latest utterance" by the mouth or pen of Canon
Wordsworth. But was that work of Canon Wordsworth an " official act?" Could he be considered as
representing the Church of England?—as, in any
sense or to any degree committing the Church of
England to his views? If so, let the Bishop apply
the same mode of reasoning to his own case; and if
not so, let him interpret the language of the friends
of the Protest as he would have his own interpreted.
It would seem, after all, he can sometimes take a
common sense view of a case, and abandon the tech-
nicalities of his special pleading, when he sees fit.

Together with the Protest, Bishop Hopkins has
printed at large in his book a list of those who signed
it ; to give them, as he says, notoriety, if he cannot
give them fame. If, in so doing, he thought to
inflict on them any pain, or sense of ignominy, he
made an egregious mistake. Their only pain proceeds from the pity which they feel for *him;* and
from their sense of the shame and contumely which
in their humble judgment he is doing his utmost to
bring upon the cause of Christ and his Church. If
they are to meet the judgment of the Christian
world and of posterity as standing in any relation
to the Bishop's political and pro-slavery letter, they
will be proud to meet it with their indignant Protest.
If their names are to be remembered hereafter, they
will rejoice to have them remembered as the names
of men who loved their country and sought to rescue
her in her hour of extreme peril, who loved the
cause of humanity and freedom, of civilization and

justice, who pitied the poor outcast, and the oppressed, who sought not to rivet but to break the
chains of the slave, and thus to cherish the spirit,
and imitate the character of Him who came to proclaim liberty to the captives, and the opening of the
prison to them that are bound, to preach the acceptable year — the Jubilee — of the Lord. The Bishop
compliments "the Christian and manly course of
those who refused to set their names to that most
unwarrantable document." That the Bishop may
have the full benefit of those names, it may not be
improper to give here a list of the Clergy of Pennsylvania, having seats in the Convention, as they
appear in the Diocesan Journal of 1863, omitting
the 164 who signed the Protest, and those who are
believed to have removed from the Diocese, or to
have been absent at the time of its issue. That list
is as follows : —

William Bacon Stevens,	R. H. Lee,
Alfred M. Abel,	T. J. Littell,
George B. Allen,	J. G. Lyons,
Thomas G. Allen,	Henry Mackay,
Hurley Baldy,	R. C. Moore,
Charles R. Bonnel,	William Newton,
William V. Bowers,	William H. Paddock,
Rowland Hill Brown,*	Edward M. Pecke,
Edward Y. Buchanan,	Alexander Shiras,
R. T. Chase,	Henry R. Smith,
J. W. Claxton,	R. S. Smith,
Alexander G. Cummins,	J. F. Spaulding,
Thomas J. Davis,	A. F. Steele,
Samuel D. Day,	C. E. Swope,
Charles P. Edmunds,	J. P. Taylor,

3

Joseph H. Elsegood,   A. Ten Broeck,
William F. Halsey,   W. P. Ten Broeck,
Chandler Hare,   C. W. Thomson,
J. A. Harris,*   A. E. Tortat,
William Hommann,   J. Townsend,
G. P. Hopkins,   H. E. Tschudy,
Joseph Jacquet,   E. M. Van Deusen,
Morris M. Jones,   William White,
B. B. Leacock,   J. Woart.
Edmund Leaf,*

It is due to the gentlemen above named to say, that many of them would undoubtedly have signed the Protest, had they had the opportunity; and that, of those who might have felt some hesitation about signing it, there are probably not five, (and perhaps not one,) who do not as fully and cordially dissent from and condemn the sentiments of Bishop Hopkins's letter, as does the Protest itself. It ought to be added that the Protest was originally intended for the Clergy of Philadelphia only; but as several of the country Clergy were very desirous of appending their names, it was eventually concluded to leave it open to their signatures also.

So much for the Protest; so much for what it contained of "reviling, vilifying, calumny, vituperation, slander, insult and libel—false, bitter, gross, groundless, scandalous, demented," etc., etc. I repeat these words, because I intend to do what I can to give notoriety, if not respectability, to the beautiful and Christian terminology of Bishop Hopkins. Again, let the reader contrast the tone and spirit of the

* Signatnres to the protest subsequently authorized.

Bishop's reply, and say which is most worthy of a
servant of Jesus Christ. The signers of the Protest
did not so much as enter into any formal expression
of what they regarded as the sophistries and ex-
travagances of the Bishop's letter; they simply
declared their dissent from, and reprobation of, its
doctrines and sentiments, and apparent aims. That
they did not refrain from a formal exposure and
refutation, because they were unequal to such a
task, I shall endeavour to demonstrate in the next
chapter.

CHAPTER II.

THE letter opens with the broad assertion that "the term 'servant' employed by our translators of the Bible has the meaning of *slave* in the Hebrew and the Greek originals, as a general rule, where it stands alone." It does not clearly appear what is meant by *standing alone*. Strictly speaking, the term never stands alone. But if we take "standing alone" to mean "without any adjective or other words accompanying it, tending to modify its meaning," the assertion above made is very wide of the truth. For the original word is applied not less freely and perhaps more frequently to the servants of God, of kings, &c., and to servants that were Hebrews, than to bondmen that were foreigners. Yet the servants of the Lord are not slaves, and the Hebrew servants went out free at the end of six years, while the definition which in the letter is immediately given of *slavery* is, "servitude for life, descending to the offspring." Moreover, one may boldly assert that the original word translated "servant" very rarely if ever means exactly what slave means in English. The ideas now by usage associated with this last word would not correspond to those connected with the original word. And finally, the

28

original word is a *general term*, and though it may sometimes include the specific sense of slave, it is ordinarily more accurately translated by our general term, servant, than it would be by the specific term, slave. The word meaning *beast* may include the *ass* in its signification, and in a particular case may be known to be applied specifically to an ass; and yet even then it is more accurate to translate a general term by its corresponding general term. Every ass is a beast, but every beast is not an ass. So every slave is a servant, but every servant is not a slave. It would be a false translation, and a solecism besides, to say "a slave of the Lord," instead of "a servant of the Lord," or to say "the slaves of the king," instead of "the servants of the king." The original Hebrew word,* in its strict etymological signification, is even more general than "servant," for it means "labourer," and this etymology undoubtedly modifies and softens the force of the word in all its applications. Still we should not propose to substitute "labourer" for "servant" in translating. Usage would again forbid it. But what we observe is that "servant" instead of being *too weak* a word to represent the original, is rather *too strong*. The pro-slavery cause will take nothing by sending us back from the English version to the original text.

The letter proceeds to state that "this kind of bondage"—*servitude for life, descending to the offspring,* —"appears to have existed as an established institu-

---

* It is true, the Greek word of the New Testament is stronger, meaning, etymologically, a *bondman*. But the servant, or bondman, of the New Testament, was one, at all events, who could have wife, children, property, and debts of his own. See Matt. xviii. 25.

3 *

tion in all ages of the world, by the universal evidence of history, whether sacred or profane."

But what evidence is there from history, "whether sacred or profane," that slavery "existed in our world" for some two thousand years, that is, from Adam till the death of Noah, or till about the time of Abraham? The "Christian Bishop" may have access to some history not generally known, or he may think that, in the first ages, the world had not become *ours*. But, in our view, those earliest ages are very important in the argument; for we may say to the advocates of slavery who argue from its permission and general prevalence, as our Saviour said to the Pharisees about divorcement,—" From the beginning it was not so." Of this the Christian Fathers were accustomed to make a strong point. "If any one ask," says St. Chrysostom, "whence came slavery into the world?—for I know many who have desired to learn this,—I will tell him. *Insatiable avarice and envy are the parents of slavery; for Noah, Abel, and Seth, and their descendants, had no slaves.* Sin hath begotten slavery,—then wars and battles, in which men were made captives." (Hom. ad Ephes. xxii.) And again : "There was no slave in the old times; for God, when he made man, made him not bond but free. (Hom. in Laz. 6.)

The Bishop admits that slavery may be a physical evil, but denies that slave-holding is a moral evil or a sin. But if enslavement is a physical evil, can a man, without moral evil, without committing sin, inflict this physical evil on his fellow man wantonly or for selfish ends?—for his own gratification, ease, or gain? If it is, on the whole, really a means of greater good to the slave himself, it hardly deserves to be called a physical evil. And if it is inflicted with due authority and for the sincere purpose of securing this greater good, it certainly is not a sin; but in this case it would be such an extraordinary kind of slavery that it would hardly deserve the name; for it could scarcely be "servitude for life, descending to the offspring." The general question whether slave-holding is a sin, I shall reserve for a separate discussion further on. But what does the "Christian Bishop" mean, when, in this connexion, he proclaims, "No blasphemy can be more unpardonable than that which imputes sin or moral evil to the decrees of the Eternal Judge, who is alone perfect in wisdom, in knowledge, and in love?" Does he mean that no blasphemy can be greater than that which calls slave-holding a sin? That seems to be the simple English of his declaration, if it has any relevancy to the question in hand, or if there is any logical connexion in his train of thought. But we may presume the Bishop knows that no man, no Christian, who calls slave-holding a sin, means to charge the sin or the moral evil upon the Eternal Judge or upon his decrees. And has the Eternal Judge anywhere so decreed slave-holding as to make it the express duty of certain men to hold their fellow men in bondage?—the duty, for example, of the Southerners to hold the poor negroes as "chattels personal?" Or, if the Eternal Judge has decreed that negroes shall be so held, for reasons which seem good in the sight of infinite wisdom and love, does it follow that it is blasphemy to impute sin to any actions of men which fulfil the decrees of the Eternal Judge? What actions of men are not in fulfilment of his decrees? Is it blasphemy to impute sin to the

traitor Judas? and to the crucifiers of our Blessed
Lord? Yet "the Son of man indeed goeth as it is
written of him, but woe to that man by whom the
Son of man is betrayed; good were it for that man
if he had never been born." "Him being delivered
by the determinate counsel and foreknowledge of
God, ye have taken and by wicked hands have cruci-
fied and slain." Were our Blessed Lord and his
Apostles, then, guilty of "the most unpardonable
blasphemy," when they thus impute sin to those who
fulfilled the decrees of the Eternal Judge? If that
be what the "Christian Bishop" says, then let the
blasphemy rebound upon his own head; or if that
be not his meaning, let him say—he is challenged to
say—distinctly to say—to what his pompous charge
of "unpardonable blasphemy" *does* apply. It cannot
apply to those who directly charge God or his decrees
with sin; for there are none such to be found—certainly none among his Christian brethren. It cannot
apply to those who charge with sin the actions of
men which are in fulfilment of God's decrees; for
then it would reach to Christ and his Apostles, as
just shown. To what, and to whom, then, does it
apply? This is a serious point, and I insist that the
Bishop should clear up the case, or disclaim and de-
sist from the wholesale charges and insinuations
against his opponents, of blasphemy, infidelity, and
ungodliness, in which he so freely indulges. It is
curious to see how the "Christian Bishop," while he
is ready to charge the word of God with approving
and upholding the institution of slavery, still shrinks
from acknowledging that he is bad enough, hard-
hearted enough, to approve it himself. He puts in
his *salvo* thus:—"If it were a matter to be deter-

mined by my personal sympathies, tastes, or feelings, I should be as ready as any man to condemn the institution of slavery; for all my prejudices of education, habit, and social position, stand entirely opposed to it." Would it not be well for the Biphop here to clear up a few things for himself? Do his "sympathies, tastes, and feelings," which lead to the condemnation of slavery, arise from the better — the more benevolent and charitable—or from the worse, the more selfish part of his nature? And if from the former, was Christianity intended to repress or to encourage and cultivate our better and kindlier feelings? Again, when these feelings lead him to condemn slavery, is it not from viewing it as an evil and a wrong? Could he be inclined to condemn what he really regarded, as he afterwards professes to regard slavery, as a blessing, a good, a thing well-pleasing to God? Were the education and habits he refers to, derived from Christian or from ungodly associations and influences? And finally, if he would leave all special pleading and chopping of logic aside, does not his inmost soul, and do not the whole tenor and spirit of the Word of God and the Blessed Gospel of Christ cry out against the institution of Slavery? Shall it be indeed necessary for a " Christian Bishop" to school down his humane instincts and sympathies, in order to bring them to a level with those of Jesus Christ?

The prediction by Noah of the servitude of Canaan, —or "the curse of Ham," as it is commonly called by the advocates of slavery, who are accustomed to make it the corner-stone of their argument, — is of course put in the front part of this defence of the peculiar institution. And this, from the general drift of the Bishop's reasoning, would seem to be the awful " decree of the Eternal Judge" above referred to. But is it seriously pretended that whatever is *predicted* is therefore right? "In the last days," says St. Paul, "perilous times shall come, for men shall be lovers of their own selves, covetous, boasters, proud, blasphemers, disobedient to parents, unthankful, unholy, without natural affection, trucebreakers, false accusers, incontinent, fierce, despisers of those that are good, traitors, heady, highminded, lovers of pleasures more than lovers of God; having a form of godliness, but denying the power thereof." Are, therefore, selfishness, cupidity, boasting, pride, blasphemy, rebellion, ingratitude, impurity, treating one's own children as mere chattels, perjury, satanic falsehood, looseness and lust, ferociousness, spite, treason, headlong obstinacy, puffed-up self-will, a loud claim of true churchmanship, of special orthodoxy and piety, with a denial of the practical power and application of Christianity; — are these all right? If so, this is a short method to justify the Southern rebellion from Scripture, without going all the way round through a defence of the institution of slavery.

But again, it was predicted that the Israelites should be enslaved and evil-entreated in Egypt four hundred years. Were the Egyptians therefore justified in holding them in bondage? "The Eternal Judge," notwithstanding his antecedent decree and prediction, seems to have decided otherwise; "for the nation to whom they shall be in bondage will I judge, said God." Perhaps, it may be said, it is not the mere prediction of the servitude of Canaan that is relied upon, but the prediction of that servitude *as a just punishment.* Canaan was punished, and, I doubt not,

justly punished, by having denounced to him the
evil that should fall on his posterity; and Ham was
punished in the same way, for Canaan's posterity
were also *his* posterity, and the punishment upon his
posterity, when it was inflicted, being inflicted, as
the Bishop says, for the sins of those who suffered
it, and not for the sins of their ancestors, was doubtless a just punishment. But the justice of a punishment does not, of course, justify those who inflict it;
and that, too, without regard to the motives from
which they inflict it. If a man has committed murder, it is just that he should suffer capital punishment; but I am not, therefore justified in inflicting
that punishment, unless I have specific authority
thereto; — to inflict it without that authority would
be murder. And still worse would be the moral
character of my act if, — instead of inflicting it with
due authority and with deep regret, and a simple,
honest view to the execution of justice, — I should
inflict it from motives of personal vindictiveness, or
to satisfy some old grudge, or for the gratification
of avarice or lust. The Israelites had specific authority for their treatment of the Canaanites, and
so far as they carried this authority into effect from
motives of obedience to the Divine commands, they
were doubtless not only justifiable, but commenda-
ble. But who else has received specific authority
for inflicting punishment upon the Canaanites?
Have the Southern slaveholders received a special
Divine precept to hold the Negroes in bondage?
Can such a precept to them be inferred from Noah's
prophecy, or the "curse of Ham," or whatever else
you may please to call it? But this curse, according to St. Chrysostom, "was removed when Christ

appeared," (Hom. in 1 Cor. XL.) If so,—and it
would seem plain enough from the very nature of
Christianity, that it is so,—then the whole fabric
built upon "the curse of Ham," vanishes into thin
air at once. And, in any event, several difficult
things would have to be established in order to make
out from it any justification of modern Negro
Slavery. It would be necessary to show, 1st. That
the Negroes are descended from Ham; 2d. Either
that the curse upon Canaan's posterity was a curse
also upon the posterity of Cush, Mizraim and the
other sons of Ham, or that the Negroes are descended from Canaan; 3d. That the Southerners
have a special Divine precept to execute the curse;
and 4th. That the poor Negroes are sinners above
all other races of men, because they suffer such
things. The first point, though it cannot be proved,
may be easily granted. The second, the Christian
Bishop has attempted to establish subsequently in
his book,—with what success we shall see in the
proper place. The third, of course, can never be
made out without some new revelation; and the
fourth is contrary to the express teaching of Jesus
Christ. Even granting the second point as well as
the first, therefore, the argument in justification of
modern Negro Slavery from "the curse of Ham,"
fails entirely; indeed, is one of the most egregious
pieces of moonshine logic that was ever invented.
But I shall expect to show that the second point is
as baseless as the rest, and, if so, the very moonshine
itself will utterly fade and disappear. So, farewell
for the present to "the curse of Ham."

Next, it is alleged that Abraham had slaves, and
that in his case "slavery was sanctioned by the

Deity." "But ye say that Abraham had slaves,"
—says St. Chrysostom, (Hom. ad Eph. XXIII.)—
"Yea, but he treated them not *as slaves.*" So it
seems this is an old pro-slavery argument; but it is
observable that St. Chrysostom, instead of adopting
it and urging it, like our "Christian Bishop," in defence of Slavery, places himself on the opposite side,
and endeavours to parry its force,—and does so
effectually; for, if there were no slavery now but
such as existed in the household of the patriarch
Abraham, and if the times and circumstances now,
were similar to those in which he lived, there would
be little reason to find fault with such domestic services. But that even this servitude, such as it was,
was "sanctioned by the Deity," does not at all appear, any more than that Abraham's polygamy or
concubinage was sanctioned by the Deity. And
even if it *were* sanctioned in this case, the desired
inference could not be made from it to Southern
Slaveholders; unless we are at liberty to infer, from
the praise that is bestowed upon Jael, the wife of
Heber, for her killing of Sisera, that the treacher-
ous murder of a confiding guest is now and always
justifiable, and laudable. The Bishop's sage conclusion from the case of Abraham and Hagar is worthy of passing recognition. It is, that the present
rebellion and civil war are chargeable upon "philanthropists, who profess to believe the Bible." Is this
meddling with politics? Is this encouraging the
Southern rebels?

The third proof alleged to show "that slavery was
authorized by the Almighty," is, the last of the ten
commandments : "Thou shalt not covet thy neighbor's house, thou shalt not covet thy neighbor's wife,

4

nor his man-servant, nor his maid-servant, nor his ox, nor his ass, nor anything that is thy neighbor's." "There," says the advocate of slavery, "you see that servants are recognized as property, side by side with houses and oxen and asses." "Nay," replies the anti-slavery man, "but if so, then wives are recognized as property in the same sense." "True," says the "Christian Bishop," not at all disconcerted by the *reductio ad absurdum*, "true, and it would be well for wives to remember it, and not take umbrage at the law which places them in the same sentence with the slave, and even the house and the cattle." I should have considered it an insult to the intelligence of my readers to expose this play upon the word *property*, had it not been gravely adopted and used by a person of such dignity and respectability. Property is commonly understood as referring to what may be bought and sold, transferred and inherited, to what is regarded as a mere passive means to serve its owner's ends. And the real question is whether men can rightly be the property of other men in this sense,—whether they can be *chattels personal*,—and whether this commandment recognizes them as such, because it puts them with oxen and houses. But the word *property* may undoubtedly be used in various other senses. The wife may be the property of the husband, and so is the husband the property of the wife. The servant may be the property of the master, and so is the master the property of the servant. My children are my property, my parents are my property, my country is my property, my God is my property;—but they are not therefore my slaves,— things,—*chattels personal*. The case is simply this: the anti-slavery man places the man-servant and the

maid-servant in the same category with the wife;
the pro-slavery man places them on a level with the
ox and the ass; the "Christian Bishop" places wife,
servant, ox, ass, and all, on one common level. Here
are the three interpretations. Which is right? Are
wives and servants to be reckoned as persons or as
things? Which was the intention of the law-giver?
"But," says the Bishop, "whatever, whether person
or thing, the law *appropriates* to an individual, becomes of necessity his property." If by "the law,"
here, he means *this law, the law of God,* we have
already answered him. If he means *the law of the
land,* will he maintain that the Almighty recognizes
as rightful property whatever the law of the land
recognizes as such, and in the same sense and degree
in which that law recognizes it as such? Is it always
right for me to hold and retain as my property whatever the law of the land secures to me as such,—for
example,—by the statute of limitations? Can there
be no unrighteous, no oppressive laws? The Israelites were held in bondage in Egypt, by the laws of
Egypt. Was it therefore all right? As the laws of
Egypt *appropriated* them to the king or to some other
individual, were they therefore his rightful *property*—
his "chattels personal?" Whatever else is meant by
man-servant and maid-servant in the commandment,
the terms undoubtedly included the Hebrew servants
who served for a term of years as a kind of apprentices. The same class of servants exist now, and
may rightfully exist always. And we are forbidden
to covet these from our neighbor. As to slaves, anti-
slavery men cannot covet them from their neighbors,
cannot desire them as their own property. It is the
pro-slavery man and he alone, who is liable to violate

the tenth commandment in this regard; or, at least, there is only one other party who can be supposed to violate it—and that is the slave himself. Will the "Christian Bishop" say that the poor slave is, in this commandment, forbidden to sigh for or even to desire his freedom? Will he say that all other men are forbidden to cherish any such desire in behalf of the slave? He elsewhere acknowledges that he desires the freedom of the slaves;—is he therefore violating the tenth commandment?

His fourth argument is drawn from the express provisions of the law of Moses in regard to the "separation of husband and wife," and to the "punishment of slaves." He cites, "If thou buy an Hebrew servant, six years shall he serve; and in the seventh he shall go free for nothing. If he came in by himself he shall go out by himself; if he were married, then his wife shall go out with him. If his master have given him a wife, and she have borne him sons or daughters, the wife and her children shall be her master's, and he shall go out by himself." (Ex. xxi. 4–6.) He then adds, "Here we see that the separation of husband and wife is positively directed by divine command." But is this really so? Is it not rather a mere arrangement that when a man had a female servant who was bound to him for a definite or an indefinite period, he was not to be deprived or curtailed of her services by her being married to one of his servants, whose term of service might expire before hers? If the master chose to make a different arrangement with his servant before the marriage, or to consent to a different course afterwards, undoubtedly he was at liberty to do so. But if the master chose not to waive his legal rights, and the servant insisted upon marrying the bondmaid, he did it with his eyes open, and must abide the consequences. The Rabbins declare that this was not a case of solemn marriage—that the woman became not a wife, but a mere *concubine*; for the children of the proper wife always followed the condition of the father. But be this as it may, this law does not *ordain* the separation of husband and wife; for though the husband went out free alone, there was nothing in the law to hinder his living as near his wife, and having as much connexion with her afterwards, as is customary among the negro slaves, even before any such separation of husband and wife as is complained of. Besides, the man was not sold to some distant plantation, and forced to go and leave his wife behind; he could remain with her if he chose; only he must continue to share her condition with her. How, then, was the " separation of husband and wife positively commanded?" Does the Bishop mean that this regulation of the Mosaic code shows that there is no sin, no moral wrong, in the separation of husband and wife, as it is often forced upon the negro slaves in the Southern States? Or does he mean that the system of concubinage or something worse and more bestial, which is said to be there established among the slaves, is authorized and sanctioned by the law of God? So it would seem. " With this law before his eyes," he exclaims, " what Christian can believe that the Almighty attached immorality or sin to the condition of slavery?" Why not say at once, " to the separation of husbands and wives," for that is the specific thing which he says is " positively directed" in this case? And what if we should answer to his whole argument, " For the hardness of your hearts

4*

Moses wrote you this precept ?" Did the Almighty attach immorality or sin to the *divorce* which he allowed and regulated ? As to the Mosaic regulations in regard to the treatment of servants, there are three : 1st, " If a man smite his servant or his maid with a rod, and he die under his hand, he shall be surely punished." That is, if under pretence of chastising his servant, he kill him, he shall, as the Rabbins have interpreted, be punished as a murderer —be put to death. And the Rabbins are plainly right; for the law for the punishment of murder is universal and absolute; it makes no distinction between bond and free. " For blood, it defileth the land, and the land cannot be cleansed of the blood that is shed therein, but by the blood of him that shed it." 2d, " If a man smite out the eye or the tooth of his servant, the servant shall go free for the eye or the tooth's sake." Which of the Southern States has adopted so humane a rule as this ? 3d, " If the servant continue a day or two after being chastised by his master, and then die, the master shall not be punished—*he is his money.*" That is, says the Bishop, " the loss of his property was held to be a sufficient penalty." But, if that were so, why not also in the first case as well as in this ? The whole distinction turns upon the question of the *intent* to kill. If the circumstances are such as to imply that intention, the murderer shall be punished—if not, not; and the fact that the servant is his master's money, added to the servant's surviving some time after the chastisement, is held a sufficient guaranty that the intention to kill did not exist. It is a rule of evidence, not a measure of penalty.

The fifth argument in defence of slavery is drawn

from the alleged fact that the regulations of the
Mosaic law in regard to the Jubilee did not apply to
foreigners who were held in bondage; since the
Israelites are expressly authorized to hold them as
"their bondmen forever." And this construction of
the law of the Jubilee is said to have been "invariably sanctioned by the Doctors of the Jewish law,
and every respectable Christian commentator." This
last statement is a little too strong, for not to mention many respectable Christian commentators, Sal-
vador, one of the most learned modern Jewish doctors, maintains the opposite view. The Hebrew
servant who had submitted to have his ear bored,
was to be a "bondman forever;" and yet most of the
Jewish doctors agree that he was to recover his freedom at the Jubilee. If so, to be a "bondman forever" was not inconsistent with going out at the
Jubilee. The terms of the Jubilee proclamation are
universal and absolute—"liberty throughout the
land, to *all the inhabitants thereof.*"

This certainly might be fairly interpreted as ap-
plying to slaves, if it applied to anybody—no exceptions are made of foreign residents or anybody else.
But I am not disposed to insist on this interpretation. The weight of authority is probably the other
way. I only insist that it is an open question. And
even supposing the other interpretation to be the
true one, what does the advocate of modern slavery
gain by it? He must admit that the Israelites were
forbidden to make slaves of their brethren; and
those of them whom they might hold, as servants,
they were to treat with mildness and release at the
end of six years. Even though it should be admitted
then, that they were allowed to have "bondmen of

the nations that were round about them," and to
retain them absolutely without limitation of time—
what is that to us Christians? Are not all men *our
brethren* now? Has any particular nation or race
now the peculiar privileges of the ancient chosen
people? Does not all the doctrine of Christ declare,
and does not every Christian heart respond, that the
measure of kindness which Hebrew owed to Hebrew
is not too great for every Christian to pay to all his
fellow men of whatever nation, race or clime?

As to the Mosaic regulation forbidding the rendition of fugitive slaves, it is alleged that it applies
only to slaves escaping *from foreign masters*. But this
is not so perfectly clear; for the terms of the law
are entirely general; and on the other hand there is
no law expressly requiring the rendition of fugitive
slaves escaping from Hebrew masters; and if it had
been intended that these should be restored, it would
seem natural to have made such an exception to the
law actually enunciated. The most probable solution
would seem to be that the law refers, not to ordinary
runaways, but to slaves escaping,—escaping for their
lives,—from the harsh treatment, or murderous assaults, or threats, of their masters. Or, if the law
be understood as referring exclusively to slaves
escaping from foreign masters, the reason would
still be similar—viz., they were not to be restored
on account of the harsh treatment and reckless
punishment to which they were liable among people
*over whose laws and usages the Hebrew legislation had no
control;* and thus this law would be on the whole a
precedent for *not* returning escaped slaves to States—
whether considered in any other relation as foreign
or domestic—in respect to whose *slave-code we could*

exercise no influence and have no voice. If the slaves are subjected to cruel treatment, under cruel and inhuman laws, this law would furnish a precedent for affording them an asylum—unless we are bound by express stipulations to the contrary; and its spirit would go against entering into or retaining such stipulations.

Then comes the argument from the New Testament, which amounts to this: that slavery existed in the time of our Saviour, but he "DID NOT ALLUDE TO IT AT ALL;" and that his Apostles taught that servants should be "obedient to their masters," and that masters should "give unto their servants that which is just and equal." Hence, as our Lord did not expressly repeal the old law, it is inferred that the regulations of the Mosaic code in respect to slavery remain in full force as a *norma* of what is right under all circumstances; and the precepts of the Apostles recognize and regulate slavery as an allowed and uncondemned institution. But are all the precepts and directions, which were given to the chosen people, and were not expressly repealed by our Lord, valid as a standard of right for modern Christian nations? Take for example the laws of war contained in Deut. xx. 10–16. "When thou comest nigh unto a city to fight against it, then proclaim peace unto it. And it shall be, if it make thee answer of peace, and open unto thee, then it shall be, that all the people that is found therein shall be tributaries unto thee, and they shall serve thee. And if it will make no peace with thee, but will war against thee, then thou shalt besiege it; and when the LORD thy God hath delivered it into thine hands, thou shalt smite every male thereof with the edge of the sword;

but the women, and the little ones, and the cattle,
and all that is in the city, even all the spoil thereof,
shalt thou take unto thyself; and thou shalt eat the
spoil of thine enemies, which the LORD thy God hath
given thee. Thus shalt thou do unto all the cities
which are very far off from thee, which are not of
the cities of these nations. But of the cities of these
people, which the LORD thy God doth give thee for
an inheritance, thou shalt save alive nothing that
breatheth."

Now here is an express and solemn *command*, which
was never repealed by our Blessed Lord. And the
case is stronger than that of slavery; for it will not
be pretended that the Israelites were *positively commanded*, that it was made their bounden duty, to hold
slaves; it can be maintained only that they were
allowed to do so. Is it, therefore, right for modern
Christian nations to wage war in this way? And
would it be " blasphemy" to maintain the contrary?
Neither our Saviour nor his Apostles have expressly
prohibited Polygamy, which is recognized and regulated in the law of Moses (see Ex. xxi. 10; Lev. xviii.
16, 18; xx. 14; Deut. xxv. 5, 7, 9, &c.); is polygamy
therefore right? Was divorce, except for one cause,
right before our Saviour forbade it? Did he forbid
it because it is wrong? or is it wrong because he
forbade it? The advocates of slavery are welcome
to all the countenance they can get from our Saviour's *silence*, if they will carry out the spirit of his
positive teaching of love and good will to all men,—a
spirit before which slavery can make but a brief
stand.

Nothing can be fairly inferred in favour of slavery
from those precepts of the apostles which require

servants to be submissive and obedient to their masters, for this is required as a matter of suffering and
Christian patience, after the example of Him, who,
when he was reviled, reviled not again, when he
suffered he threatened not. (See 1 Peter ii. 18–24.)
From the command to obey magistrates it does not
follow that the tyranny of Tiberius and Nero was
sanctioned. From the command, "if a man smite
thee on the one cheek offer also the other," we may
not infer that a man is justified in smiting thee on
one or both cheeks; or that a third person would be
justified,—even though a "Christian Bishop,"—in
compelling thee to submit to the infliction. And as to
the precept to masters—"give unto your servants
that which is just and equal—or rather that which
is just, and *equality*—knowing that ye also have a
master in heaven," "neither is there respect of persons with him:"—if this precept were carried out
honestly and fully, how long would slavery stand
before it? Those masters are presumed to know
what is required, by justice and equality from their
own enlightened reason and Christian conscience—
as our Lord said to the Pharisees, "wherefore of
your own selves judge ye not what is right:"—and
not by blunting their moral sensibilities, and entan-
gling their consciences with perverse interpretations
and misapplications of a Divinely given but now
obsolete code of civil regulations. Is it not plain
that, among other things, "justice and equality"
would require masters to desire and seek, by intellectual, moral, and religious culture, to prepare their
servants for freedom, and when so prepared, gladly
and willingly to emancipate them? Could a sense
of justice and equality allow them to retain them as

slaves, as "chattels personal," and that with a view and purpose of perpetuating their bondage and that of their children and children's children, at all hazards?

But St. Paul, it is said, sent back Onesimus, a fugitive slave, to his master, Philemon. This is uniformly the grand climax of the pro-slavery argument from the Bible, as the "curse of Ham" is its invariable foundation stone. Yes, St. Paul sent Onesimus back to Philemon, with these words:—"Receive him that is mine own bowels ... receive him forever, not now as a servant, but above a servant, a brother beloved .... receive him as myself .... Having confidence in thy obedience I have written unto thee knowing that thou wilt also do more than I say."—Is it supposable that Philemon should have retained Onesimus as a slave, as a "chattel personal," after such a letter as that? Observe, he was to receive him, "not now as a servant, but above a servant, a brother beloved."—I take the words just as they stand, in their simple force, without any gloss, or paraphrase, or emendation,—he was to receive him *as the Apostle himself.* Would he receive the Apostle as a slave, as a "chattel personal," to be condemned to ignorance, and held in perpetual bondage? But as if to clench the point, the Apostle adds, "I know that thou wilt do more than I say;" and what could that *more* be, which the Apostle insinuates, but to emancipate the slave? It appears from ecclesiastical tradition that Philemon did emancipate Onesimus; for the latter is subsequently spoken of as Bishop of one of the churches. Why the advocates of slavery should have such a fancy for the Epistle to Philemon, it is indeed difficult to comprehend. The more frequently parallel cases should occur in these times, the better. As often as a Philemon can be found as a master, by all means let his fugitive slaves be returned to him, to be treated as St. Paul requested that Onesimus should be treated;—it will not delay the progress of emancipation. And let the ministers of Christ among slave-holders collect the slaves together as often as they can, and present them to their masters with these words: "Sir, receive these poor slaves that are mine own bowels, receive them forever, not now as servants, but above servants, as brethren beloved, receive them as myself. In saying this I have confidence in you that you will also do more than I say." Or let those ministers take the slaves one by one, as, upon sufficient instruction, and evidence of piety, they may be admitted to the Holy Communion, and present them to their masters with that address. Surely it is enough that the slaves should be made Christians; it is not necessary that they should run away and rob their masters, in order to have a claim to such a commendation. What a strange sermon this would be to the ears of Southern masters! What a gospel to the poor slaves! Let it be often preached, the oftener the better. I only fear that such church communion would be voted a nuisance, and such preaching would be silenced, and that the Epistle to Philemon would soon be regarded by the abettors of chattelism and perpetual slavery as an "incendiary document."

Before the abolition of slavery in the British West Indies, it was made a charge against a Wesleyan missionary that he had read an inflammatory chapter of the Bible to his congregation.

5

The denunciation of anti-slavery preachers as persons " calling themselves Christians," and the charge against the " numerous and respectable friends of this popular delusion" that they are " not accustomed to study the Bible half as much as they read the newspapers, the novel, and the magazine,"—is of course an argument unanswerable. As to the alleged duty of Christian ministers to rebuke the anti-slavery movement and preach down the war, it is plain that this would be political preaching and introducing slavery into the pulpit, as much as preaching on the other side would be ; and the Bishop condescends not to " judge" those who take, in this matter, a different view from himself ; though he hesitates not to represent them as " strangely regardless of their highest obligations."

The " Christian Bishop" next proceeds to carp at the doctrines of the Declaration of American Independence. To this he devotes a large part of his letter, which furnishes one of the best specimens, perhaps, of elaborate special pleading contained in his whole book. It is fitting that American freemen should know that he who would make chattel-slavery a Divine Institution and pervert the word of God and the authority of Jesus Christ and his apostles to its support, scouts at the doctrines and political opinions of the Fathers of the American Republic, and pronounces the " self-evident truths" which are placed at the head of the Declaratien of Independence to be in his judgment " no truths at all." I shall not follow him at present through all his argument, as the subject will come up again in its proper place. A few words here must suffice. He gives an essay of considerable rhetorical merit ranging through heaven and earth and sea and sky, and all the kingdoms of nature, to show the wonderful variety and diversity in the Creator's works. The thing is well done. But what has it to do with the Declaration of Independence? He reminds us that "all men are born *unequal* in body, in mind, in social privileges. Their intellectual faculties are unequal. Their education is unequal. Their associations are unequal. Their opportunities are unequal." But what has all this to do with the Declaration? Who ever supposed the authors of the Declaration such downright fools as to assert that there was no variety in Nature's works, or that all men were born equal in the respects just named? But are we to suppose, therefore, that they were raving, and had no meaning at all? If the Bishop had taken as much pains to show what, as reasonable and intelligent men, they probably *did* mean, as he has to show what they could not have meant without the most egregious stupidity, he would have performed the more appropriate office of a critic. Suppose that when they proclaimed and laid at the very foundation of our American Commonwealth, "the self-evident truths, that all men are created equal; that they are endowed by their Creator with certain unalienable rights; that among those are life, liberty, and the pursuit of happiness;"—suppose, I say, they meant, that all men are created equally men — *men*, not brutes, *persons*, not things, — equally moral beings, beings capable of and possessing rights; that these rights inhere in their very nature, and though capable of being politically forfeited by personal fault, yet incapable of being transferred to another, or in idea annihilated; that, by virtue of their very hu-

manity, all men have equally the rights of personal
security, of personal liberty, of marriage, of property,
of seeking happiness in the free and full development
of their moral being :—in short, just this, *that human
slavery is contrary to nature, and to the design of the
Creator of mankind?* Would this be absurd? Something like this they probably did mean; and when
the *facts* of the well known inequalities, political and
social, which actually exist among mankind, are set
forth by the Bishop to show that their doctrine is
false, he entirely misses the mark. They were not
dealing with the visible facts, but with fundamental
ideas. And when the Bishop would suggest that the
actual facts are the best proof of the original design,
he would use the word design in a peculiar predesti-
narian sense. Man was designed for holiness and
happiness, whether he actually attains them or not.
The seeds of plants may actually perish or be destroyed in various ways, but if we examine their
construction, we shall find that each one, in its very
constitution, was designed to produce a new plant
after its kind.

But, says the Bishop, " since the fall, men *have no
rights to claim at the hands of their Creator.*" And what
of that? Who ever said they had? If he really
thinks that the authors of the Declaration meant to
make such claims, meant to say that men have an
"unalienable right" to claim " life, liberty, and the
pursuit of happiness," at the hands of their Creator,
he must be even vastly more stupid than he supposes
those authors to have been. I shall not follow his
example so far as to charge such stupidity upon him.
But unless he is amenable to that charge, he must
mean, and it is to be presumed he *does* mean, that

fallen men have, by virtue of their humanity, no mutual rights, no rights in relation to one another, no rights as men in distinction from brutes, as persons in distinction from things, no rights which as brethren they are bound to respect in one another, no rights which are not the creature of mere might, of the *purely arbitrary enactments of positive law*—in short, no rights at all in any true and proper sense. For, unless there are *natural rights of man*, there can be no *positive rights*. There is nothing to make them out of; in that case the very idea of *rights* is wanting; they could no more be created by positive enactment *for man*, than they could *for brutes*. Wherever there is a rational and moral nature, there are also of necessity *natural rights*.

The "Christian Bishop" seems to have a special spite, and very naturally from his position,—against the so-called *natural rights of man*. According to him, the fathers and founders of American Freedom either did not know what they meant, or the doctrines of their famous Declaration were all wrong. And consequently the American Revolution was all wrong in principle and unchristian from beginning to end. For the authors of the Declaration certainly appealed for justification to the *rights of man*,—appealed to them, just like Infidels and Atheists, as the Bishop would say,—and, without admitting such an appeal, no justification of their course can be found, but on their heads must rest all the blood that was shed, and all the misery that was borne, during those seven years of a fratricidal or parricidal war,—for "fallen man has no rights" to claim — still less to fight for. At the successful close of the Revolution, the Continental Congress, in a solemn address to the

5 *

people, uttered the following declaration : " Let it be remembered that it has ever been the pride and boast of America *that the rights for which she has contended were the rights of human nature. By the blessing of the Author of those rights*, they have prevailed over all opposition, and form the BASIS of thirteen independent States."

An effort is made to attach odium to the doctrine of the *natural rights of man*, by connecting with it all the excesses of the French Revolutionists. This procedure is characteristic of the " Christian Bishop's" logic. But is Christianity chargeable with all the crimes and cruelties that have been committed in her name ? If the doctrine of natural rights and freedom and equality is liable to abuse and extravagance, will any abuse of it lead to worse consequences than will follow from its rejection ? If from a love of freedom men may be led into excesses, would not its eradication from their minds end in their utter debasement and degradation ? Does not Christianity teach men that it is a beautiful thing to be *free? free* in the highest sense ;—but that highest sense is understood only as illustrated by the lower. And does not Christianity teach that all men are *equal* in the sight of God ? Is equality then such a dangerous or such an absurd idea ? They certainly are not all equally tall, equally strong, equally healthy, equally intellectual, equally wise, equally rich, equally powerful, equally happy, in his sight. In what sense are they then *equal* before him, consistently with the vast variety and diversity of his works ? " *God is no respecter of persons.*"

But, says the letter, " the Revolution produced no effect on the institution of slavery." Let Benjamin

Franklin, and the Legislature of Pennsylvania who abolished slavery in 1780, answer that allegation. The preamble to that act of emancipation — in a somewhat abridged form, and as quoted by the Hon. John Sergeant, in his speech on the Missouri question, runs thus:—

"When we contemplate our abhorrence of that condition, to which the arms and tyranny of Great Britain were exerted to reduce us, when we look on the variety of dangers to which we have been exposed, and deliverances wrought, when even hope and fortitude have become unequal to the conflict, we conceive it to be our duty, and rejoice that it is in our power, to extend a portion of that freedom to others which hath been extended to us, to add one more step to universal civilization, by removing, as much as possible, the sorrows of those who have lived in undeserved bondage. Weaned by a long course of experience from those narrow prejudices and partialities we had imbibed, we conceive ourselves, at this particular period, called upon, by the blessings we have received, to manifest the sincerity of our profession. In justice, therefore, to persons who, having no prospect before them, whereon they may rest their sorrows and their hopes, have no reasonable inducement to render that service to society which otherwise they might; and also, in grateful commemoration of our own happy deliverance from that state of unconditional submission to which we were doomed by the tyranny of Britain—Be it enacted, that no child born hereafter shall be a slave, &c."

Did the Revolution, then, "produce no effect on the institution of slavery?"

Those beautiful words seem to me to be a sort of quiet, gentle refutation of the Bishop's whole book. When they are read, I confess I do not envy the man who can feel more sympathy with his harsh Draconian defence of slavery than with those humane, grateful, and truly Christian sentiments. I do not envy the Christian who can meet them with the cry of "Infidelity," "Atheism," "rebellion against the authority of the Almighty," "blasphemy against the decrees of the Eternal Judge," or can cast in the teeth of that abolition Legislature the shout of "liberty, equality, fraternity," as made by the godless revolutionists of France.

But the "Christian Bishop" insists that the "negro race were not included in the Declaration." If so, its authors took a very singular way of leaving them out. "We hold these truths to be self-evident that all men are created equal," &c. If the Bishop has any proof that the authors of the Declaration denied that negroes are men, let him bring it forward. Until that is done it must be plain that they are included in the proposition; and this is said not merely in view of its grammatical construction, but in virtue of a logical necessity; for, how could such a proposition be "self-evident," unless it were universal, founded in the very nature of man as man? The "Christian Bishop" endeavours to prove that "the signers of the Declaration did not take the negroes into the account at all," because they held slaves themselves, and continued to hold them to the end of their lives. This is a question of *consistency* which he may settle with those signers as best he can. But as to the inference he makes from their conduct, one might as well say, since they continued to use profane oaths, they did not believe profane swearing is a sin, or that since every Christian violates God's commands from day to day, therefore no Christian believes such violation to be wrong. Meantime abundant positive evidence from their own language, some of which I may hereafter produce, may be brought to show that Franklin, Jefferson, Washington, Madison, and most of the leading men of those times, from both North and South, believed negro slavery to be an injustice and a wrong.

The Declaration, so far from being, as the Bishop would represent it, a *brutum fulmen*, not only meaningless or false at that time, but now quite obsolete and null, is rather the doctrinal principle and the historical basis on which our Constitution and the whole frame of our government rest. True, it is not a statute; it has no direct legal force; but it embodies the fundamental ideas of the framers of our political fabric, and furnishes the key for the interpretation of their subsequent language. When, therefore, in the Preamble to the Constitution, they say, "We the people of the United States," the "*we*" certainly includes the Free blacks, for they were embraced in the free population to be represented in Congress, and they continued to vote even in North Carolina, till the year 1832.* Nor is there any reason

* I have found the following statements made on good authority; but I have not had an opportunity to verify their accuracy in all particulars:

By reference to the Constitutions of New York, New Hampshire, Massachusetts, New Jersey, Virginia, Maryland, and North Carolina, formed before the date of the Constitution of the United States, and in force at its adoption, and also to the Constitutions of Georgia and Pennsylvania, formed soon afterwards, it appears to suppose that it does not also include the slaves prospectively; for it is notorious that the framers of the Constitution generally presumed that slavery was rapidly dying out—an expectation which would probably have been verified but for the invention of the Cotton Gin. To suppose that "we the people of the United States" means only those who have a right to vote, is preposterous; for when the Preamble goes on to say—"to secure the blessings of liberty to ourselves and our posterity"—is it possible it should mean that the blessings of liberty were to be secured only to voters? What would an Englishman at that time have thought of restricting "we the people of England"—"we the free people of England," exclusively to those few who possessed the elective franchise?

The charges of cruelty in the punishment, and barbarity in the treatment of slaves, are rebutted by à priori considerations; the Christian principle, the natural kindness, and, above all, the pecuniary interest of the master—and well may he give the

that in respect to the qualification of electors for the most numerous branches of the State Legislatures, *there was no distinction on account of colour* in those nine States. Connecticut and Rhode Island, being under the old royal charters, could have none. South Carolina, by its Constitution of 1776, allowed negroes to vote, but in 1778 the privilege was restricted to every "white man," &c. In Delaware, by act of February 3, 1787, emancipated slaves and their issue were debarred "the privilege of voting at elections or being elected." And even this seems to have been a violation of the letter of the Constitution of the State. It is well known among intelligent men, that the practice of admitting free men of colour to vote obtained universally at first among all the original "old thirteen." In Virginia, *negroes voted side by side with white men until* 1830!

chief place to this last consideration—forbid it. And then our Lord Jesus Christ cleansing the temple with his scourge of small cords is brought forward, side by side with the whipping-post, to encourage the slave-driver and the overseer as they ply the lash upon the backs of the poor slaves, male and female, and to illustrate the functions of their office!! And the whole is wound up with the characteristic interrogatory: "Are our modern philanthropists more merciful than Christ, and wiser than the Almighty?" I will not trust myself to characterize such a train of thought. I might be led to use much stronger language than that of the "reviling, vilifying, insulting, vituperative, calumnious and slanderous" Protest itself.

In answer to the charge that slavery leads to *immorality*, it is replied that there is no evidence that it leads to more immorality "in the slave population of all the fifteen slave States, than is found in the single city of New York, in Sabbath breaking, profane cursing and swearing, gambling, drunkenness and quarrelling, in brutal abuse of wives and children, in rowdyism and obscenity, in the vilest excesses of shameless prostitution—to say nothing of organized bands of counterfeiters, thieves and burglars." But who, what "servant of Jesus Christ," undertakes formally to defend such vices or their causes in the city of New York? And suppose the slaves are saved from many of them, from gambling, counterfeiting, burglary, and abuse of wives and children, for example,—what is gained by it in the moral elevation of the mass, when, to accomplish it, they are all deprived of their very humanity—of all freedom of action and development as moral beings?

If they were transformed into a herd of beasts, they would be guilty of no immoralities at all. Besides, the regular normal results of a system, on the one hand, and its abuses and perversions on the other, have very diverse bearings in determining its proper character. In some of the slave States, and perhaps in strictness it is true in all, the slaves have no legal *wives* at all; and suppose there is as much of looseness of sentiment and practice in connexion with the marriage relation among the mass of the population of New York as among the Southern slaves— which is unquestionably a gross exaggeration—still, how great the difference between its being systematically established, encouraged and protected *by law*, and its irregular existence in spite of the law? But it is curious and almost ludicrous to see the Bishop gloating with such evident logical and rhetorical satisfaction over the vices, crimes, and debasement of the "lower class" of the population of the city of New York, when they are precisely the best friends of his cause; they are his true constituents as a pro-slavery political leader; they, and not the virtuous country population, whether of New York or of Vermont, are his true disciples as a pro-slavery apostle. The most rabid pro-slavery fanatics, and the most ferocious haters of the negro race, are precisely the New York mob. Let him collect the Sabbath breakers, the profane swearers, the gamblers, drunkards, and street-fighters, the abusers of wives and children, the rowdy, obscene and grossly licentious, the counterfeiters, thieves and burglars of the city of New York; and ask them their sentiments on the slavery question. He will then find, perhaps, that there are some associates whom a good man

might wish to avoid, besides Garrison, Beecher,
Emerson and Parker. And suppose there are some
cases of licentiousness among the higher classes of
Northern society to set off against the licentiousness
of slaveholders among their helpless slaves; is it
nothing that in the one case the immorality is protected by the law, and in the other the crime is
punished by the law? But though the poor negro
woman is not allowed to testify in court against her
ravisher, her offspring testifies, " before this sun," in
a language that cannot be misunderstood, and which
leaves no suspicion of perjury. Let the increase of
mulattoes in the Southern States bear witness to the
comparative licentiousness or purity of a slave-holding population.

As to *property in man*, the " Christian Bishop"
gravely tells us that " no slaveholder pretends that
this property extends any further than the *right to
the labour of the slave.* . . . The intellect and the soul,
which properly constitute the MAN, are free in their
own nature from all human restraint." Thus he
would resolve slavery into a peculiar form of a very
general human relation which is perfectly right and
proper; and taking into account the assumed intellectual inferiority of the negroes, he would justify
this peculiar form of that relation in their case. But,
says the South Carolina code, " slaves are deemed,
held, taken, reputed and judged in law to be *chattels
personal* in the hands of their owners or possessors,
and their executors, administrators and assigns, to
all intents, constructions and purposes whatsoever."
And the Louisiana code declares that " a slave is one
who is in the power of a master to whom he belongs.
The master may sell him, dispose of his person, his
6

industry, and his labour. He can do nothing, possess nothing, nor acquire anything, but must belong to his master." These are specimens of slave laws. Were the authors of the Carolina and Louisiana codes "slaveholders?" If so, slaveholders seem to have taken especial pains to show and claim that the property of the master in the slave extends to something beyond "his labour." But if the Bishop wishes to refine upon the case and speak philosophically, I am ready to admit that the slaveholder has no use for the person, the soul, or intellect of the slaves, except with a view to the labour he can get out of them; that they are for him merely producing machines,—the intellect, the soul, being regarded simply as the driving force,—that his grand object is work, work, gain, money. To this end all the rest is made to converge. Give him the full control of the body of the slave and all its activities, and he cares not how free his soul may be in its unapproachable sanctuary. And provided he can extract from him the greatest amount of labour here on earth, I suppose he is perfectly willing that his soul should afterwards have its rest in heaven. But if he "cannot bind the intellect," he can keep it in enforced darkness and ignorance; if he "cannot bind the soul," he can stint and stop its moral development by systematically cutting off from it all means of moral growth and culture. Having for generations precluded the blacks, by strict legal provisions, from all opportunity of intellectual enlightenment and improvement, he can turn around and talk philosophically of the intellectual inferiority of the African race, and give that as a reason for keeping them in perpetual bondage. If they have not an intellect

equal to that of the whites, it is thus practically con-
fessed that they have an intellect *superior to their
condition as slaves,* and which needs to be restrained
and repressed in order to secure the master in reap-
ing the fruits of their " labour." Shame on such a
system and its impious defenders! For I speak of
the system and not of the practice or character of
every individual slaveholder.

But " God has wonderfully adapted the race to
their condition," devoutly adds the " Christian
Bishop." That is to say, men have found a race of
their brethren so weak and gentle, so docile and pa-
tient, so submissive and affectionate, that they can
conveniently, safely and profitably make them their
slaves ;—one would suppose that to do this was crime
and baseness enough — but no, they are not content
without adding impiety to oppression, and urge the
blasphemous excuse that " God has wonderfully
adapted the race to their condition !"

The Bishop alleges that " emancipation has, in a
majority of cases, failed to benefit the negro, and
has, on the contrary, sunk him far lower in his social
position;"—that is to say, the sporadic cases of emancipation under the laws, customs, and social influences and prejudices of the slaveholding States, such
as they are. But what shall we say of the laws and
customs, the moral and social tone, of a people,
where a man,—a veritable man, made in the very
image of God,—but being in a greater or less degree
of a certain hue, is, by becoming a freeman, sunk
far lower than the slave *in social position ?*

In his attempt to answer the *argumentum ad hominem,* " how should you like to be a slave ?" the Bishop
entirely misses the point. The question is not at all

" how he should like to be *another* man, or to practice
another profession?" but, being a man, " how he
should like to be a *slave?*" It is not, whether he
would be a shoemaker, or a sheriff, or a stevedore,
or a lawyer, or a scavenger,—but how he should
like to be deprived of his liberty, and *compelled* to be
any of those or anything else, at the arbitrary will
of another man, and as a mere instrument and tool
for his profit? The love of liberty is presumed to
belong to man, as man,—to be a natural sentiment
if not a " natural right" of humanity. Does the
" Christian Bishop" suppose that it is no more a
general attribute of human nature, than is a taste or
aptitude for some particular employment or trade?
It is presumable that a slave may love liberty as
passionately as even the learned and refined Bishop,
just as the shoemaker or the " Irish labourer" may
love his wife and his children as much as " the mer-
chant-prince," "the American statesman," or " the
British peer;" and, if you would forcibly deprive
him of either, he may fairly ask " how you would
like to have your children torn from you?" And if,
on the other hand, any social system can actually
succeed in divesting men, any race, or class of men,
of their love of libery, their love of parents, of
wife, of children, and thus eradicating from their
hearts the very affections and character of humanity,
—who would not consider it the most withering and
damning charge under which any social system could
rest? Who would not consider the defence of such
a system "unworthy of any servant of Jesus Christ?"
There can be no more utter and fatal condemnation
of slavery than its oft repeated excuse—" the slaves
no not desire to be *free*,—they are happy as they

are."* But, says the "Christian Bishop," there are
thousands in our land, free according to law, who
are quite unfit for freedom. "They are in bondage
to Satan." Would it be right, then, for us to enslave
them, in imitation of their present master? The
oldest slaveholder is undoubtedly Satan himself.

In the "Christian Bishop's" view, it is no valid
objection to the system of American slavery that it
involves the frequent compulsory separation of husband and wife, of parents and children. On this

* We will grant, notwithstanding, that many slaves are happy;
habit is so powerful and God so good! The poor girl has in her
garret a holy image of her mother's ring; the lonely orphan
tending goats or swine on the slope of the mountain knows of
unknown springs and bird's nests hidden in the rock, which belong to him and to him alone; and even in the dungeon's depths
the prisoner at length creates to himself a little world apart,
peopled by an insect, a flower, a sunbeam, a name cut in the
wall. God does not suffer a blade of grass to lack a drop of
water, nor a human being to lack a gleam of happiness. The
poor slave, if he does not divert his thoughts from life, ends by
becoming accustomed to it, consoled for it; he thinks of death,
then of heaven! But he is happy *in spite of* slavery, not *on account of* it; his happiness he finds in the little liberty of which
he dreams, or which he gives himself. The master knows it
well. What recompense does he promise the slave at the end of
a life of devotion? Liberty. Besides, is there not veritable
confusion in all this discussion? Do we rightly comprehend ourselves, and are we speaking of the same thing? *To be happy, to
be free,*—are these synonymous? I tell you that the slave should
be free, and you reply to me that he eats, that he drinks, that
he sleeps, that he dances, that he is happy. I speak to you of
liberty, which is the happiness of the soul, and you tell me of
enjoyment, which is the servitude of the senses. I speak to you
of a birthright, and you answer me with a dish of pottage! Let
us have done with this misunderstanding. (*Cochin, Results of
Slavery*, p. 90.)

6*

point, his zeal for his favourite institution has carried him beyond even the slaveholders themselves; for the Southern Bishops, in their so-called "Pastoral Letter" a few years since, distinctly admitted such separations to be wrong, to be "unchristian," to be an evil in the system which ought to be forthwith remedied. But the "Christian Bishop's" argument on this point is as extraordinary for a logician as his conclusion is for "a servant of Jesus Christ." By the slavery of circumstances, says he, it comes to pass not unfrequently in the ordinary course of life, that husbands and wives, parents and children, are separated from each other; and "is it wise to declaim against this necessity in one form when we are forced to submit to it in so many other kinds of the same infliction?" But because husband and wife may be separated in various ways in the course of Providence, is the slaveholder justified in separating them by *force*, at his will, and for the sake of gain, of money, of mean and miserable money — which only the thrifty and infidel abolition Yankees are supposed to seek? The husband and wife may have no more occasion to "complain" of Divine Providence in one case than in the other, but they may have occasion to complain of human oppression and wrong. Indeed there is no crime which the Bishop's reasoning will not excuse, or charge upon the Providence of God. The thief may say, "why, it is no uncommon thing for men to lose their property by flood or fire; is it wise, then, to complain just when it is stolen?" And the murderer may say, "men often die of disease, why complain just when they are murdered?" Suppose the king of Dahomey, having slaughtered his hecatomb of human victims, should stand up amidst the reeking sacrifice and lift his bloody hands and say, "let no man wag his blasphemous tongue against what I have done. 'Wo to him that striveth with his maker.' 'There can be no greater blasphemy than imputing wrong to the decrees of the eternal Judge.' Be it known to all, that I am fully justified in butchering these men; *because it is no uncommon thing for men to die, and these very persons would soon have died in some way or other, if I had not killed them!"*

Like all pro-slavery reasoners, the "Christian Bishop" is evidently gravelled by the parallel case of Polygamy. He makes the best of it. He endeavours to show that Polygamy is forbidden in the New Testament; but, after all, it is not from direct texts, but only in an *inferential way.* And as much as that has been done over and over again in the argument against slavery. It is equally true of slavery and of polygamy that our Saviour never mentioned them in his instructions, nor have his apostles expressly forbidden them. As to the Hebrew right of divorce, the Bishop represents it as " *an indulgence granted by Moses,"* which, says he, " is a very different thing from an authoritative decree of the Almighty." This curious idea of his, that the allowing of divorce was a part of the law of Moses, but not a part of the law of God, he elsewhere insists upon. We shall recur to this subject of divorce and polygamy in the sequel.

" In regard to the slavery of Ham's posterity, God issues his commands distinctly," says the " Christian Bishop;" and this seems to be that "decree of the Almighty" to which he referred above as superior to the law of Moses. He had before spoken of the "prediction" or "prophecy" of Noah, and the "curse of Canaan," which he had enlarged into a "curse of Ham," a curse upon Ham's posterity in general. Now he enlarges it still more into a "distinct command" of the Almighty. But God predicted the bondage of the descendants of Abraham in Egypt. Were the Egyptians, therefore, "distinctly commanded" to enslave them? Noah cursed Canaan. Are all the "servants of Jesus Christ," therefore, "distinctly commanded" to curse all the descendants of Ham to the end of time? And are we all, the sons of Japheth, "distinctly commanded" to make them slaves, wherever and whenever we can find them, and to hold them in perpetual bondage? What *can* be meant by this "distinct command," this "authoritative decree of the Almighty?"

The "Christian Bishop" expressly urges his views "in the interests of Union and Peace," and declares that "the question of slavery lies at the root of our present difficulties." Yet he insists that he is "no politician," and he elsewhere, in the most scornful terms, scouts at the idea of "expediency," of "political expediency," as a principle of action.

He declares that slavery has been an incalculable blessing to the negroes, the most effective agent for Christianizing and civilizing them that has ever existed; "and thus," says he, "the wisdom and goodness of God are vindicated." But this is not the real end and object of his letter; and besides, if it had been, who has called "the wisdom and goodness of God" in question? When slavery is assailed, *it is not God that is complained of, but man.* The true upshot and aim of the letter had been stated just before, in the words which we have already quoted: "The slavery of the negro race, *as maintained in the Southern States*, appears to me fully authorized, both in the Old and the New Testaments." Thus no mere abstract doctrine, but this concrete fact, is the true and practical conclusion of his whole argument. Has that conclusion been established?

The "Christian Bishop" claims great credit for his hearty desire and his former labours for the abolition of slavery. Yet he tells us that all along he has believed and taught "that the plain precepts and practice of the apostles sanctioned the institution, although, as a matter of *expediency*, the time might come when the South would prefer, as the North had done, to employ free labour." Thus its abolition was with him purely a question of *expediency* and Political Economy; and no wonder that, while the profits of cotton, and the lust of dominion stood in his way, his labours on such a platform produced such MEAGRE results.

CHAPTER III.

"THE Scriptural, ecclesiastical, and historical View
of Slavery," taken as a whole, is, perhaps, one
of the most characteristic and elaborate specimens
of the fallacy or sophism which the logicians have
denominated *ignoratio elenchi*, or substitution of a
false issue for the true one, which can be found in
the whole range of polemic authorship. It refutes,
or attempts to refute, at large, the extreme *doctrines*
of the "ultra-abolitionists;" and then quietly assumes
that the signers of the " Protest" are utterly routed
and annihilated, together with all anti-slavery men
who condemn the positions taken in the letter to
which that Protest refers. But by what right is it
taken for granted that all anti-slavery men,—all men
who reject the pro-slavery doctrines of Bishop Hopkins, are " ultra-abolitionists ?"

The stale pro-slavery arguments from the Scriptures, which have already been alleged, answered,
and refuted a score of times, are served up again
and garnished with episcopal authority ; the indexes
of the Fathers and of Ecclesiastical councils are ran-
sacked ; doctors, commentators, publicists, historians,
are quoted — and what do they prove ? — why, that
the relation between master and servant is not
wrong ; that Christianity does not expressly con-

demn slavery or formally require its immediate and
total abolition; that slavery existed in connexion
with the Church, and under the protection of Christian legislation for many centuries; that the American Constitution "is not a covenant with death and
hell;" that certain good results have incidentally
flowed from slavery; and that certain infidels have
been ultra-abolitionists. And what of all this? Does
it prove that the principles, the genius and spirit
and practical influence of Christianity are not and
have not always been against slavery, slavery in the
concrete, slavery proper, slavery as distinguished
from other forms of service? Does it show that *that*
slavery which is intended to be perpetual, which
separates husbands from wives, and parents from
children, which reduces men to chattels, which forbids their instruction, and uses them as mere instru-
ments of gain to their masters, is all right? Does
it show that "slavery as it is maintained in the
Southern States,"—in the Cotton States, where the
slaves are sent out to work in gangs under the lash
of the overseer, or in the other States which sell
men and women in the open market as their staple
product,—is authorized and approved by the Christian religion, the Christian Church, and Christian
history? These are the conclusions which should
have been established, and which are coolly assumed
to be established, by the elaborate argument. Any
intelligent reader can judge, when the question is
fairly brought before his mind, whether they have
been established. To the less learned portion of our
readers, however, it may be proper to say,—lest they
should be dazzled or confounded by the immense
array of lore gathered together in defence of sla-

very,—that the simple statements of the Scripture, after all, furnish the strongest of the arguments alleged; statements which Fathers, Councils, Doctors, and Commentators, do little more than repeat; statements which the author of the "View" must be aware are as well known, as cordially received, and as earnestly loved by the signers of the Protest as by himself; statements which are familiar to the ordinary readers of the Bible, and, with a full knowledge of which, they will be able to say, whether, on the whole, the Bible leaves on their minds the impression that it is, in principle and spirit, a Pro-slavery Bible or an Anti-slavery Bible, *a Bible approving or condemning such slavery as "is maintained in the Southern States?"*

As the "Christian Bishop" has taken some pains to define his position and his personal relation, present and past, to the subject in hand, I may, perhaps, be allowed to indulge in a little egotism also. Let me say, then, that I have always rejected the extreme doctrines of the ultra abolitionists, and in former times have earnestly contended against their practical aims and measures,—but in respect to the practical question, times have now changed; when slaveholders professed to fear the knife at their own throats, it was one thing; when they aim the knife at mine and my country's, it is another. I have never belonged to an abolition society, or gone to hear an abolition lecture, or read Uncle Tom; but have clung to the Church, heard the Gospel, and studied the Bible. I had never before the rebellion preached an abolition sermon, and I have never published a pamphlet on the subject of slavery; but I have always exercised the elective franchise according to the dictates of my conscience and as a solemn duty I owed to my country. Nor do I see how any American citizen of Christian principles can consider it a matter of boast that he never voted at an election;—unless he means that, if he had voted, he would have voted wrong; in that case, and only in that case, were it certainly better for him not to have voted at all. I have always accepted and adhered to the Federal Constitution and every provision contained in it, the fugitive slave clause so-called included; but I have always abominated the fugitive slave *law* and the insulting, barbarous, and unconstitutional features of its enactments. I have ever been an ardent friend of African Colonization, as an anti-slavery measure, and am so still. I know that some slaveholders supported it as a pro-slavery measure, as a means of amusing the anti-slavery philanthropists, and getting rid of the incumbrance of the free blacks:—whether the views of the "Christian Bishop," in his advocacy of Colonization, were more anti-slavery or pro-slavery, one may judge from his present position. But I never accepted the wild notion that African colonization was to put an end to American slavery by transporting all the blacks to Africa; my view has rather been that it would prove by a visible example that the blacks, notwithstanding all their alleged inferiority, are capable of governing themselves, developing industrial resources, educating themselves, elevating themselves, and making reasonable progress in civilization; and thus would prepare the way for the amelioration of the condition of the race on this side of the Atlantic. The example, I think, has already been developed, and the time has come for making the application of the ar-

7

gument, if it is to have any practical application at
all. But if, after all this, no minister or accredited
agent of this new negro state is to be allowed to
pollute the soil of our free republic, while they are
welcomed by other Christian governments; if we
are still to be told that negroes are an inferior race,
fitted only to be slaves, made to work under the lash,
that "God has wonderfully adapted them to their
condition," that the "curse of Ham" is upon them,
and that he who would aim at their liberation is
"contending with his Maker," opposing the "designs
of Providence, and blasphemously resisting the decrees and the express commands of the Eternal
Judge,"—if we are still to be told this by the colonizing slaveholders, and if the colonizing "servants of
Jesus Christ," and the colonizing "Christian Bishops"
are not only to sustain but to lead them forward in
such views,—what good is to be expected from African Colonization? And what credit should such
"servants of Jesus Christ" claim for their advocacy
of the Colonization scheme?

I am ready cordially to admit and fully believe
that there are, among those reckoned as slaveholders,
men incomparably superior to myself in Christian
spirit, in Christian character, in all the virtues and
graces which adorn the Christian heart;—men who
mourn over the evils and the wrongs of slavery with
unspeakable and desponding sadness; men who do
not hold or treat their slaves as slaves, but recognize
and love them as brethren; who care not only for
their bodies, but for their minds and souls, as they
who must give account; who would gladly see them
happily free; who are disposed to give them all the
instruction and preparation for freedom they can,

and to set them at liberty as soon as the laws of the State will allow it to be done consistently with their good,—men, in short, who detest the sentiments of the " Christian Bishop's" letter as cordially as do any of those who protested against it. And shall I condemn such men? By no means. I would as soon think of condemning the Christian martyrs.

If the legislature of any slaveholding State, instead of obstructing emancipation and aiming at the perpetuation and extension of slavery, encourages emancipation in all possible ways, and honestly aims at the eventual abolition of slavery, providing for its ultimate and gradual yet certain extinction, securing to the slave the rights of person, marriage, and property as far as possible in his present condition, and to the freedmen the means of mental, moral, social and religious improvement, — I should hardly call such a State any longer a slaveholding State; 1 should consider it in spirit, character, and purpose, a Free State. It would not be chargeable with the *moral* guilt of slavery. Or if it must be called a slaveholding State, I should not go out of my way to condemn such slaveholding as that. But where was there ever in the memory of man, a slaveholding State *with a government controlled by the slaveholding oligarchy,* whose legislation was of that character? Slavery, as it is in general " maintained in the Southern States," I hold, and have ever held, as a system, to be bad, morally bad,—not merely in extreme cases of abuse and outrage—but in its law, in its purpose, and in its use,—in its theory and in its practice.

While slavery beseechingly cried, " have patience with me and I will set all right as soon as possible," I was not disposed to take it by the throat. But slavery has changed her tone. "She was at first humble, then apologetic, then respectable, then justifiable, then necessary, then a blessing, then divinely appointed, then ambitious, then aggressive, then domineering, then insulting, then rebellious." Slavery is, at last, *established and sanctioned by the decree of the Eternal Judge and the distinct command of the Almighty, is a fundamental condition of the purest Christianity, and the highest civilization, and the true corner stone of a Christian State.*

Such is the new Gospel Slavery,—a Gospel preached now by " Christian Bishops," who ascribe its origin to Jesus Christ, and his apostles, its propagation to the Christian Church, and its constitutional establishment in this country to the fathers and founders of American freedom; and who denounce all its opposers as blasphemous atheists and anti-Christs.

Now it is a great mistake to suppose that there is no middle ground between these new gospellers and the " ultra-abolitionists."

" Slavery is a wrong and a sin ;" therefore, say the ultra-abolitionists, " it ought to be abolished universally, absolutely, and instantly—no compromise, no degrees, no delays, this very moment and everywhere." On the other hand, the new gospellers say, "it is manifest that this universal, absolute, and instantaneous abolition, is not required either by the Holy Scripture, by Christian doctrine, or by sound reason ; and *therefore* slavery is neither a wrong nor a sin." Now both parties are wrong, and both are right. They are both right in their premises and both wrong in their conclusion ; and the difficulty arises from the term " slavery" being used in different senses in the different propositions. In its

concrete and practical sense, in which slavery means
the denial of human rights to the slave, and the corresponding motive and purpose of the master, and
his corresponding treatment of the slave, it is a
wrong and a sin, if there be any such thing as wrong
or sin in human conduct, and ought universally,
absolutely, and instantly to be abolished. In the
sense in which slavery may mean a mere formal,
legal, and temporary relation existing for the good
of the slave and with a view to his preparation for
freedom, its universal, absolute and instant abolition
is not required by reason, scripture or humanity, and
it is neither a wrong nor a sin. But when the ultra-
abolitionist draws his conclusion, he means it must
be abolished in this latter sense, though his premise
is true only for the former sense, and when the new
gospeller says it is neither a wrong nor a sin, he
means in the former sense, though his premise is
true only in the latter.

But, says the New Gospeller, "slavery is one thing,
and the treatment of the slave is manifestly another
thing." To this I answer, I know of no slavery, I
am concerned about no slavery, under the sun, *ab-
stracted from treatment*. If the law makes the slave a
chattel, and his master treats him as a man and not
as a chattel, then he does not treat him *as a slave*.
If the law divests the slave of all rights, and his
master recognizes and respects all his rights and
claims, as a man and a brother, he does not treat him
as a slave. And when no men are treated *as slaves*,
slavery is virtually abolished; and this is the abolition which the New Testament expressly requires.
The New Testament does not meddle with the legislative functions of government; it issues no formal

7 *

commands to rulers. But if the slaveholding legislators do not intend to treat, or to authorize any
others to treat, any men as chattels, or to deprive
them of their natural rights as men, why retain such
laws on the statute book? Are there, were there
ever, on the face of the earth, any legislators so
stupid as that? Such laws, if they intend such results, are wrong; if not, they are unaccountably
foolish.

Whether slavery is a sin, will be further discussed
in an appropriate chapter. But what I have to insist
on now is, that, in this discussion, we have to do with
no abstractions, but with a concrete, practical thing.
Abstract slavery exists nowhere. Slavery is a *fact*,
and as a *fact* we have to deal with it. What we have
to do with is, moreover, the definite *fact* of "*slavery
as it is maintained in the Southern States.*"

As I have said, I have strongly objected heretofore
to the aims and measures and oftentimes intemperate
language of the ultra-abolitionists. But while I
earnestly opposed their doctrines and sentiments
and expressions, I as earnestly maintained, and still
maintain, their right of *free speech*, and in defending
it I should be ready to suffer any indignity or violence. I hold that every American has, and always
has had, the right to discuss the subject of slavery,
like any other moral or political question, to his
heart's content,—a right expressly guarantied to
him by the Constitution. Some men seem to think
that the only thing solemnly guarantied by the Constitution, and made absolutely sacred, is *property in
slaves*, and hence they are amazingly enamoured of
the Constitution. They had not until quite recently
discovered that Free Speech is guarantied also—

they never imagined it was guarantied to ultra-abolitionists, but they have at last discovered that it is guarantied to sympathizers with treason and rebellion. It was undoubtedly the intention of the slaveocracy, if they could have retained control of the government, utterly to stop the mouths of all prating abolitionists from one end of the Union to the other, that then they might hold their chattels in peace. I have myself been told to my face by one of their Northern abettors, a man of high political consideration, and at that time a Judge of a State Supreme Court, "Sir, you have no right to lecture about slavery, you have no right to print about slavery, you have no right to preach about slavery, you have no right to talk about slavery, you have no right to think about slavery—it is a crime." He said "about," but of course meant "against." This was just before the Southern rebellion burst out.

I have no doubt that if the deliberate designs of the slavocrats and their Northern allies could have been carried out, free America would soon have been the place, and the only place, on the face of the earth, where no anti-slavery man would have been allowed to wag his tongue, and where to condemn slavery would have been punished as "a crime." But it may be said, it is the reckless, violent, slanderous and outrageous language of the abolitionists that it was proposed to restrain. The Judge went further than that; and undoubtedly his Southern masters meant to make thorough work of it if they could. It ought not to be forgotten, however, that all the abusive, insulting, reckless and outrageous language did not come from the side of the abolitionists. On the contrary, they were far more than outdone by the fana-

tical virulence and studied insolence of their adversaries. Witness the following language of one of
their number who has been supposed to have been
really attached to the Union, and to have clung to
it to the last moment, Alexander H. Stephens, now
Vice-President of the so-called Confederate States,
then a member of Congress from Georgia. It is
from a speech which he delivered in the House of
Representatives upon the Kansas-Nebraska bill,
and I give it as reported in the newspapers at the
time. It is true, as the author published his corrected
speech in the Congressional Globe, it is considerably
softened and diluted; but it remains substantially
the same. "Well, gentlemen, you make a good deal
of clamour over the Nebraska measure, but it don't
alarm us at all. We have got used to that kind of
talk. You have threatened before, but you have
never performed. You have always caved in, and
you will again. You are a mouthing white-livered
set. Of course you will oppose the measure; we
expected that; but we don't care for your opposition. You will rail, but we don't care for your rail-
ing. You will hiss, but so do adders. We expect it
of adders, and we expect it of you. You are like
the devils that were pitched over the battlements
of heaven into hell. They set up a howl at their
discomfiture, and so will you. But their fate was
sealed, and so is yours. You *must submit* to the yoke,
but don't chafe. Gentlemen, we have got you in our
power. You tried to drive us to the wall in 1850,
but times are changed. * * * * You went a wooling,
and have come home fleeced. Don't be so impudent
as to complain. You will only be slapped in the face.
Don't resist. *You will only be lashed into obedience.*"

Now let the place, the time, the circumstances and the person be remembered; and then let us hear no more from pro-slavery men about the violent and abusive and *sectional* language of abolitionists.*

* Should the fact that this speech of Mr. Stephens is not, in these precise words, acknowledged by him in the text of the Congressional Globe, be alleged to prove that he did not utter these words on the floor of the House;—in the first place I think it does not prove the point; in the second place I refer the reader to the Congressional Globe, where he will find the speech, too much extended for insertion here, but containing the same matter and spirit which are condensed into the briefer form above cited; in the third place I find in the Congressional Globe itself a record of the following interruptions of Mr. Lovejoy of Illinois, when speaking in the House on Slavery, in the Session of 1860 :—

By Mr. Barksdale of Mississippi: "Order that blackhearted scoundrel and nigger-stealing thief to take his seat."

By Mr. Boyce, of South Carolina, addressing Mr. Lovejoy: "Then behave yourself."

By Mr. Gartrell, of Georgia, (in his seat): "The man is crazy."

By Mr. Barksdale, of Mississippi, again : "No, Sir, you stand there to-day an infamous, perjured villain."

By Mr. Ashmore, of South Carolina: "Yes, he is a perjured villain, and he perjures himself every hour he occupies a seat on this floor."

By Mr. Singleton, of Mississippi: "And a negro-thief into the bargain."

By Mr. Barksdale, of Mississippi, again: "I hope my colleague will hold no parley with that perjured negro-thief."

By Mr. Singleton, of Mississippi, again: "No, Sir, any gentleman shall have time, but not such a mean, despicable wretch as that."

By Mr. Martin, of Virginia: "And if you come among us, we will do with you as we did with John Brown—hang you as high as Haman. I say that as a Virginian."

I cannot forbear reminding the reader, that these very men,

It has been usual for many years past for South
Carolinians and slaveholders generally to decry and
disparage New England. Their venom and spite
against New England could never be sufficiently
vented. This bitter and virulent anti-New England
feeling has become a marked characteristic of the
rebellion, and very naturally commands the sympathy and imitation of all those who are at heart disposed to side with the rebels. But loyal men may
well stop and consider how far such petty sectional
antipathies can be encouraged or entertained, consistently with a patriotic regard for the Union of the
country. New England is loyal, thoroughly loyal;
will loyal men therefore cast her off and treat her
with contempt? New England may have boasted
of herself quite too much ; but, in the first place, she
really had something to boast of; and, in the second
place, *she does not envy or disparage others.* She rejoices
in the greatness and prosperity of the Empire State
of New York, and of her magnificent metropolis,
though they have both vastly outstripped her own
States and cities in the race of wealth and civic
grandeur. She rejoices in the noble history, the vast
resources, and the rapid growth of Pennsylvania; and
makes her pilgrimages to Independence Hall. She
looks upon the other States as but parts of her common country ; and she shares in their prosperity and
renown. She has no jealousy or contempt for any
State in the Union. Even the great men of South
Carolina she has been accustomed to regard as her

who were thus insolently accusing Mr. Lovejoy of "perjury,"
were, notwithstanding their solemn oaths to support the Constitution of the United States, plotting treason and secession then,
and had been plotting it for years !

own. And Washington, the Virginian, she reveres, and will ever revere, with filial regard, as the purest and noblest name in a history which she is proud to share in as the history of her country. New England may boast of herself, but it is not her habit to detract from others. She may have her faults in her past history and in her present character; and happy the State which has none, or even which has no greater. But for a New England Bishop to join in the crusade against New England, in the effort to heap contempt upon New England, is peculiarly odious. It is an ill bird that fouls its own nest. To decry the Puritans is not enough to make a good churchman; and to decry New England will not suffice to make a generous and patriotic American. But, perhaps, it could hardly be expected that an "Irishman" should have any appreciation of the old Puritans, or of the Puritan stock. For myself, I claim to be a Yankee, the son of a Yankee, and the grandson of a Yankee,—a Yankee to the backbone; and if there are any among us who, in the face of traitors and rebels, are ashamed for their loyalty to be called Yankees, I am sorry for it. Any name is an honour which distinguishes me from the enemies of my country.

The "Christian Bishop" fights the "*Ultra*-Abolitionists" as he calls them, and would seem disposed to claim to be himself an abolitionist. I also disclaim the positions of the "ultra-abolitionist," and might seem to occupy substantially the same ground as he. But the difference is as great as that between the twilight of the morning and the twilight of the evening. The tendencies are contrary. We may stand on the same ground, but he looks one way, and I look the other; he looks against emancipation and in favour of slavery; I look against slavery and in favour of emancipation. The same premises may be so arrayed and used as to lead to opposite conclusions. It is said that on a certain occasion, Mr. Pitt being about to make a speech on Indian affairs, and directing his secretary to prepare for him the statistics relating to the subject, the secretary asked: " On which side does your Lordship desire the argument to come out ?"

But while I contend for ultimate abolition, I will not say how rapidly, in a normal condition of things, the process of emancipation ought to go on. Nor must I be understood to maintain that the negroes should be placed at once upon a social and political equality in all respects with the whites. Personal liberty and other civil rights, as the rights of marriage, of property, of contracts, are one thing; and the elective franchise is another. The elective franchise is a matter of public expediency, not of private right. Multitudes of free Englishmen, not to say the mass of free Europeans, possess no elective franchise. Social position and intercourse must be settled, not by legislation, or as a matter of proper right, but by the prevailing spirit and habits of society, the tastes and preferences of individuals. Only give the negro an open field, a fair opportunity; and then let him have whatever he can earn; whatever he shows himself worthy of, let him be allowed to receive. As to amalgamation, *miscegenation*, and that stuff, which so provokes the pretended horror of some persons, the surest way to stop it completely is to emancipate the slaves at once. That these processes are going on much more rapidly among the domestic slaves than among the free blacks, let the children's faces testify.

The "Christian Bishop" claims to be an abolitionist; but nobody will call him so. The abolitionists will not claim him. The slaveholders will not denounce him. I expect to be denounced as a Yankee and an abolitionist, with all the terms of obloquy, spite and odium, contempt, contumely and cursing, which the friends of slavery are accustomed to connect with those names. It has long been their well known policy to undermine the social position, degrade the character, and bring into disrepute and contempt the names, of all their earnest and outspoken opponents. I am prepared for it all. The "View of Slavery" may serve as a somewhat dignified and reticent specimen of the insolence and abuse in which they are prone to indulge. But the insolence and abuse are nothing to me. The doctrine itself is the main thing. And it is with a sense of unspeakable humiliation and sadness that I find such doctrines as constitute this new gospel of slavery—promulgated by a "Christian Bishop" in the nineteenth century of the Christian era. Let us humbly pray that they may be retracted by their author for his own sake; or, at least, that the overdose may prevent any pernicious effects upon others.

8

CHAPTER IV.

SLAVERY AND THE SCRIPTURES.

ONE of the stereotyped methods by which the apologists and eulogists of slavery have always endeavoured to bring odium on their opponents, has been, to class them with rationalists, infidels, and atheists. So the Southern Bishops in their so-called Pastoral Letter. So the "View of Slavery." In several places the effort is made, and in one chapter, systematically made, to associate the opponents of slavery with those who say, " down with a pro-slavery Bible," and particularly with Emerson and Parker, and men of similar Theological proclivities. Now it is a curious fact that it is precisely the New Gospellers and not the Christian anti-slavery men, who agree with that school of rationalists and infidels, and continually play into their hands. The "View of Slavery" *adopts the premises* of the Infidel, and then denies his conclusion. *The anti-slavery men deny both.* The Infidel says, " the Bible sanctions slavery; then the Bible is not the word of God." The " View of Slavery" says, " the Bible sanctions slavery; but the Bible is the word of God." The anti-slavery Christian says, " the Bible does not sanction slavery; and the Bible is the word of God." But so long as you give the Infidel his premise he will infallibly draw his conclusion; and, until the

(86)

reason and conscience of men can be remodelled, he
will succeed in leading multitudes more to draw the
same conclusion. Neither the Infidel nor the New
Gospeller could assume a more damaging concession
or make a more calumnious and blasphemous charge
against the Bible than this :—that it is a pro-slavery
Bible, that it sanctions holding one's fellow men as
chattels, that it authorizes slavery "as it is maintained in the Southern States," in the Cotton States,
and in States where men and women are systematically bred for the market as a staple product. Let
this point be yielded, let this charge be established,
and infidelity exults in the confidence of a speedy
and certain triumph—a confidence not unfounded.
But it may be said, if it be really true that the Bible
sanctions slavery, we are bound as Christians not to
deny the fact or pervert the Scriptures, but humbly
to bow to their instructions. Yes, if this be really
true; but that is a question of fact, and as a question
of fact, it should be investigated candidly, dispas-
sionately, and impartially ; and no odium should attach to the conclusion reached on the one side or
the other. And, in like manner, the infidel's conclusion also, "that the Bible is not the word of God,"
if it be true, ought to be admitted, and no odium
should attach to its admission or assertion. But, if as a
Christian I may shrink with horror from the infidel's
conclusion, so as a Christian I may detest the infidel's
premise, especially when I see it put forward and
peremptorily insisted on by a professed "servant of
Jesus Christ" in the interest of such an abominable
and effete institution as American chattel slavery,
and in utter disregard of the odium and infamy thus
heaped upon the Christian religion.

The "View of Slavery," like the "Letter" to which
it is a sequel, makes the "curse of Canaan" one of
its principal arguments. It first recurs to the original position, that the "curse of Canaan" was intended
for all the posterity of Ham, and makes an effort to
impose this dogma upon all Episcopalians by the
authority of Bishop Newton, as though, because the
House of Bishops have prescribed "Newton on the
Prophecies" as a part of the course of study for
Theological students, therefore all good churchmen
were bound to accept every interpretation and suggestion of Newton as infallible truth, even though
it might eventually be found to involve palpable
falsehoods or horrible and blasphemous consequences;
all which the good Bishop, in his simplicity, never
dreamt of. Even if history had shown it to be true
of all the descendants of Ham that they have been
slaves to the posterity of Shem and Japheth, this
would not prove that Noah predicted it. And then,
what shall we say to Nineveh, and Babylon, and
Phenicia, and Egypt? These all belonged to Ham's
descendants; but were they servants to Shem and
Japheth? Were they not rather the first conquerors
of the world, the founders of commerce and letters
and arts and civilization, and the teachers of mankind? Nimrod, a son of Cush, was probably the first
man who enacted the petty tyrant, and held his fellow men as his slaves. But the author of the "View
of Slavery" seems at length to have seen reason to
distrust this his former interpretation, an interpretation which would require the original Hebrew text
of our Bibles to be changed, without the slightest
authority except that of one solitary version; and
which has against it almost all the critical learning

of the world. He resorts to another theory, of which, so far as appears, he has the credit of being the author. It is, that *the Africans are the descendants of Canaan himself.* For, in the exuberance of his Christian and Episcopal charity, he is determined, at all hazards, that the poor negroes shall be accursed. If the curse cannot be brought to bear upon them in one way, he will try another. And the way attempted is very curious.

1. "Canaan had eleven sons,—more than either of his brothers; therefore his descendants must be presumed to have been more numerous than those of either of them; and probably they went and settled in Africa."—But Isaac had two sons, and Jacob had twelve; were therefore the descendants of Jacob more numerous than those of Isaac? Benjamin had ten sons, Judah three, and Dan one; were these the proportional numbers of their posterity in the wilderness, and afterwards in the times of Samuel and David? The Benjamites were at one time very few in Israel; had the balance probably gone to Africa?

2. "The Bible accounts for but seven tribes or nations of the Canaanites who were to be destroyed by the children of Israel in the promised land; leaving four more to be accounted for, who, with the remnants that escaped of the seven, probably went to Africa."—But Sidon and Hamath are among the four, and they are accounted for as well known places; while Sodom and Gomorrah, and the cities of the plain, may well account for the other two, without going to Africa. It is true that from Sidon came Tyre, and Tyre sent a colony to Africa. But there is no reason to suppose—rather the contrary—

8 *

that the Carthaginians, who were descendants of Canaan, were, or ever became, African negroes. Or, if Hannibal were of the race of African negroes, then history has shown us one man of this negro race who exhibited no small degree of intellectual ability. Any nation might count itself happy if, in its hour of need, it could be sure of finding among the foremost of its sons, a military genius equal to the son of Hamilcar.

3. "Abulfaragi says that, in the division of the earth made in the time of Peleg, Palestine was assigned to Shem, and India and Africa to Ham.— This division was made by divine authority, and has the force of a divine appointment.—The families of the Canaanites were spread abroad; but they did not hold Canaan as their land in the time of Abraham; but Moses calls it 'the land of Canaan' at that time by way of anticipation. Melchizedek, a priest of the most high God, and who probably was no other than the patriarch Shem himself, was king of Salem at that time. Many of the Canaanites who were in the land at the time of Joshua's invasion probably escaped and wandered abroad.—Therefore the Canaanites probably 'spread themselves abroad' in Africa."

Now the division of the earth in the time of Peleg may have been by divine appointment under the direction of Noah; but Abulfaragi was not there as the clerk of that court; and it is only a piece of deception, not intended, I presume, to represent that the division as described by Abulfaragi was made by divine appointment. On the contrary we have an authentic record of this division on the authority of divine inspiration in the 10th chapter of Genesis,

wherein Palestine is expressly assigned to the Canaanites, and not a word is said about India—at
least as far as we know. " The families of the Canaanites were spread abroad, and the border of the
Canaanites was from Sidon, as thou comest to Gerar
and Gaza; as thou goest unto Sodom and Gomorrah,
and Admah and Zeboim, even unto Lasha." So runs
the text. And this unquestionably was very nearly
the boundary of what we call Palestine. But the
author of the " View" has a very simple device for
removing out of his way the difficulty arising from
this text. In the original, says he, the word for
border is without the definite article; it should be
translated, therefore, " *a* border of the Canaanites,"
and not " *the* border of the Canaanites." If this were
so, it does not appear how it would hinder that the
Canaanites should have possessed Palestine—Abulfaragi to the contrary notwithstanding. But what
the author expects to gain by this device is, to leave
the doors open for the Canaanites to spread elsewhere, viz., into Africa. But in truth the device
itself is one of the most astonishing pieces of grammatical criticism that ever proceeded from the pen
of a learned Bishop. Why, every tyro in Hebrew
syntax knows that the Hebrew article is regularly
omitted—its force being implied—in constructions
similar to that in question, *i. e.*, before substantives
rendered definite by a following genitive; as, " the
word of God," " the border of Canaan,"—unless the
substantive, having occurred before, is repeated.
The instances in illustration are innumerable. I select a few, and these exclusively connected with the
use of this particular Hebrew word for " border :"
Joshua xiii. 23, " the border of the children of Reu-

ben," and "the border thereof;" xv. 1, "the border
of Edom;" xvi. 5, "the border of the children of
Ephraim," twice; xvii. 8, "the border of Manasseh;"
also in xix. 10, xviii. 25, xxxiii. 41, &c. &c. Now in all
these cases the Hebrew has no article, and in all but
one the Septuagint has it, as well as the English.
Such are the facts. What then can it mean that a
learned Theologian, an astute and practised polemic,
a Doctor of divinity, a Bishop of the Church, should
gravely tell his confiding readers that, as the article
is omitted before the Hebrew word for *border*, it
should be translated "*a* border" instead of "*the* border?" Did he learn this new rule of the Hebrew
article from "reading newspapers and novels," or
from conning his Hebrew "Bible?" Will he, peradventure, prove it by the authority of the Early
Fathers? Is he really ignorant of the first principles of the language in which he undertakes to offer
his magisterial criticisms, or ——? It is most charitable to adopt the former alternative.—And thus
the Canaanites are left in Palestine, in spite of Abulfaragi; and shut up there too, in spite of the absence
of the Hebrew article from their "border." How
are they to spread into Africa?

If Palestine was not called "the land of Canaan"
in Abraham's time, it certainly was so called some
hundred years afterwards; for Joseph's brethren expressly describe themselves as coming from "the
land of Canaan," (Genesis lxii., &c.); and could not
have called it so by *anticipation*. Moreover, when
Abraham was there, "the Canaanite was then in the
land," and the cities of the plain were cities of the
Canaanites; and we are told on good authority that
Abraham did not have possession of it,—even if it

had been assigned to Shem,—" for God gave him none inheritance in it, no not so much as to set his foot on." And when Sarah died, Abraham found himself without even a spot of his own wherein to bury his dead; and he purchased a lot for a burying place—of whom ?—of the sons of Heth, who was a son of Canaan. The story of the purchase presents a most exquisite picture of primitive and patriarchal courtesy and gentleness, on the one side and on the other. Nothing can exceed the dignified self-respect of one party, the kindly sympathy of the other, and the gentlemanly politeness of both. Abraham evidently had not got into his head the idea that these sons of Heth were an utterly accursed race.

As for Melchizedek, king of Salem, after all is said, there is nothing whatever beyond the sheerest conjecture and *petitio principii*, to show that he was not, as his residence would indicate, and as Dr. Hales thought, a Canaanite. I can easily conceive the horror that any contemner of negroes and retailer of the " curse of Ham" must feel, at the suggestion that he who was greater than the patriarch Abraham, and to whom the patriarch paid tithes, was a veritable descendant of Ham, an accursed Canaanite. Yet on the face of the history, this would seem the most likely conclusion; and it is confirmed by the fact that in Joshua's time the name of the king of *Jerusalem* was *Adonizedek*, meaning "lord of righteousness." The similarity of this name to Melchizedek, " king of righteousness," is striking and suggestive, — the more so, if the commonly received conjecture be well founded, that Salem and Jerusalem were the same place. Still it must be admitted, not only in respect to this but to all other conjectures as to Melchizedek's kindred, that, in fact, the Scripture leaves him without assigning father or mother, genealogy, birth or death.

Let Melchizedek therefore pass. It will hardly be denied that Rahab the harlot was a Canaanitess; and, if she was, then some of the Canaanitish blood flowed in the veins of our Blessed Lord—one of the accursed race was his mother. What more horrible than that? Moreover, it seems that Judah married a Canaanitish woman; and that it was only the severest Divine threatenings that could stay the frequent intermarriages of the Israelites with the tribes of Canaan. If the Canaanites were indeed negroes, the antipathy of colour and the horror of amalgamation seem not to have arisen at that early period.

Of any wandering abroad of the Canaanites who escaped the sword of Joshua, there is not the slightest mention or intimation in the Scripture. We might admit, however, that some of them may have taken refuge at Sidon or among the Philistines; but that they peopled Africa, except as a few perhaps among the Carthaginian colonists, is a pure fable, as sheer and original an invention as the new rule for the use of the Hebrew article.

And thus, whether the negroes are the descendants of Ham or Shem, it cannot be shown either that the curse of Canaan attached to any of the other posterity of Ham, or that the negroes are descended from Canaan himself. Neither of these propositions has any reasonable degree of evidence or of probability. And if either or both of them *were* true, it would not reach the point in question, which is, whether the Southerners are justified in holding the negroes in slavery. Now, even though the negroes were cursed ten times over, it would not follow that we or anybody else should have a right to make them our slaves, and thus fulfil the curse.

God had threatened Israel and Judah with punishment and captivity. Was, therefore, the king of Assyria justified in destroying the kingdom of Israel and desolating Judea? God himself declares that he will punish him for these very deeds of pride and cruelty, because, while he thus fulfilled God's righteous purpose, "yet he meant not so, neither did his heart think so, but it was in his heart to destroy and cut off nations not a few." Isa. x. 5-15.

Many fearful curses were denounced by Moses against the Israelites, in case they should forsake their God. Were European Christians therefore justified in fulfilling them by the cruel and inhuman oppression of the Jews in the middle ages? Joshua cursed the rebuilder of Jericho, saying :-"Cursed be the man before the Lord, that riseth up and buildeth this city Jericho : he shall lay the foundation thereof in his first born, and in his youngest son shall he set up the gates of it." Would any man, therefore, have been justified, who should have taken it into his head, either wantonly, or from malice or selfishness, to murder the sons of the man whom he might see rebuilding that city? Clearly not; and neither is the " curse of Ham," or the " curse of Canaan," whatever it may have meant, and to whomsoever it may have applied, any authority or justification for " slavery as it is maintained in the Southern States."

But an argument is drawn for its justification from the example of Abraham and the provisions of the Mosaic law. Before examining the validity of this argument, let us see more exactly what it is which

is to be thus justified. What is Southern slavery?
Let it answer for itself, and let the answer be in the
words of the unanimous decision of the Supreme
Court of North Carolina, solemnly delivered by
Judge Ruffin, in 1829 :

" The question before the Court has indeed been
assimilated at the bar to the other domestic relations; and arguments drawn from the well established principles which confer and restrain the authority of the parent over the child, the tutor over
the pupil, the master over the apprentice, have been
pressed on us. The Court does not recognize their
application. There is no likeness between the cases.
They are in opposition to each other, and there is
an impassable gulf between them. The difference
is that which exists between freedom and slavery,
and a greater cannot be imagined. In the one, the
end in view is the happiness of the youth, born to
equal rights with that governor. . . . With slavery it
is far otherwise. The end is the profit of the master,
his security, and the public safety ; the subject, one
doomed in his own person and his posterity, to live
without knowledge, and without the capacity to
make anything his own, and to toil that another
may reap the fruits. . . . The obedience of the slave
is the consequence only of *uncontrolled authority over
the body. . . . The power of the master must be absolute,
to render the submission of the slave perfect.* I must
freely confess my sense of the harshness of this proposition. I feel it as deeply as any man can. And
as a principle of moral right, every man in his retirement must repudiate it. But in the actual condition of things it must be so. There is no remedy.

This discipline belongs to the state of slavery. It is inherent in the relation of master and slave."

There you have Southern slavery, in its true character, *in puris naturalibus*, as depicted by its own hand. All those analogies—as that of husband and wife, parent and child, tutor and pupil, master and apprentice, master and servant,—by which the advocates of slavery so often sophistically attempt to hide its deformity, to soften down its inhuman and immoral features, or to throw dust into the eyes of those who are looking to see what it is, are here formally and authoritatively, — and I must add, honestly,—cast off and utterly rejected. "There is no likeness between the cases; there is an impassable gulf between them," says the Court. Yes, "an impassable gulf," — the same difference as between paradise and hell. Slavery is a thing *sui-generis*. Now let the moralist look at it, and say whether such an institution is right and just, or whether it is a wrong and a sin. Let the Christian look at it, and say whether he can believe that such a system is consistent with the principles of the gospel of Jesus Christ. Yet such is slavery, as *"maintained"*—maintained by law,—in North Carolina; and the same principles are adopted, more or less expressly, in all the other slave States. "As a principle of moral right," says the North Carolina Judge, "every person in his retirement must repudiate it." But, says the "Christian Bishop," "it is fully authorized by both the Old and the New Testament;" and, from his retirement in Vermont, he is ready to anathematize all those who protest against such a sentiment.

Compare such slavery, with the kind of servitude exemplified in the following scene from the history of

9

Abraham: "And Abraham was old and well stricken in age: and the Lord had blessed Abraham in all things. And Abraham said unto his eldest servant in his house, that ruled over all that he had, Put, I pray thee, thy hand under my thigh: And I will make thee swear by the Lord, the God of heaven, and the God of the earth, that thou shalt not take a wife unto my son of the daughters of the Canaanites among whom I dwell: But thou shalt go unto my country, and to my kindred, and take a wife unto my son Isaac." Genesis xxiv. 1–4. "And the servant took ten camels, of the camels of his master, and departed; (for all the goods of his master were in his hand;) and he arose, and went to Mesopotamia, unto the city of Nahor. And he made his camels to kneel down without the city by a well of water, at the time of the evening, even the time that women go out to draw water. And he said, O Lord, God of my master Abraham, I pray thee, send me good speed this day, and show kindness unto my master Abraham. Behold, I stand here by the well of water; and the daughters of the men of the city come out to draw water. And let it come to pass, that the damsel to whom I shall say, Let down thy pitcher, I pray thee, that I may drink; and she shall say, drink, and I will give thy camels drink also: let the same be she that thou hast appointed for thy servant Isaac; and thereby shall I know that thou hast showed kindness unto my master." Genesis xxiv. 10-14.

If Judge Ruffin has defined what slavery is, most certainly St Chrysostom was right in saying that Abraham did not treat his domestics *as slaves.*

As to Hebrew servitude under the Mosaic law, not

much need be added to what has been already said. The author of the "View" tells us that "the Jewish doctors have the best right to be heard in the interpretation of their own law." Of the precept, in Deut. xxiii. 15, 16, against returning fugitive slaves, Maimonides observes: "Beside the act of mercy, it has this further beneficial result—that it teaches us to accustom ourselves to virtuous and praiseworthy actions, not only by succouring those who have sought our aid and protection, and not delivering them into the hands of those from whom they have fled, but also by promoting their comfort, doing them all manner of kindness, and not injuring or grieving them even in word." How different this from the spirit of one who cautions us against listening to the stories of fugitives, or showing them any sympathy! Which spirit would most become "a servant of Jesus Christ?"

The wisest and best among the Jews have been accustomed to construe the Mosaic code as, in spirit, forbidding slavery. "Our sages," says Maimonides, "ordered us to make the poor and orphans our domestics, instead of employing slaves. . . . Every one who increases his slaves does day by day *increase sin and iniquity in the world.*"

The Rabbi Mielziner, one of the best modern Jewish authorities, says: "No religion and no legislation of ancient times could, in its inmost spirit, be so decidedly opposed to slavery, as was the Mosaic; a religion which so sharply emphasizes the high dignity of man as a being made in the image of God, a legislation based upon that very idea of man's worth, and which, in all its enactments, insisted not only upon the highest justice, but also upon the ten-

derest pity and forbearance, especially towards the
necessitous and unfortunate; a people, in fine, which
had itself smarted under the yoke of slavery, and
had become a nation only by emancipation, would
necessarily be solicitous to do away wherever it was
practicable with the unnatural state of slavery, by
which human nature is degraded." It is remarkable
that the beautifully humane and gentle features
which abound in the Mosaic institutions, and which
are thus urged by the Jewish Rabbi to show that a
law of such a spirit cannot be supposed to authorize
such a system as slavery, slavery proper, modern
chattel slavery, Judge Ruffin's slavery,—the very
same exquisitely refined and delicate touches of
kindly sentiment are alleged by the "Christian
Bishop" to show that such a law having authorized
slavery, slavery cannot be so very harsh and inhuman a thing! Suppose he should undertake to prove
to me from the word of God that there is no pain in
the toothache; should I believe him while my head
was throbbing with the agony? or should I not
rather as a good Christian—not to say a pious Jew—
presume that his interpretation of God's word must
somehow or other be wrong?

According to the current tradition, the Greek
translation of the Old Testament, called the Septuagint, was made by seventy-two of the most learned
of the Jewish elders in the time of Ptolemy Phila-
delphus. If, therefore, the authority of Jewish doctors
is to be regarded, that of the Septuagint must be
allowed great weight in determining the proper
meaning of the original text in relation to the matter
in hand. Now the Septuagint version does not re-

cognize Hebrew servitude *as slavery at all*, either in the case of Hebrew or foreign servants.

The original Hebrew word for "servant," as I have said, means etymologically *a labourer;* and has a variety of applications,—to slaves, to bondmen from other nations, to Hebrew bondmen, to household servants, to waiting men and women (especially young), to the ministers and officers of kings, &c., to the priests, prophets, ministers and worshippers of God. Its proper meaning, therefore, is expressed, not by the specific term *slave*, but by the general term *servant*.

The force of this statement would not be diminished if, in the tenth commandment and throughout the Pentateuch, the Septuagint had used, for this Hebrew word, the stronger, but still *general*, Greek term, meaning etymologically *bondman*. Indeed this is what we should naturally have expected them to do.* The reader will find, however, in the note be-

---

* But this they have not done. It is remarkable that, in their version of the Pentateuch,—while they have freely used the Greek δουλος as the translation of the Hebrew *Ebed*, when referring to Egyptian bondage, or to bond-servants among the heathen,— they have always employed παις (boy, lad, garçon) or παιδισκη (girl, maid) or οικετης (domestic) when referring to the servants of the Hebrews, whether of foreign or of Hebrew origin, and never δουλος or δουλη. To this I have found but one, and that only an *apparent*, exception. It occurs in Lev. xxv. 44, 46. "Both thy bondmen and thy bondmaids which thou shalt have, shall be of the heathen that are round about you; of them shall ye buy bondmen and bondmaids." (46.) "And ye shall take them as an inheritance for your children after you to inherit them for a possession; they shall be your bondmen forever."

Here, in verse 44, "bondmen and bondmaids," in the first clause, are παιδες and παιδισκαι, and, in the last clause, after "buy,"

9*

low, the evidence from which it will appear.that the Septuagint regarded Hebrew servitude as of a peculiarly mild type; that is, in their judgment, there

they are δουλοι and δουλαι. But this exception only proves the rule; for it plainly proceeds upon the implication that they have been the servants of others before, and are bought as being already δουλοι and δουλαι. In verse 46 they are called neither παιδες nor δουλοι, but κατοχοι, which simply regards them as a confirmed possession. It is moreover observable that the Septuagint, in conformity with the etymology of the original word, very frequently use εργα instead of δουλεια for bondage, even for Egyptian bondage; —thus in Ex. i. 14, &c., &c., we have, for "hard bondage," εργα σκληρα—"hard works,"· or "hard labour."

It is true that, when the Septuagint have translated the Hebrew word for "serve" by a *verb*, they have commonly employed δουλευω, when the service was paid to *men*, (and another word when it was paid to God.) But this is apparently for want of any softer *verb* in the Greek language appropriate to their purpose. Thus, Gen. xv. 13, "Thy seed shall serve them four hundred years;" Gen. xxv. 23, "The elder shall serve the younger," [where *slavery* is not meant]; Gen. xxix. 18, "I will serve thee seven years for Rachel." In verse 27, this service is called by Laban εργασια ; and, in Gen. xxx. 26, it is called by Jacob δουλεια;—it being presumed by the translators that Laban would be disposed to extenuate, and Jacob to magnify its hardship. Ex. xxi. 2, "A Hebrew servant, παις, shall serve, δουλευσει, six years," So Deut. xv. 12. Lev. xxv. 39, "Thou shalt not compel him to serve as a bondservant," —ου δουλευσει σοι δουλειαν οικετου. But in verse 40, they have returned to the etymology of the original word. "He shall serve εργᾶται— (work for) thee, unto the Jubilee." It is hardly necessary to add that, in the tenth commandment, the Septuagint always use, not δουλος and δουλη, but παις and παιδισκη. In the "curse of Canaan," also, they translate by παις, οικετης, and not δουλος.

It is not intended here to intimate that παις is never applied in Greek to designate a slave, but it is a milder term than δουλος,— just as, in English, man, or lad, or servant, is a milder term than slave,—and as such was chosen by the Septuagint to indicate the milder character of Hebrew servitude or domesticity.

was, properly speaking, no such thing at all as Hebrew *slavery*, certainly no such slavery as that char-
acterized by Judge Ruffin. It should be called, not
even Hebrew *servitude*, but rather Hebrew *domesticity*.

By the law of Moses, the murder of a servant was
punished, and the punishment for murder was death.
As much might be said for the laws of the Southern
States; but all such nominal protection of personal
rights becomes a practical nullity and a mockery,
since no evidence of slaves or of blacks is admitted
against a white person.

By the law of Moses the testimony of servants was
valid; at least, no exceptions are made to the precept
that the testimony of two men is true. And if any
of the Jewish doctors have held a different view, it
has been under the influence of the prejudices and
customs of the Roman law.

The Hebrew law treated the servant as a person,
and vindicated for him the rights of a husband and
a father. But, after the precedent of the Roman
legislation, a slave's marriage, in the Southern States,
is, in law, a nullity; and, in practice, husbands are
sold away from their wives, children from their parents. There " the human cattle are bred like sheep
or swine for the market; in short, the whole system
is a standing defiance of nature and humanity."

The Hebrew servant had the Sabbath infallibly
secured to him for a day of complete rest. Not so
with the Southern slave. There may be some " law"
for it, but " no testimony" annuls it.

The Hebrew servants shared in the religious rites
and festivities of their masters. They were circumcised; they ate the passover, which no stranger or
hired man was allowed to touch. They took part,

side by side with their masters, in the most solemn acts of national worship. What an instructive picture is the following: "And thou shalt keep the feast of weeks unto the Lord thy God with a tribute of a free-will offering of thine hand, which thou shalt give unto the Lord thy God, according as the Lord thy God hath blessed thee. And thou shalt rejoice before the Lord thy God, thou, and thy son, and thy daughter, and thy man-servant, and thy maid-servant, and the Levite that is within thy gates, and the stranger, and the fatherless, and the widow, that are among you, in the place which the Lord thy God hath chosen to place his name there. And thou shalt remember that thou wast a bondman in Egypt: and thou shalt observe and do these statutes. Thou shalt observe the feast of tabernacles seven days, after that thou hast gathered in thy corn, and thy wine. And thou shalt rejoice in thy feast, thou, and thy son, and thy daughter, and thy man-servant, and thy maid-servant, and the Levite, the stranger, and the fatherless, and the widow that are within thy gates: seven days shalt thou keep a solemn feast unto the Lord thy God in the place which the Lord shall choose: because the Lord thy God shall bless thee in all thy increase; and in all the works of thine hands, therefore thou shalt surely rejoice. Three times in a year shall *all thy males* appear before the Lord thy God in the place which he shall choose; in the feast of unleavened bread, and in the feast of weeks, and in the feast of tabernacles: *and they shall not appear before the Lord empty: Every man* shall give as he is able, according to the blessing of the Lord thy God which he hath given thee." Deut. xvi. 10–17.

"The bondman came up to stand with the freeman

before the Lord. The gift of the bondman"—and it seems he could have something of his own to give—"was mingled with that of the freeman, and was equally accepted. Perfect religious equality was thus proclaimed, and that in a commonwealth of which religion was the foundation, and of which Jehovah was king. No cruel division of classes, no aristocratic pride on one side, or degradation on the other," not to say chattel-slavery,—"could well hold its ground against such a law." Compare this picture with that drawn by Judge Ruffin, and say whether the law of Moses "fully authorizes slavery as it is maintained in the Southern States." In the words of Cochin: by the Mosaic code, "the servant could have recourse to the law for all wrongs; his testimony was received; he could hold property and redeem himself; he was instructed; his rights were respected. No slave-trade, no fugitive slave law, no enslaving of natives; a year of Jubilee; the purity of women, the weakness of childhood, the rights of manhood placed under the provident protection of the law; equality professed, fraternity preached. Such was Hebrew servitude. Let the partisans of modern slavery cease to seek arguments from it; let them rather pattern after it."

But, in fact, whatever may have been the character of the bondage in which the Israelites were allowed by the Mosaic code to hold persons from the nations round about them,—it does not follow from it that under the new dispensation, and under the circumstances of the present time, we are authorized to hold our fellow men even in similar bondage. In connexion with this proposition, two points remain which I have promised further to examine. The first is, the common brotherhood of mankind under the Christian dispensation; the second is, the analogy of the law of divorce.

As to the first point, I understand the author of the " View" stoutly and earnestly to deny it;—and well he may, if he is to find any support for his pro-slavery position in the Mosaic code; for, otherwise, the service of Hebrew to Hebrew would be the *extreme* precedent of the service now authorized between man and man; and that was neither " a servitude for life" nor " a servitude descending to the offspring,"— not to speak of chattelism or of the slavery of Judge Ruffin. This is a vital point. We do well to examine it carefully. Says the author of the " View," " nothing can be more false than the assertion that Christianity has made the heathen *savage* any more *our* brother than he was the brother of the Jew under the Mosaic dispensation." May not one be pardoned for expressing his amazement and mortification that such a sentiment should be uttered by a Christian Bishop? Can it be in the spirit of him who said: "Go ye into all the world and preach the Gospel to every creature?" of him " who *hath broken down the middle wall of partition,* having abolished in his flesh the *enmity* even the law of commandments contained in ordinances . . . . . having slain the *enmity* by his cross, and came and preached *peace* to them who were *afar off* and to them that were nigh?" If it be said that " Christian brotherhood is by no means denied, but that Christian brotherhood is a brotherhood in the Christian Church, and not a brotherhood of humanity,— that this latter is left just as it was under the Mosaic economy;" I answer in the words of St. Peter: " Ye

know that it is an unlawful thing for a man that is a
Jew to keep company or come unto one of another
nation; but God hath showed me that I should not
call any man common or unclean." As I look upon
the savage and remember that Christ died for him—
that he was purchased by the same blood whereby
my soul was redeemed,—shall I regard him no more
as my brother, than, by the Mosaic law, the Jew was
taught to regard him as *his?**

" Thou shalt love thy neighbour as thyself." But
who *is* my neighbour? This is the question. The
Jew found him only in his brother Jew. But our
Lord told the Jew that the hated Samaritan was his
neighbour;—told us that whoever is suffering, oppressed, or in want, is our neighbour, if we can reach
him with our aid. Thus he established the common
neighbourhood, if not the common *brotherhood* of mankind. And if it be said that this is but an interpretation of a previously existing law, in its original
sense, and no enlargement of that original sense, I
answer that it could not have been so understood in
the Mosaic code; for that code expressly makes distinctions between Hebrew "servants" and foreign
" bondsmen;" so that, if both were equally *neighbours*, the Israelites were either required to love the
Hebrews more than themselves, or permitted to love

* As to "spiritual brotherhood,"—was there no "spiritual
brotherhood" under the old economy as well as under the new?
The difference is this: as the spiritual brotherhood of the old
economy was related to a worldly brotherhood confined to a single
tribe or people, so the spiritual brotherhood of the new economy
is related to the worldly brotherhood of all mankind. The Jewish
brotherhood was gathered from the Jews; the Christian brotherhood is gathered out of every nation and people under heaven.

the foreigners less. But even granting that the only change which Christianity wrought in this respect, was a change from the brotherhood of the Hebrew commonwealth to the brotherhood of the Christian church; what shall we say, after all, to *a Christian's holding his brother Christian in slavery, in perpetual bondage?* Is that fully authorized by the analogy of the Mosaic code?

When we allege that the Christian dispensation is an improvement upon the Mosaic, or that it does not follow that what was allowed under the Mosaic is also allowed under the Christian; and instance in proof our Lord's express abrogation of the Mosaic law of divorce;—the author of the " View" replies that that law of divorce was no part of the law of God, but that " Moses wrote it in his human discretion," while the law of slavery is of God's own positive enactment. How he ascertained this important fact, one is curious to know. Of the law of divorce our Lord had said: " For the hardness of your hearts Moses wrote you this precept." On this statement alone, as far as appears, his proposition rests for its verification. " Moses wrote you this precept;"—but does it follow that because *Moses* wrote it, God did not command it? It seems to me that a Christian who believes in the divine legation of Moses would infer just the contrary. " Moses wrote of me," said our Blessed Lord; are we therefore to presume that what he wrote was not by divine inspiration, but " in his human discretion ?" Did our Saviour or his apostles ever make a distinction between the writings of Moses and the word of God, between the law of Moses and the law of God? In St. Luke our Lord is represented as ascribing the words uttered at the burning bush to the authorship of Moses; in St. Matthew he ascribes them to God himself. Thus, unless there is other evidence from some other quarter to support the assumption that Moses wrote the precept of divorce "in his human discretion," the words of our Lord cannot be tortured into any authority for it, or even as giving any colour to it. If other evidence existed, it might then be possible that those words should be so interpreted. Is there any such evidence in the original text? In the fifth chapter of Deuteronomy, Moses rehearses the ten commandments, and adds: " These words the Lord spake unto all your assembly in the mount, out of the midst of the fire, of the cloud, and of the thick darkness, with a great voice : and he added no more : and he wrote them in two tables of stone, and delivered them unto me." The rest of the law, as Moses goes on to relate, was given not directly to the people, but through the mediation of Moses, so that if one chooses to make a distinction of dignity between the Decalogue and the rest of the Mosaic law, there may be some reason for it. But neither the law of divorce nor that of slavery is found in the ten commandments. No such distinction, however, can be taken in such a sense as that the rest of the law of Moses should not have been also the law of God. For as to the rest, Moses declares that God said to him : "As for thee, stand thou here by me, and I will speak unto thee all the commandments, and the statutes and the judgments, which thou shalt teach them, that they may do them in the land which I give them to possess it." " Ye shall observe to do, therefore," he adds, " as the Lord your God hath commanded you." Deut. v. 31, 32. Then in the sixth

10

chapter Moses goes on to say : " Now these are the commandments, the statutes, and the judgments, which the Lord your God commanded to teach you ;" whereupon he proceeds to lay down the law of supreme love to God, which our Saviour declares to be the first commandment of all. He afterwards sets before the Israelites a blessing and a curse, " a blessing if ye obey the commandments of the Lord your God which I command you this day ; and a curse if ye will not obey the commandments of the Lord your God." " Ye shall observe to do all the statutes and judgments which I set before you this day." Deut. xi. 27, 28–32. And then he proceeds to say : " These are the statutes and judgments which ye shall observe." Deut. xii. 1. And again : " If thou shalt keep all these commandments to do them which I command thee this day." Deut. xix. 9. And then follows a continuous series of precepts up to the twenty-fourth chapter, where the law of divorce is inserted ; followed again continuously by others, until chapter twenty-sixth, verse sixteen, where the whole is clenched with the declaration : " This day the Lord thy God hath commanded thee to do these statutes and judgments." And again, " Moses, with the elders of Israel, commanded the people, saying, keep all the commandments which I command you this day." " Thou shalt therefore obey the voice of the Lord thy God, and do his commandments and his statutes which I command thee this day." "And it shall come to pass, if thou shalt hearken diligently unto the voice of the Lord thy God, to observe and do all his commandments which I command thee this day, that the Lord thy God will set thee on high above all nations of the earth." Then follow the blessings. "But it shall come to pass, if thou wilt not hearken unto the voice of the Lord thy God, to observe to do all his commandments and his statutes which I command thee this day;"—and then follow the curses. Deut. xxvii. 1–10, and xxviii. 1–15. Now the law in regard to the *Hebrew servant* is indeed given, in Exodus, in almost immediate juxtaposition with the ten commandments, Exodus xxi. 2. But it is given also among the other statutes and judgments in Deuteronomy xv. The law in regard to foreign bondmen is given only in Leviticus. But nothing can be inferred from juxtaposition in regard to the relative importance of laws in the Mosaic code. And now, after all these express asseverations of Moses in the book of Deuteronomy—"these are the commandments, the statutes, and the judgments of the Lord your God, which I command you this day,"—shall a "Christian Bishop," who finds one of them lying in the way of his pet theory, take it out, and boldly declare that Moses wrote it "in his human discretion?" And shall such a Bishop denounce his opponents for their want of reverence for the "word of God," and claim to be superlatively orthodox? Shall he rebuke Colenso even? How much else of what "Moses wrote" did he write "in his human discretion?" For, observe, our Lord merely says, "Moses wrote this precept," not that he wrote it "in his human discretion." Is it not abundantly evident that if the inspired authority of Moses can be relied upon as proof that any of the statutes and judgments contained in the book of Deuteronomy are from God, then the law of divorce is among them? But because our Lord says, "Moses wrote it," therefore he wrote it "in his human discretion!" Is it not admitted that Noah uttered the curse upon Canaan? But suppose it should be argued that because Noah, recovering from the effects of the wine, uttered that imprecation, therefore he uttered it "in his own discretion;" what a fluttering there would be in the camp! What a zeal for the "word of God!" What a cry of "Colenso!" But I submit that this suggestion would be as plausible as the other; unless the word of God is allowed to be wrested in no direction except in favour of slavery.

If God could have directed Moses to give the people the precept about divorce "for the hardness of their hearts," so may he have directed him to give other precepts; as, for instance, those in relation to slavery, for a similar reason; and that, with a view, in both cases, not to establish an evil, but to correct a greater one. For in neither case is the thing *commanded*; it is only suffered, restrained and regulated.

And this is in perfect accordance with God's ordinary proceeding with mankind, and with the gradual character of the unfolding of his instructions and revelations. The divine legislation, even, as a development of divine Providence, when intended for the formal regulation of man's social and civil relations, must be suited to his character, condition, and circumstances; and in that sense will partake of man's imperfections, and may itself become more perfect as man makes progress in moral culture and social improvement. Not only may the law of divorce, therefore, have been given "for the hardness of men's hearts," but those of war also (in Deut. 20) and of the Goël,—and of *servitude*.

We come now to the New Testament. And here we need add but few words to what has been already said in answer to the "letter;" for the "View" adds little to the argument, unless it is in the shape of a formal defence and eulogy of the whipping-post as an eminently Christian institution.

The argument drawn by the partizans of slavery from the New Testament, is chiefly of a negative character. When carefully analyzed, it is reduced substantially to this: "*The New Testament does not expressly abolish or prohibit slavery.*" Now it is to be remembered that the New Testament is throughout addressed to individuals and never to governments. Slavery, therefore, as a political or civil institution, as a system established and maintained by law, of course was not abolished. But it does not follow from this that the general principles of Christianity, if applied by legislators and governments, would not lead to, and require, its abolition. Unlike the men to whom our Saviour and his apostles preached, *we*, —*i. e.* men in these times, and in this country, stand towards slavery in a twofold relation, as individuals and as legislators. As individuals, our duty, now as then, is resolvable chiefly into a question of treatment, of motive, and of personal feeling. As legislators, we are responsible for the system, for its legal character, its tendency and its working. And when slavery is now condemned, it is regarded as well in its latter aspect as in the former. It is the system that is condemned. It is the law of slavery that is pronounced wrong. We are responsible for it in this aspect; for, in this country, "we the people" make the constitution and the laws as well as keep them. We have claimed certain rights ourselves, as the very foundation of our civil system; and we are bound by the simplest principles of the gospel and of justice

10 *

to accord the same rights to others. Of all people
on earth Christianity especially forbids *us* to hold
our fellow men as slaves. This is applicable to the
people of the several States in their legislative capacity. They profess to be Christian people, and those
who hold slaves profess to justify the system by the
principles of Christianity. As moralists and Christians, we have a right to judge the system, the legal
system, by those principles; and if it is inconsistent
with them, to condemn it. The general principles
of Christianity are modified and determined in their
application by the mental and moral condition of
those who are to apply them, by their views of rights
and notions of happiness, and wherein it consists.
What they claim for themselves as rights, what they
regard as constituting happiness, these things they
are to claim and labour to secure for others as well
as for themselves. Now among the general principles of Christianity are—" Thou shalt love thy neighbour as thyself;" and " all things whatsoever ye
would that men should do to you, do ye even so to
them;" and " have not the faith of our Lord Jesus
Christ, the Lord of glory with respect of persons."
Are these consistent with holding our neighbour,
our fellow man, our fellow Christian as a slave? If
we are asked, as we often are, why we apply these
refined principles exclusively to the system of slavery, while they are violated as often by non-slaveholders as by slaveholders? We answer, that we do
not apply them exclusively to slavery, but we say
that every violation of them, whenever and wherever
it is committed, is wrong, is unchristian. " If there
come into *any* Christian assembly a man with a gold
ring, in goodly apparel, and there come in also a

poor man in vile raiment, and they have respect to him that weareth the gay clothing, and say unto him, sit thou here in a good place; and say to the poor, stand thou there, or sit here under my foot-stool,"—I say, with the apostle James, that they violate the Christian law of impartial regard and love, whoever and wherever they may be. But now suppose that assembly should proceed to enact a law that any person might take this poor man, drive him to the field to work like an ox without wages, deprive him of his rights as a man, a husband and a father, reduce him to the condition of a chattel, a *thing*, for the profit of his master, to be " doomed in his own person and his posterity to live without knowledge, and without the capacity to make any-thing his own, and to toil that another may reap the fruits;" and suppose that other assemblies and other men professing to be Christians, and even a " Chris-tian Bishop," should approve the act, and gravely and pertinaciously defend it as "fully authorized" by the doctrine and religion of Jesus;—what then ? If I condemned before, what shall I do now ? Shall I restrain my expression of " indignant reproba-tion ?" Even though all actual treatment were left out of the question, though no man were found bad enough to carry such an enactment into effect, could we fail to denounce the enactment itself as utterly unchristian and abominable ? And would it mend the case if those Christians should add the mockery of admitting that man to come by himself to the Holy Communion ; while they gravely enact that, though a communicant in the church, his testimony upon oath is not worthy to be believed ? When it was proposed to receive such testimony even in the Ecclesiastical courts of the Protestant Episcopal Church, the proposition was rejected through the urgency of the slaveholding interest, who treated it as a piece of "dirty business."

Now, all the immense array of citations in exposition of the Scripture, from the Fathers, the doctors of the church, and the commentators, collected by the author of the "View,"—with a single exception, perhaps,—go not an iota further, than a defence and justification of the New Testament in not abolishing the law of slavery. That it sanctioned and approved of that law as such, they do not pretend; it only required the law to be obeyed while it existed. Their address, too, is made to individuals. Of course they aim, therefore, at treatment, at practice under the law. They, too, require servants to obey their masters; and they require masters to treat their servants *not as slaves* but as brethren.

If the New Testament approved and sanctioned any slavery, as a legalized system, it approved and sanctioned Roman slavery. Hebrew slavery no longer existed to be either sanctioned or abrogated. Now the system of Roman slavery was perhaps the most outrageously cruel and inhuman that ever existed. Moreover, it was a slavery of *whites*. Can a Christian believe that Christ and his apostles approved and sanctioned such slavery as that? Approved and sanctioned it, moreover, in such a sense, as fully to authorize and justify it among Christians, at the present day? If I understand the author of the "View," he believes it; believes that the Southerners would be fully authorized by the doctrine of the New Testament in reducing to slavery any whites—of an inferior race to themselves, perhaps, — whom they might judge proper; and takes great credit for them in having restrained this large Christian liberty of theirs within such narrow bounds as to content themselves with having for their slaves only the still more degraded and vastly inferior race of the blacks! Though after all, if slavery is so good a thing, and withal so perfectly right and Christianlike, one does not see why there should be any credit due to its restriction.

But let us remember that the exigence of the argument required him to maintain that holding white men in slavery is fully justified by the New Testament, and that he accepts the consequence. The author of the "View" quotes Aristotle. Compare St. Paul with Aristotle.

As good an argument could be made, and has been made, from the precepts of the New Testament, in favour of the duty of passive submission even to the most tyrannical governments, as can be made in favour of the right of slavery. When St. Paul declared that "the powers that be are ordained of God," and required all Christians religiously to obey them, the government actually existing was the tyranny of Nero. That tyranny he neither undertook to abolish nor even to condemn. Did he therefore fully authorize and justify it? Or, because he did not condemn it, are we also, in a free country, forbidden by the apostle to criticise the laws of the land and the acts of the government, and to condemn them, if in our judgment they are wrong? Or, still more, has he established the doctrine that the government

can do no wrong, that the idea or judgment of wrong
cannot attach to its acts, that if the law establishes
anything—slavery, for example—that this, by virtue
of the very fact that it is established by the law, is
right? Has the apostle announced any such monstrous doctrines as these? Certainly not. Simply
he did not address governors, or judge governments,
or criticise laws. It was not the time to do so. Our
circumstances are different. We have, as I have said,
responsibilities in our capacity of law-makers as well
as of law keepers. We are the governors as well as
the governed. The apostle does indeed give his commands to masters as well as to servants, and enjoins
them in substance, not to treat their servants *as
slaves*. But, it is quickly urged, " he does not require
them to emancipate them." True, he is willing that
the relation of *master and servant* should practically
as well as legally remain. He sanctions it, I have
no doubt, and it will always continue a rightful relation. But from this it no more follows that the
apostle sanctions slavery than from his declaring
government to be a divine institution, it follows that
he sanctions tyranny.

In short, all these negative arguments from the
New Testament in favour of the law and practice
of slavery, vanish away as smoke before the general
spirit and tendency of its teaching. Let any one
place distinctly before his mind a picture of Roman
slavery, or such an idea of Southern slavery as is
given in the delineation of Judge Ruffin, and let him
compare them — compare those concrete, practical
realities, and not any carefully analyzed and expurgated abstractions — with the tone and character of

the doctrine of Christ and his apostles; and let him ask himself whether the two agree, whether they are compatible, whether such ruthless systems are "fully authorized" by this doctrine;—and I cannot doubt as to what will be his answer. He will say, *no*, with all the energy of his soul;—and, it seems to me, he cannot fail to stamp any opposite view with his "indignant reprobation."

CHAPTER V.

THAT the Christian Church has not adopted or acted upon the doctrines of the "ultra-abolitionists," *i. e.*, of those who insist upon the immediate, universal, absolute, and formal abolition of slavery as the first and greatest commandment of Christianity, is freely admitted. But that either the teaching, the spirit, or the practical working of the church, has been opposed to emancipation, and in favour of maintaining and perpetuating the system of slavery, either as right, as good, or as a divine institution,— is utterly denied. The church has attacked slavery not in the abstract but in the concrete, not in its totality but in its details, not by storm but by a gradual undermining, not at first by an open declaration of war, but always with a consciousness of real antagonism, as in the presence of a gigantic evil, of a monstrous and almost unmanageable wrong.

Before Constantine the church stood in the same position towards slavery and the Roman government in which the apostles had left it. That is to say, the church could not meddle with the law; she had no control over the legislative function, and it were useless as well as dangerous formally to have pronounced the law to be wrong. She therefore attacked, not the law, not the system, but the practice.

(120)

She still required Christian masters to treat their slaves, not as slaves, but as equals and as brethren, and strongly favoured emancipation. For, as Wallon says, in his history of slavery, within the pale of the church, "the slave passed from the category of things which the right of property placed at the disposal of the master." Said Clement of Alexandria, "Our household servants are to be treated like ourselves, for they are men as well as we."* And Cyprian thus taunts his Pagan adversary: "You compel to be your slave a man who was born as you were, who dies as you do, whose body is made of the same substance with your own, whose soul has the same origin with yours, who has the same rights and is under the same law." (Cyp. ad Dem.)

"That these principles were carried into practice in the church, we have the evidence of credible history. For though the number of slaves set free by individual masters may be exaggerated — as when Ovinius of Gaul is said to have emancipated five thousand and Melanius eight thousand,—that very exaggeration in the popular tradition shows the tendency of Christianity towards universal emancipation."†

"A Roman prefect, Hermas, converted in the reign of Trajan, 98–117, received baptism at an Easter festival with wife and children, and twelve hundred and fifty slaves, and on this occasion gave all his slaves their freedom and munificent gifts besides. So in the martyrology of St. Sebastian, it is related

* Pædag. 3. 12. de famulis quidem utendum est tanquam nobis ipsis ; sunt enim homines sicut nos.
† Thompson's Christianity and Emancipation.

11

that a wealthy Roman prefect, Chromatius, under Diocletian (284–305), on embracing Christianity, emancipated fourteen hundred slaves, after having them baptized with himself, because their sonship with God put an end to their servitude to man. In the beginning of the fourth century, St. Cantius, Cantianus, and Cantianilla, of an old Roman family, set all their slaves, seventy-three in number, at liberty, after they had received baptism. After the third century the manumission became a solemn act, which took place in the presence of the clergy and the congregation. The master led the slave to the altar; there the document of emancipation was read, the minister pronounced the blessing, and the congregation received him as a free brother, with equal rights and privileges. Constantine found this custom already established, and African councils of the fourth century requested the Emperor to give it general force;"* for as the law stood then, the rights of the freedman were quite insecure.

As a further indication of the tone of Christian feeling on slavery, take the following from Lactantius: " We call ourselves brethren, for no other reason than that we hold ourselves all equal. . . . We have, notwithstanding the difference of outward relations, no slaves, but we call and consider them brethren." . . . . " God would have all men equal."

Such was the spirit of early Christianity. But to have required all Christian masters to emancipate their slaves would have been unreasonable; for as several laws were then made to restrain and prevent emancipation, it might have been impossible.

* Schaff: Hist. Church.

After the conversion of Constantine the case was different. But Constantine, though converted to Christianity, was, like most other Christian princes, controlled in his government, more by political than by moral or religious considerations. And the leaders and governors of the church, who had now become in no small degree corrupted by a worldly spirit and the prospect of increasing power, fell in, quite too readily, with the political views of the Emperor, and even stood ready to take their share of the gain and spoil.

Still, the spirit of Christianity could not be entirely stifled, and its influence is seen in the changes made by Constantine in the imperial laws; ameliorating the condition of the slave; encouraging emancipation by a solemn decree that masters wishing to free their slaves might resort to the churches and perform the act before the altar, and in the presence of the congregation; and issuing a charter for the protection of freedmen, which surrounded their rights with all possible means of defence. And thus, as the Duke de Broglie finely says, "the church was invested with a sort of official patronage for the enfranchisement of mankind. The places consecrated to the Christian faith became the asylums of liberty—the inviolable free soil. The church at this solemn moment accepted from God and from Constantine the task of emancipating the world without overturning it."*

Whatever the Fathers may have said, and rightly said, in imitation of the apostles, guarding against encroachment upon the legal rights of the masters, and enjoining obedience upon the servants, none of

* Thompson's Christianity and Emancipation.

them ever wrote expressly in favour of the system of slavery, none of them ever could have been, without a revolution of his whole Christian being, the author of such a book as this modern "View of Slavery." I propose to pass in rapid review the citations from the civil law, the Councils, the Fathers and Doctors of the Church, upon which the author of the "View" relies. I will take them in his own order.

In his citations from the civil law, I observe (1.) that liberty is called a "*natural* faculty;" (2.) slavery is declared to be a "constitution of *municipal law*, whereby, *contrary to nature*, one man is subjected to the dominion of another;" (3.) "manumission is a thing which has its origin in *municipal law;* for, since by the *law of nature* all would be born free, both slavery and manumission would have been unknown;" (4.) "manumission takes place in various ways, either *by the sacred constitutions in the holy churches*, or by will," &c. (5.) "In case of the intolerable cruelty of masters, the slave shall be sold," &c.

That men, by the law of nature, "*jure naturali*" are free—are born free, is here asserted almost as plainly as in the Declaration of Independence; and slavery is declared to be an artificial distinction, contrary to nature, *contra naturam*, a creature of positive law.

Again, I observe, the same constitution of the civil law which rejects the testimony of slaves, rejects alike the testimony of all immoral persons, or slaves to vice; those who "in illicitarum actionum servitutem subiguntur"—a point which the author of the "View" found it convenient, in his text, to omit. Also, which strongly shows the leaning of the later civil law in favour of liberty, it is declared in a decree of Leo—that the selling of one's self into slavery is *void, criminal* in both parties, and the act of one demented and mad.

As to the doctrine of Aristotle, which has always been a favourite text with oligarchists, that " some men are *free by nature,* and others *are slaves,* and that, in the case of the latter the lot of slavery is both advantageous and just;" it is manifestly at war not only with the teaching of the Scriptures but with the principles of the civil law and with the dictates of humanity; and even Aristotle relented so far as elsewhere to indicate that if a slave were mentally cultivated so far as to be fitted for freedom he ought to be set at liberty. On this philosophy of the Stagirite the Southern slaveholders rest their plea. "The general emancipation of the negroes," say they, " would not only be ruinous to the masters, but cruel to the last degree towards the slaves themselves; because it would thrust into the dangers and difficulties of freemen millions of human beings who are entirely unfitted *by nature* for freedom, and who need the protection and government of their masters even more than the masters need their labour. And therefore they resist the policy of abolition,"—and therefore these millions of negroes are, generation after generation, to be raised, bought, sold, and treated like cattle, carefully kept in universal ignorance, and sunk in one vast system of concubinage, so that men and wives, parents and children, may be separated without compunction ! What insufferable mendacity and hypocrisy ! Have these slaveholders arranged their laws with a view to improve and elevate " the nature" of these millions of human beings and thus fit them for freedom ; or to prevent, rather,

11 *

any such elevation or improvement, and to proscribe any attempts towards it? And can they really pretend to say in the face of heaven, that their *motive* in opposing abolition, and perpetuating, at all hazards, the system of slavery, is more to secure the highest good of the slave than the gain to be derived from his labour?

Let the Supreme Court of North Carolina answer this question: "The difference," say they, "is that between freedom and slavery, and a greater cannot be imagined. In the one, the end in view is the happines of the youth," &c. . . . "with slavery it is far otherwise. The end is the profit of the master, his security and the public safety; the subject, one doomed in his own person and his posterity to live without knowledge and without the capacity to make anything his own, and to toil that another may reap the profits."

Yet the author of the "View" expressly subscribes to the Southern Aristotelian argument as unanswerable. "Am I justified," says he, "in assuming that I have a vast deal more of intellect and Christian principle than the Southern clergy, who defend their domestic institution on these grounds, of scripture, of law, and of sound philosophy? Can I say to them, Stand by, for I am holier than you? Stand by, for I am more intellectual than you! Stand by, for I have more philanthropy than you! Stand by, for I have the *master mind* by nature, and your minds ought to be, in justice, the *slaves of mine*, by reason of my superiority! . . . . I must be excused if I dare not occupy a position which seems to me the very reverse of common sense, of sound argument, and of Christian moderation." What beautiful Christian humility!—one is ready to exclaim. But unfortunately the rule does not work both ways; for it makes a vast difference whose ox is gored, yours or mine. Could it have been expected that such a lowly-minded person would denounce the expressed judgment of a large body of his brethren as "false, bitter, insolent, unjust, vituperative, calumnious, violent, aggressive, demented?" Is it credible that, being a Bishop, and differing in judgment from the House of Bishops in regard to the performance of a certain official act, he should, publicly and alone, have separated himself from the body of his brethren and official equals, as much as to say, "Stand by, for I have the *master mind* by nature, and your minds ought to be, in justice, the *slaves of mine*, by reason of my superiority!" Of course, this must be an utterly groundless and slanderous report.

I proceed with the citations. The words of Philo are clearly in favour of freedom, and the rights of humanity as *natural* rights. "The divine law," says he, "accommodates the rules of *right*, not to fortune but to *nature*."

Tertullian, in speaking of the stealing of a slave, has clearly in view the taking him from one man to make him — not free — but the slave of another; — "*domino eripiatur ut alii vindicetur.*" This he condemns;—and who does not?

Jerome (Note 17*) represents the slave as the equal of his master — yet not to despise him : "*Ne sibi aequalem contemnant.*"

The remaining two quotations from Jerome require

---

* The numbering of the note in the Appendix to the "View" is followed, for the sake of easy reference.

no comment; and I shall omit others of a similar character without further remark.

The supposititious Ambrose (No. 20) derives slavery " from the iniquity of the world;" but adds that the real, *natural*, proper slave is the sinner. Anti-slavery men will subscribe to that.

Augustine (No. 22) says that the church makes masters more disposed to " consult for the good of their slaves than to chastise them,"—*ad consulendum quam coercendum*—which the author of the " View" rather whimsically translates, " more inclined to consult than to coerce them."

In the next quotation (No. 23) Augustine shows only the natural effect of stripes, not the right of inflicting them.

When he says (No. 24) that " it is either adversity or iniquity that has made one man the slave of another," and afterwards refers to Joseph, does he mean that the enslaving of Joseph was just? When slavery is the punishment of crime duly ascertained, it is not objected to by abolitionists; only the children should not suffer for the crimes of their parents.

His saying (in No. 26) is striking, and very much to our purpose. " Masters and servants are diverse names; men and men are equal names." * Thus Augustine recognizes the *existence of slavery;*—that is not at all denied. But he turns his face against it;— that is to be remembered. And this is but an instance of the common fact with the Christian fathers.

Does Basil mean (No. 29) that those who are " oppressed by power," as well as those who are

---

* Sunt domini, sunt et servi, diversa sunt nomina; sed homines et homines paria sunt nomina.

"reduced to servitude by reason of poverty, as the Egyptians under Pharaoh," are rightfully made slaves; so that the Israelites also were rightfully made slaves to the Egyptians?

A specimen of Chrysostom's over-refinement is given (in No. 30) in reference to the apostolic injunction "use it rather;" 1 Cor. vii. 28. But Chrysostom frankly admits a diversity of opinion on the question, and candidly gives, not his authority, but his reasons. Of the sufficiency of these we are left to judge. He has himself given sufficient proof, as we shall show elsewhere, that he was no friend to slavery, but that he decidedly favoured emancipation. But what use would there have been in emancipating Christian slaves, if it was their Christian duty rather to remain in slavery? If the injunction "use it rather" means "use slavery rather," it must be given by the apostle, either, as Poole suggests, in the sense of "prefer to continue a slave rather than be guilty of *fraud*," or with a view, as the apostle elsewhere says, "of the present distress," and must be put by the side of his injunction to avoid marriage.

Prosper (No. 31) says expressly, "slavery comes from *crime* (*culpa*), not from *nature*." How will Aristotle stand with the Fathers of the Church?

Gregory (No. 32) simply makes maids and matrons *equally* slaves, for he makes them both *fear*. And what of it?

This Father (No. 33) teaches natural equality in the clearest terms. "Servants," says he, "should be admonished in one way, and masters in another; servants that they should always regard in themselves the humility of their condition, but masters that they should not forget *their nature*, whereby they were *created on an equality* with their servants. . . . . Masters are also to be admonished that against God they do not wax insolent with his gift, by refusing to acknowledge that those whom they hold in present condition as their slaves are *by the fellowship of nature their equals.**

Now here are the so much decried propositions of the Declaration of Independence in almost express terms; and that at once in spite of Aristotle, and of the charges of extravagance and nonsense so often indulged in against them by those who think themselves exceedingly clear headed and wise.† It has often been charged upon the Declaration that all that is true in its first proposition is the bald and empty statement that " all men are equally created." Yet this unmeaning statement the author of the " View" does not hesitate, in his translation, expressly to father upon Gregory. I submit that the connexion shows, and, without the connexion, the supposition that Gregory was not a simpleton would

---

* Aliter admonendi sunt servi, atque aliter domini. Servi, scilicet, ut in se semper humilitatem conditionis aspiciant: domini vero, ut naturæ suæ qua æqualiter sunt cum servis conditi, memoriam non amittant. . . . . Domini quoque admonendi sunt quia contra Deum de munere ejus superbiunt, si eos quos per conditionem tenent subditos, æquales sibi per naturæ consortium non agnoscunt.

† The charges do not always stop with "extravagance and nonsense." Dr. Smyth, a prominent rebel of South Carolina, in a pamphlet upon this subject, says: "What is the difficulty and what is the remedy? It is found in the atheistic, red republican doctrine of the Declaration of Independence! Until that is trampled under foot, there can be no peace." With which does the "Christian Bishop" more nearly coincide, with the primitive St. Gregory, or with the rebel Dr. Smyth?

show, that he meant something more than that. By "æqualiter conditi sunt," he must have meant that men are made of equal condition, or on a footing of equality.

As an offset to the deed (No. 34) by which Gregory renounces in favour of Felix all legal right to a slave who had already been a long time in possession of the latter, I may insert another and far more significant deed of the same Gregory manumitting two persons who had been his slaves : "As our Redeemer, the Maker of every creature, was pleased in his mercy to put on human flesh, that by the grace of his divinity he might break the bonds that hold us captive, and restore us to our pristine liberty, it is fitting and salutary that men whom nature in the beginning made and brought into the world free, but whom the law of the land has subjected to the yoke of servitude, should be restored by the benefit of manumission to liberty in that nature in which they were born.   Moved by this consideration and as a *dictate of piety*, you, Montana and Thomas, I have made free," &c.*

Isodore tells us (No. 35) that "for the sin of the

---

* Cum Redemptor noster totius conditor creaturæ ad hoc propitiatus humanam voluerit carnem assumere, ut divinitatis suæ gratia diruto quo tenebamur captivi vinculo servitutis, pristinæ nos restitueret libertati; salubriter agitur, si homines quos ab initio natura creavit liberos et protulit, et jus gentium jugo substituit servitutis, in ea natura in qua nati fuerant, manumittentis beneficio, libertati reddantur.   Atque ideo pietatis intuitu, et hujus rei consideratione permoti, vos Montanam atque Thomam famulos Sanctæ Romanæ Ecclesiæ cui Deo adjutore deservimus, liberos ex hoc die civesque Romanos efficimus, omneque vestrum vobis relaxamus servitutis peculium.

Greg. I., v. Ep. 12.

first man the punishment of servitude was divinely
imposed, so that to those for whom God sees that
liberty is not congruous he may more mercifully ap-
point servitude. . . .　Hence, also, among nations,
princes and kings have been chosen that by their
terror they might restrain the people from evil, and
subject them to laws to the end they should live
rightly.　Better is the subjection of slavery than the
elation of liberty."*

Of course servitude for the good of the servants,
as government for the good of the governed, is
right; but this will justify neither all systems of
government, nor all systems of slavery.

The canon (No. 36) that slaves should not be ordained without the will of their masters, implies that
ordinations of slaves to the ministry not unfrequently
took place, and that the consent of Christian masters
would be gladly given of course, in all proper cases.

The canon (No. 37) which enjoins, "let the master
love his servant, and although he is above him, yet
let him acknowledge that there is equality in so far
as he is a man,"† contains another clear recognition
of human equality, of the natural equality of man
as man.

The anathema of the council of Gangra only assumes the *duties* of slaves,—the same duties which
the apostle had expressly enjoined, and which Christian anti-slavery men are far from denying.　Only,

* Propter peccatum primi hominis humano generi pœna divi-
nitus illata est servitutis, ita ut quibus aspicit non congruere
libertatem, his misericordius irroget servitutem. . . . . Inde et in
gentibus principes, regesque electi sunt ut terrore suo populos a
malo coercerent, atque ad recte vivendum legibus subderent.

† Judicet tamen esse aequalitatem, vel quatenus homo est.

perhaps, the injunction might be strained too far in its application; as to say, for example, that a Christian being a slave to a Turk, and treated with outrageous cruelty, he should not leave his master's service though he had an opportunity to escape. Even the law, "thou shalt not kill," yields to the necessity of self-defence.

The decree of the council of Agde (No. 39) implies that the manumission of deserving slaves by the Bishops of churches is presumed as the regular thing. The churches, it is to be presumed, took slaves for this purpose, *i. e.*, for the training and benefit of the slaves, not from motives of cupidity; consequently, even while they were held, they were not held *as slaves*,—Judge Ruffin's slaves :—or, if any churches did otherwise, they certainly did wrong.

The canon of Orleans* (No. 40) is translated in the "View" as follows : "The slave who has taken refuge in the church for any transgression, if he has received the sacrament after the admission of his fault, shall be compelled to return immediately to the service of his master." Thus *a domino* is entirely ignored, and *pro* is translated "after." But suppose the slave has not received and refuses to receive the sacrament, "after the admission of his fault," what then? Shall he find an asylum in the church? If so, it would not seem difficult for him to avoid being sent back to his master. I suspect the sense to be, "provided he has received an oath from his master for the fault he has committed;" *i. e.*, a solemn promise of forgiveness on the master's part, and of

* Servus qui ad ecclesiam pro qualibet culpa confugerit, si a domino pro admissa culpa sacramenta susciperet, statim ad servitium domini sui redire cogatur.

amendment on his own, confirmed perhaps by a common participation of the sacrament.

As to two years' excommunication for killing a slave (No. 41); is it a precedent for us? Is it just and equal? Estimating men's lives at different values was a barbarous custom of the Middle Ages. Does Christianity or the church require it to be restored? If not, what is the value of this decree of the council of Epone? What else does it show except that the church was then degraded and corrupt, and her moral judgment not to be relied upon?

In translating the canon of Orleans (No. 42), what the author means by "the masters' sustaining the benefit of redemption," I am quite too dull to apprehend. I suspect the meaning of the canon is, substantially, " that the slaves of the church or of the priests should not be allowed to plunder or take captives, because it is not reasonable that the ecclesiastical discipline should be stained by an excessive accumulation of slaves, while the masters are accustomed to afford them the favour of redemption." If something like this is the sense of the canon, of which I would not be sure, it shows that it was usual for masters to emancipate their slaves, or to redeem slaves that they might set them free.

When a slave was to be ordained (No. 43), nothing was more reasonable than to require the consent of the master as a proof of proper character. And observe that in the case of a *freedman* the consent of his former master is required, for a similar purpose.

The canon of the council of Macon (No. 44) allowing the Christian slave of a Jew to be extorted from his master at a fixed price, is as clear a departure by the church from the apostolic precept, as any act of emancipation with nominal compensation could ever be.

The canon of Toledo (No. 45) proves nothing but that, in the corruption of the times, the churches themselves held slaves, and that they were sometimes disturbed in their possession by civilians.

The canon of Narbonne (No. 46) also recognizes undoubtedly the existence of servitude. It forbids a slave to yoke oxen on Sunday. But what if his master should require it? Is there any danger that the Southern slaves should yoke oxen on Sunday if not required? How strange for such a mandate to be issued to the slave and not to the master, threatening the slave himself with punishment for disobedience!

The council of Berghamsted in 697 (No. 47) recognizes manumission at the altar, *i. e.*, as a religious act.

The canon of Aix la Chapelle (No. 48) is largely copied from Isidore (see No. 35). Divine Providence is vindicated; which may be well in answer to any who are disposed to charge the Almighty with the sin of slavery. But is, or is not, "liberty congruous" for those who are true Christians? Is it right that such should be held in perpetual, hopeless bondage?

The Capitulary of Louis the Pious (No. 49) is harmless. Slaves were not to be Christian ministers. That was felt to be dangerous; therefore they were to be set free before ordination. *Fraud* was, of course, enough to show that a man was unfit for the ministry.

The canon of Worms (No. 51) contains an express provision for the emancipation of slaves *by the church,*

without the consent of the masters.*   Which was
right, this, or the earlier canons which forbade it?

Next comes the famous canon of the council of
London in 1011, in the following words:

"Let no one by any means presume henceforth to
engage in that nefarious traffic, by which, hitherto,
men have been accustomed to be sold, like brute
beasts, in England."

The Bishop of Oxford had appealed to this canon
as "the rule of *the church*" on both sides of the Atlantic; but the Bishop of Vermont, in his zeal to
show that the church has never committed herself
against "the nefarious traffic whereby men are sold
as brute beasts," contends that this canon has no
binding force; for he has discovered that Anselm,
then Archbishop of Canterbury, in sending to the
Archdeacon William a statement of the matters
treated of in this council, has omitted this alleged
canon altogether.   Whether this omission was acci-
dental or designed does not appear.   If it was designed, either Anselm meant to give a list of such
canons only as he himself officially sanctioned ("*nos
decrevisse*"), or this omission can scarcely be reconciled with the simple truth.   But, in any event,
although the precise point of the Bishop of Oxford,
touching the legal validity of the canon, may be
parried, its weight in the present argument is
scarcely at all diminished.   Its moral force still remains, as an expression of a feeling which must have
been widely prevalent in the church to have found
utterence in this form, even though it were not expressly confirmed by the authority of the Archbishop.

* Si servus, absente vel nesciente domino suo, *episcopo autem
sciente quod servus sit*, diaconus aut presbyter fuerit ordinatus,
ipse in clericatus officio permaneat.

Gregory Nazianzen (No. 54) makes provision in his will for either the speedy manumission of the slaves or their enjoying the comparatively comfortable service of the church.

Saint Perpetuus (No. 55) directly liberates his slaves, and gives his books to the church.

"Alcuin (No. 56) had the disposal of the revenue of his abbeys, and as their estates were peopled with serfs, Elipand of Toledo reproaches him with having as many as twenty thousand." This surely does not imply that the prevailing Christian sentiment regarded it as any credit to a Bishop to have even this class of bondmen.

The request of the council of Soissons (No. 57) aims at an episcopal encroachment upon the temporal lords; but, after all, demands the right to punish only for *crime*. Would it, in the view of the Bishop of Vermont, be particularly desirable for Bishops now to have the right to "scourge the peasantry with rods?"

Pope Benedict, in his decree (No. 58), would manifestly, as his primary object, punish the clergy for having wives or concubines, by making their children slaves,—certainly a most unchristian proceeding in motive and in means. Benedict did not imagine, probably, that there would ever arise men who, of their own accord, would hold, sell, and bequeath their own children as slaves. But of what authority is this decree? What does it prove?—that the churches held slaves? That is admitted. The question is, is it any authority for justifying that fact? At all events, it recognizes slavery as an evil—as a punishment for crime; every principle of justice

12*

must therefore pronounce it a wrong when inflicted
upon the innocent.

The general principle of Melanchthon (No 59) we
may still adopt without hesitation. But he evidently
goes too far—farther than he himself really thought
of going—when he says that "slavery was approved
(by the apostle Paul) *such as it was then described in
the laws.*"* I trust that even the author of the
"View" will not admit that the apostle *approved* of
the system of Roman slavery as it was maintained
by law. "It is in vain one looks for anything like
common human feeling in the Roman slave-law of
republican times and that of the early empire,"—
and this was the time of St. Paul. "The slave was
a chattel, had no individuality or 'caput,' his union
with a wife was no marriage, his master might torture or kill him at will, the modes of torture were
various and cruel, and the ordinary punishment of
death was crucifixion. The breaking up of slave
families was entirely in the hands of the merchant
or owner; husband might be separated from wife,
and mother from children, all dispersed and sold off
into the houses of strangers and to foreign towns.
In the eye of the law slavery was equivalent to
death, for the law does not recognize the existence
of the slave; it entirely avoids and annuls the contract of a master with his slave, gives the slave no
action at law against him, and *compels female slaves
to surrender themselves to their master's lust against their
will;*"† and, it may be added, that, in case a master was

---

* Approbari servitutem, qualis tunc in legibus descripta fuit.

† *Döllinger,* on the Roman Law, in "The Gentile and the Jew,"
Vol. II., p. 259.

See also *Dr. Taylor's Elements of the Civil Law,* p. 429; and
Cooper's Justinian.

killed by unknown hands, it required all the slaves
of his household, which were sometimes several hundred in number, without trial and without distinction, to be put to death.   Surely Melanchthon never
meant that St. Paul *approved* such a legal system as
that.   And I should be equally sure that the author
of the " View" does not in his heart and conscience
approve it, or think that St. Paul approved it,
were not some misgiving created by the fact that
this system so closely resembles the system of Southern slavery, which he has declared to be, in his
opinion, " fully authorized by the New Testament."
Melanchthon may have been led to express himself
too strongly by the tendency which prevailed among
the Protestants at that time, and which arose naturally from their zeal against the spiritual and temporal tyranny of the Pope, to go quite to an extreme
in courting the civil power.   But who will now go
with Luther in sanctioning the double marriage of
the Elector of Hesse, or even in his doctrine that a
Christian slave had no right to escape from a Turkish
master?

Calvin only suggests (No. 60) what may or may
not have been the apostle's reasons for his well-
known injunction.

His exposition (in 61) is good; that even unbelieving masters — even those who are themselves
slaves to the devil, are to be obeyed;—but to what
purpose is this towards justifying those who serve
the devil in holding Christians in slavery?

According to Calvin (No. 62), it was not only as a
runaway slave, but as having been a *thief*, that Onesimus was sent back to his master to be forgiven.

So Poole (No. 63), " Servants believing in Christ

are not taken from unwilling masters," is freely admitted. But should not believing masters be willing?
willing to receive them "no longer as servants, but
as brethren beloved ?"

That "Christian liberty (No. 64) is consistent with
political servitude, and that by Christ political states
are neither destroyed nor changed," will scarcely be
denied even by the "ultra-abolitionist."

The father (Ham) (No. 66) was undoubtedly punished by the curse upon the son (Canaan); but the
suggestion of the commentator, about Moses' having
omitted a part of Noah's imprecation *for certain political reasons*, is, to say the least, not very respectful
to Holy Scripture.

Probably the Israelites (No. 68) may have bought
slaves of the Cuthæans (Cushites) as well as of other
nations. But Maimonides must not be supposed to
mean that the Israelites had (especially) *negro* slaves.
He is speaking of the *circumcision* of servants; and
he specifies the Cushites, because they were uncir-
cumcised, while the Egyptians, Edomites, &c., were
circumcised already. There is no reason to suppose
that the Israelites or Maimonides thought particularly of Ham or of the descendants of Ham, in connexion with the purchase of slaves.

" Thou shalt not covet," &c.—" By these words of
the law," says Poole (No. 70), " are especially established the dominion and property of the things which
it is not lawful to covet; servitude, moreover, and
the master's power." Yes, the right of a man to his
ox (*as an ox*), to his servant (as a servant), and to
his wife (as a wife), is doubtless hereby recognized
and established; but *property* in the servant is no
more recognized than in the wife; neither is reduced

to the level of the ox and the ass; neither is made a chattel. Observe Poole says *property in things* (proprietas rerum), but the *power* of the master (herilis potestas).

Poole's interpretation (No. 71) of Deut. xxiii. 15, forbidding the surrender of fugitive slaves to their masters, may be correct. That is to say, the Israelites were not to deliver up the fugitive slaves of those over whose laws of slavery they had no control.

The interpretation (No. 72) of Exod. xxi. 16, forbidding man-stealing, is not so clear. It by no means follows, from the more restricted precept of Deut. xxiv. 7, that this general statute has no wider an application. The two are not at all inconsistent, and both can be understood literally just as they stand, the one forbidding the stealing of an Israelite, the other forbidding the stealing of any man. Or is it insisted upon, that, though the Israelites were forbidden to steal any of their brethren, they were nevertheless allowed, by the clear implication of the Divine law, to *steal* as many as they pleased of other nations? To suppose this is hardly consistent, at least, in those, (if there be any such,) who maintain that the precept, "thou shalt love thy neighbour as thyself," was originally intended to be understood by the Jews in the same broad and impartial sense in which our Saviour interpreted it.

Poole gives (No. 73) a very strange comment or reflection, in noting as a proof of the poverty of those who returned from the captivity, the small number of their servants. But it by no means appears that even these servants were all slaves. They may have been Hebrew domestics, reduced to service in consequence of their poverty, so that the

more of them there should have been, the greater
the proof of the poverty of the returning Jews. See
Jer. xxxiv. 11. The Hebrew words in Jeremiah for
man-servants and maid-servants—these all being
Hebrew servants—are the same as in the tenth commandment.

Thus I have examined all the authorities relied
upon by Bishop Hopkins to prove his conclusions
that slavery—such slavery as is maintained in the
Southern States—is right, is a blessing, is approved
and sanctioned, and defended by the church in all
ages. I have not intentionally omitted any citation
or any point that seemed to me particularly to favour
his views, and I confidently appeal to the reader for
the result. Do these authorities bear out the allegations? Observe they are the best and strongest that
could be picked and culled from all ecclesiastical
history. Is it not abundantly evident, after all, that
the spirit of the church, and of her great writers,
has been always anti-slavery? I have cross-ques-
tioned the Bishop's own chosen witnesses; and I
might safely rest the cause here. But I will summon
a few testimonies on the other side, and they need
be but few.

I begin with Chrysostom.—" Think not," he said,
Hom. ad Ephes. xxii., " that God will forgive you an
injury done to a slave, because he is a slave. The
laws of this world draw distinctions between men,
because they are made by men; but the law of our
common Lord knoweth no such distinction, and dis-
penseth the same blessings equally to all. But if any
one ask whence came slavery into the world?—for I
know many who have desired to learn this,—I will
tell him. *Insatiable avarice and envy are the parents of*

slavery; for Noah, Abel, and Seth, and their descendants, had no slaves. Sin hath begotten slavery,
—then wars and battles, in which men were made
captives. But ye say that Abraham had slaves. Yea,
but he treated them not as such."

Hom. in Lazar. 6. " There was no slave in the old
times; for God, when he formed man, made him not
bond but free."

Hom. in 1 Cor. 40. " Slavery is the punishment of
sin, and ārose from disobedience. But when Christ
appeared, he removed this curse; for ' in Christ Jesus
there is neither bond nor free.' "

Hom. in Tit. 4. " It is usual to say that slaves are
a shameless race, difficult to be governed or led, and
not fit to be instructed in godliness. It is not their
nature which rendereth them such, God forbid! but
the negligence of their masters, who care for nothing
but that themselves should be well served; or, should
they ever attend to the morals of their slaves, only
do so for their own advantage, that less trouble may
be thereby occasioned them, not really caring whether they be given up to fornication, theft, or drunkenness."

Hom. in 1 Cor. 40. When rebuking the rich and
the noble, who sought to make a display by keeping
a number of slaves, and who appeared surrounded
by a swarm of them in the market-places, theatres,
and baths, which at times gave them the appearance
of supporting so many slaves from philanthropy, he
said: " If ye cared for these men, ye would buy them;
let them learn trades, that they might support themselves; *and then give them freedom.*"

In another place, while representing the communion of possessions of the first apostolical congrega-

tion at Jerusalem as an example for the Christians
at Antioch, and supposing the case of their following
it, he said : (Hom. in Act Apost. 11) " How much gold
would be collected together, if every one sold his
lands, possessions, and houses, and brought the prices
of them hither,—I *speak not of the sale of slaves, for
that did not exist in those times, though perhaps their
masters were pleased to set them free."*

In a discourse on pride and avarice, St. Augustine
says : "A Christian ought not to exalt himself above
other men ; for God gave thee to be over the beasts.
You ought to seek to have all men equal to yourself.
But man transgresses the bounds of moderation ;
and, in his excessive greed, he who was made over
the cattle seeks to be over men ;—and this is very
pride."†

In another sermon, describing a manumission in
church as if it were a thing of course, he says :—
" What thou canst do for thy servant, thou doest,
thou makest him free."

Addressing a friend who held a part of an undi-
vided estate in which certain slaves were included,
he says : " This is the business, let this be carried
through without delay, let those slaves be divided
and manumitted," &c.

In a discourse on the Sermon on the Mount, he em-
phatically declares : "A Christian ought not to hold
a slave like a horse or like money. For *man* ought
to *love man* as himself."—Who is my neighbour ?

---

* Εἰ παντες και πασαι αυτων ενταυθα εκενωσαν χρηματα, και χωρια και
κτηματα και οικιας απεδοντο (ανδραποδα γαρ ουχ αν ειποιμι, ουδε γαρ τοτε ην
τουτο, αλλ᾽ ελευθερους ισως επετρεπον γενεσθαι). — *Neander's Chrysostom,*
pp. 413–416.

† Aug. op. Tom. III. 2040, V. 145, 1576, III. 1260, VII. 243.

In his Civitus Dei, he says: "In the house of the just man who lives by faith, even those who command are servants to those whom they seem to command; for they govern neither from a lust of enacting the master but as an opportunity of doing good, nor from domineering pride but from provident pity." And again: "This natural order prescribes, for so God made man (Gen. i. 26); he would not that a rational being made in his own image should have dominion (be master) over any but irrational creatures, not man over man, but man over cattle." And once more: "As regards the worship of God, wherein eternal goods are to be hoped for, the just Fathers consulted for all the members of their households with equal love."

Said Gregory of Nyssa: "God said, let us make man in our image. Him who is made in the likeness of God, who rules over the whole earth, who is clothed by God with power over all things on the earth; tell me, who is it that sells or buys such an one? ... How shall that be sold which is above the whole world and all that it contains? For it is necessary also to sell his faculties; and at what price will you estimate the mind of man, that rules the world? Though you should have named the whole world you would not have told its price; for he who knows man hath said, that the whole world is not enough to give in exchange for the soul. When, therefore, a man is exposed for sale, nothing less is brought into the market than the lord of the earth."

Gregory goes on to argue the equality of masters and servants: "They have the same affections of mind and of body, the same joy and sorrow, the same pleasure and pain, the same anger and fear,

13

and are subject to the same sickness and death. They breathe the same air, behold the same sun, have the same vital organs, are nourished by the same food. After death, master and slave become alike dust; they stand before the same judge; their heaven and hell are the same."*

St. Isidore of Pelusium, like Clement of Alexandria, says that "servants should be treated even as ourselves, because they are men like ourselves." And again, in his epistle to Ironis: "For I know not how one who loves Christ, who has known and experienced that grace which has secured freedom for us all—*can hold a slave.*"†

In the eighth century, Theodore Studita, who was at the head of a monastery, writes: "A monk should never possess a slave, either for his own service or for the service of the convent, or to cultivate its lands; *for the slave is a man created in the image of God.*"

And in the twelfth century, at the council of Armagh, in Ireland, "the Bishops declared that the misfortunes of their country were the just punishment of the perpetuated crime of slavery," and freed all captives held as slaves. What a lesson this for us! and it comes from Ireland.

A bull of Pope Gregory XVI. interdicts all ecclesiastics from venturing to maintain that the traffic in blacks is permitted under any pretext whatever; and from teaching in public or in private, or in any way whatever, anything to the contrary."

* Works of Gregory, p. 406.
† Neque enim Christi amantem Ironem, qui cognitam et exploratam eam gratiam habeat, quæ omnes in libertatem vindicavit, famulum ullum habere arbitror.

Las Casas, the stout champion for the freedom of the Indians, is often charged with having favoured the slavery of the negroes.

Las Casas, unfortunately for his reputation, added to a scheme which he proposed, the provision that each Spanish resident in Hispaniola should have license to import a dozen negro slaves.

The origin of this suggestion was, as he informs us, that the colonists had told him that, if license were given them to import a dozen slaves each, they, the colonists, would then set free the Indians; and so, recollecting that statement of the colonists, he added this provision. Las Casas, writing his history in his old age, thus frankly owns his error: " This advice that license should be given to bring negro slaves to their lands, the Clerigo Casas first gave, not considering the injustice with which the Portu- guese take them and make them slaves; which ad- vice, after he had apprehended the nature of the thing, he would not have given for all he had in the world. For he always held that they had been made slaves unjustly and tyrannically."

Hear the following abolition sermon from a very renowned Portuguese preacher, Vieyra, in 1653: " But you will say to me, this people, this republic, this State cannot be supported without Indians [i. e., slaves.] Who is to bring us a pitcher of water or a bundle of wood? Who is to plant our mandioc? Must our wives do it? Must our children do it? In the first place, as you will presently see, these are not the straits in which I would place you; but if necessity and conscience require it, then I reply, yes! and I repeat it, yes! you and your wives and your children ought to do it. We ought to support ourselves with our own hands; far better is it to be supported by the sweat of one's brow [to be "mud-sills"] than by another's blood. O ye riches of Maranham! What if these mantles and cloaks were to be wrung? they would drop blood."* What if such sermons had been ringing from every Christian pulpit North and South for the last thirty years, instead of the church being gradually muzzled by "political expediency?"—Perchance our slaveholders would think such preaching to savour of abolitionism or of politics, or even to be absolutely incendiary.

Hear Las Casas announcing as his "authorities" for a sermon on "the Feast of Pentecost," the following from the thirty-fourth chapter of Ecclesiasticus:

"He that sacrificeth of a thing wrongfully gotten, his offering is ridiculous; and the gifts of unjust men are not accepted.

"The Most High is not pleased with the offerings of the wicked; neither is he pacified for sin by the multitude of sacrifices.

"Whoso bringeth an offering of the goods of the poor doeth as one that killeth the son before his father's eyes.

"The bread of the needy is their life,—he that defraudeth him thereof is a man of blood.

"He that taketh away his neighbour's living slayeth him; and he that defraudeth the labourer of his hire is a blood-shedder."

I think the clerigo might have dwelt upon one of the remaining verses of the chapter with great profit:

* Quoted in Southey's History of Brazil, vol. ii., p. 479.

" When one prayeth and another curseth, whose voice will the Lord hear ?"

When the priest and the Levite pass by denouncing the "curse of Ham," and the poor negro sends up his heart-cry amidst his toils and stripes and miseries, which, think you, will Jehovah hear?

At the end of one of Las Casas's sermons, "all were amazed; some were struck with compunction; others were as much surprised to hear it called a sin to make use of the Indians as if they had been told it were sinful to make use of the beasts of the field."

Such is the blinding and hardening effect of slaveholding. And had a certain Northern Judge of the present day been there, he would have told Las Casas that he knew of no Scripture which declares it a *sin* to hold either Indians or negroes as slaves.

But facts speak louder than words; and, whatever may have been the dicta of fathers, or councils, or doctors, and although the church was powerless to influence the government, before Constantine, and rapidly corrupted in its moral sense by its contact with a slaveholding aristocracy, afterwards,—still, the actual result was, that Christianity had not only greatly mitigated, but to a large extent abolished Roman slavery before the downfall of the Western Empire.

After that, Christianity had her work to do over again with the barbarian conquerors. They established a new system of bondage under the form of serfdom. But again, though the church was quite too much in sympathy with the feudal lords, the silent influence of Christianity had almost entirely

13*

abolished this new form of slavery in Western Europe before the sixteenth century.*

Then appeared a third form of slavery—that of negroes—introduced gradually, and almost surreptitiously, into the European settlements in America, and enlisting on its side, for a time, and to a large extent, the mistaken advocacy of the church herself. But here again the native spirit of Christianity at length prevails; and now, with the exception of Spain, Brazil,† and our Southern States, all the Western Christian World has declared itself openly and decidedly opposed to slavery. The abolitionists are not a mere knot of infidel malcontents, or New England fanatics, or Puritan Yankees, but the great mass of enlightened Christendom. The clergy and the dignitaries of the church may often have lagged behind, under the influence and the incubus of a conservative, and oppressive, and selfish aristocracy—(all aristocracies are intensely selfish,

---

* Russia, coming up somewhat behind, in the progress of Christian civilization, has completed the abolition of serfdom in Europe, in this nineteenth century.

† The laws of slavery in Brazil are far more humane than in most slave countries. One provision enables the slave to have his name registered and his price fixed by a magistrate, and then pay that price as he can get small sums—the sale of the slave being no bar to counting previous payments—so that when the price is paid he is free. In 1850 the slave trade was prohibited in Brazil. Since the present reign commenced the number of slaves has decreased one million, while the products of the soil have increased thirty-five per cent. The Emperor seems anxious to bring the system to an end, but indications in the northern part of the empire threaten him with a rebellion like ours, to perpetuate the system. Perhaps our sufferings may be the means of mitigating those of Brazil.—*Spirit of Missions.*

as well as unscrupulously cruel,)—but the spirit of
Christianity has lived in the hearts of the Christian
people, and has wrought out, thrice in succession,
these triumphant results in favour of liberty. To
what other cause than the influence of Christianity
can they be ascribed? If Christianity is friendly to
slavery, whence has it come that precisely in the
most enlightened Christian countries it is, and in
Christian countries alone, that slavery is abolished
and abhorred?*

Goldwin Smith, the learned Professor of History
at Oxford, states the case thus:

"No sooner did the new religion gain power in the
world, than the slave law, and the slave system of the
empire, began to be undermined by its influence. In
conscious alliance with stoicism, to which among
all the ancient systems of philosophy it had the most
affinity, Christianity broke in upon the despotism of
the master, as well as upon the despotism of the
father and the husband. The right of life and death
over the slave was transferred from his owner to the
magistrate. The right of correction was placed
under humane limitations, which the magistrate was
directed to maintain. All the restrictions on the
enfranchisement of slaves were swept away. The
first Christian Emperor recognized enfranchisement
as a religious act, and established the practice of
performing it in the church, before the bishop, and
in the presence of the congregation.

"The liberties of the freedman were at the same

* The appeal made, on the other side, by the author of the
"View," to the Greek Church, the Nestorians, the Copts, and
Abyssinians, may be regarded as one of the strongest confirma-
tions of my position.

time cleared of all odious and injurious restrictions. This remained the policy of the Christian Empire. The Code of Justinian, the great monument of Imperial Jurisprudence, is highly favourable to enfranchisement, and that on religious grounds.

" The facility of enfranchisement, and the prospect of enlarging that facility, would conspire with political prudence to prevent Christianity from coming into direct collision with Roman slavery.

" Hope was not denied to the Roman slave. But hope is denied, or almost denied, to the American slave. In most of the Southern States the law withholds the power of enfranchisement from the master, against whose benevolence and generosity it seems the State is more concerned to guard, than against his cruelty and lust.

" A slave can be emancipated only by the authority of the legislature, or by a court of law, and upon special cause shown; and further, the condition of a Negro, when emancipated is such as to make freedom at once a very qualified and a very precarious boon. The free Negro is still to a great extent excluded from the rights of a citizen and a man. His evidence is not received against a white man; the law does not secure to him the safeguard of a trial by a jury of his peers; he has no vote or voice in framing the laws by which he is governed, and degrading restrictions are imposed even upon his religious worship. He is liable to be brought back into slavery many ways,—among others, by being married to a slave; and if his freedom is challenged, he must bring white witnesses to prove himself free. By the Roman law the presumption was in favor of freedom, and, under the Empire, freedmen not only enjoyed full liberty, but from their industry and pliancy often engrossed too much power in the State.

"But the Roman world was doomed; and it was doomed partly because the character of the upper classes had been deeply and incurably corrupted by the possession of a multitude of slaves.

"The feudal age succeeded; the barbarian conqueror took the place of the Roman master, and a new phase of slavery appeared. Immediately Christianity recommenced its work of alleviation and enfranchisement. The codes of laws framed for the new lords of Europe under the influence of the clergy, show the same desire as those of the Christian Emperors, to break in upon the despotism of the master, and assure personal rights to the slave. The laws of the Lombards, for instance, protected the serf against an unjust or too rigorous master; they set free the husband of a female slave who had been seduced by her owner; they assured the protection of the churches to slaves, who had taken refuge there, and regulated the penalties to be inflicted for their faults, instead of leaving them subject to an arbitrary will.

"In England, the clergy secured the slave rest on the Sunday, and liberty either to rest or work for himself on a number of holidays. They exhorted their flocks to leave the savings and earnings of the predial slave untouched.

"They constantly freed the slaves who came into their possession. They exhorted the laity to do the same, and what living covetousness refused, they often wrung from death-bed penitence. This they did constantly and effectually during the early part of the Middle Ages, while the church was to a great

extent in a missionary state, and had not yet been
turned into an establishment allied with political
power. Afterwards no doubt a change came over
the spirit of the clergy in this as well as other respects. The church became an estate and part of a
feudal system. Her Bishops became Spiritual Lords.
And these Spiritual Lords, in the time of Richard II.,
voted with the Temporal Lords for the repudiation
of the King's promise of enfranchisement to the vil-
lains, and the last serfs who remained in existence
were found on the estates of the church.

"Twice vanquished, in the shape of Ancient
Slavery, and in the shape of Feudal Serfdom, the
enemy rose again in the shape of Negro Slavery,
the offspring not of Roman or Barbarian conquest,
but of commercial avarice and cruelty. And again
Christianity returned to the struggle against the
barrier thus a third time reared by tyranny and
cupidity in the path of her great social hope and
mission, the brotherhood of man. By the mouth of
Clarkson and Wilberforce, she demanded and obtained of a Christian nation the emancipation of the
slaves in the West Indies. And if, in the case of
American slavery, the upper classes of this country,
from political considerations, have shown a change
of feeling, and the clergy of the Established Church
have gone with the upper classes, the Free Churches,
more unbiassed organs of Christianity, have almost
universally kept the faith.

"If, then, we look to the records of Christianity
in the Bible, we find no sanction for American
slavery there. If we look to the history of Christendom, we find the propagators and champions of the
faith assailing slavery under different forms, and in

different ages, without concert, yet with a unanimity which would surely be strange if Christianity and slavery were not the natural enemies of each other." *

Neander, the most learned of modern ecclesiastical historians, thus states the result of his investigations : " Christianity effected a change in the convictions of men from which a dissolution of the whole relation of slavery, though it could not be immediately accomplished, yet by virtue of the consequences resulting from that change, was sure eventually to take place. This effect Christianity produced, first of all, by the facts to which it was a witness, and next by the ideas which, by means of these facts, it set in circulation. By Christ, the Saviour for all mankind, the differences among men, resulting from sin, were reconciled; by Him the original unity of the race was restored. These facts must now operate in transforming the life of mankind. Masters as well as servants were obliged to acknowledge themselves the servants of sin, and must alike receive, as the free gift of God's grace, their deliverance from this common bondage,—*the true, the highest freedom.* Servants and masters, if they had become believers, were brought together under the same bond of a heavenly union destined for immortality ; they became brethren in Christ, in whom there is neither bond nor free, members of one body, baptized into one spirit, heirs of the same heavenly inheritance."†

The measured judgment of Guizot is given in the

* Goldwin Smith, "Does the Bible sanction Slavery?" pp. 202–205.

† Church History, Vol. I., p. 372.

following terms : " The church combated with much
perseverance and pertinacity the great vices of the
social condition, particularly slavery. It has been
frequently asserted that the abolition of slavery in
the modern world must be altogether carried to the
credit of Christianity. I believe this is going too
far : slavery subsisted for a long time in the bosom
of Christian society without much notice being taken
of it—without any great outcry against it. To effect
its abolition required the co-operation of several
causes—a great development of new ideas, of new
principles of civilization. It cannot, however, be
denied that the church employed its influence to restrain it ; the clergy in general, and especially several
popes, enforced the manumission of their slaves as a
duty incumbent upon laymen, and loudly inveighed
against the scandal of keeping Christians in bondage.
Again, the greater part of the forms by which slaves
were set free, at various epochs, are founded upon
religious motives. It is under the impression of some
religious feeling—the hopes of the future, the equality of all Christian men, and so on—that the freedom of the slave is granted. These, it must be con-
fessed, are rather convincing proofs of the influence
of the church, and of her desire for the abolition of
this evil of evils, this iniquity of iniquities."*

On the other hand, Balmes. a Spanish Roman Catholic writer, in his great work on European civilization, is not at all content with the moderate judgment of the Protestant Guizot. " What abolished
slavery among Christian nations ? Was it Christianity ? Was it Christianity alone, by its lofty ideas
in human dignity, by its maxims and its spirit of

* Guizot.   Civilization in Europe.   Lect. 6.

fraternity and charity, and also by its prudent, gentle, and beneficent conduct? *I trust I shall prove that
it was.*

"M. Guizot is much mistaken if he expects to
prove that the abolition of slavery was not due exclusively to Christianity, by the mere representation
that slavery existed for a long time amid Christian
society. To proceed logically, he must first see whether the sudden abolition of it was possible, if the
spirit of peace and order which animates the church
could allow her rashly to enter on an enterprise
which, without gaining the desired object, might
have convulsed the world. The number of slaves
was immense; slavery was deeply rooted in laws,
manners, ideas, and interests, individual and social;
a fatal system, no doubt, but the eradication of which
all at once, it would have been rash to attempt, as
its roots had penetrated deeply and spread widely in
the bowels of the land.

"It is not even necessary to suppose that the first
Christians understood all the force of the tendencies
of Christianity with respect to the abolition of slavery. What requires to be shown is, that the result
has been obtained by the doctrines and conduct of
the church.

"The first thing that Christianity did for slaves,
was to destroy the errors which opposed, not only
their universal emancipation, but even the improvement of their condition; that is, the first force which
she employed in the attack was, according to her
custom, *the force of ideas.* This first step was the
more necessary, as the same thing applies to all
other evils, as well as to slavery; every social evil
is always accompanied by some error which pro-
14

duces or foments it. There existed not only the oppression and degradation of a large portion of the human race, but, moreover, an accredited error, which tended more and more to lower that portion of humanity. According to this opinion, slaves were a mean race, far below the dignity of freemen; they were a race degraded by Jupiter himself, marked by a stamp of humiliation, and predestined to their state of abjection and debasement,* a detestable doctrine no doubt, contradicted by the nature of man, by history and experience; but which, nevertheless, reckoned distinguished men among its defenders, and which we see proclaimed for ages, to the shame of humanity and the scandal of reason, until Christianity came to destroy it, by undertaking to vindicate the rights of man.

"We may inquire of M. Guizot what were the *other causes,* the *other ideas,* the *other principles of civilization,* the great development of which, to avail myself of his words, was necessary ' to abolish this evil of evils, this iniquity of iniquities.' Ought he not to explain, or at least point out, these causes, ideas, and principles of civilization, which, according to him, assisted the church in the abolition of slavery, in order to save the reader the trouble of seeking or divining them? If they did not arise in the bosom of the church, *where* did they arise? Were they found in the ruins of ancient civilization? But could these remains of a scattered and almost annihilated civilization effect what that same civilization, in all its vigour, power, and splendour, never did, or thought of doing? Were they in *the individual inde-*

* How much this is like the " curse of Ham !"

pendence of the barbarians? But that individuality, the inseparable companion of violence, must consequently have been the source of oppression and slavery.* Were they found in the *military patronage,* introduced, according to M. Guizot, by the barbarians themselves; patronage which laid the foundation of that aristocratical organization which was converted at a later period into feudality? But what could this patronage — an institution likely, on the contrary, to perpetuate slavery among the indigent in conquered countries, and to extend it to a considerable portion of the conquerors themselves—what could this patronage do for the abolition of slavery? Where, then, is the idea, the custom, the institution, which, born out of Christianity, contributed to the abolition of slavery? Let any one point out to us the epoch of its formation, the time of its development; let him show us that it had not its origin in Christianity; and we will then confess that the latter cannot exclusively lay claim to the glorious title of having abolished that degraded condition; and he may be sure that this shall not prevent our exalting that idea, custom, or institution, which took part in the great and noble enterprise of liberating the human race."†

The celebrated German theologian Möhler, also a Romanist, has written a whole treatise to show that *slavery was abolished by Christianity.*

I cheerfully set the authority of Balmes and Möhler against that of Bishop England, to whom the author of the "View" appeals, and whose see was no

* Just as with our modern "chivalry."
† Balmes, European Civilization, pp. 91, 95, 114.

other than Charleston, S. C.—as an exponent of the position of the Roman Catholic church in relation to this question.

In the face of all these authorities, what shall we say to such allegations as the following: " The causes which led to the extinction of slavery in Europe were secular and not religious;" " no statement can be more unsupported by the facts of history than that the extinction of slavery in Europe was owing to the influence of Christianity." Did not the early Christians make emancipation a solemn religious act? And, as Guizot says, was it not all along, " under the impression of some religious feeling—the hopes of the future—the equality of all Christian men, and so on, that the freedom of the slave was granted ?"

The friends of Wilberforce will be amazed to hear it intimated that he did not really aim at the *abolition* of slavery in the West Indies, and that he was not prompted in his efforts by Christian principle and religious motives. And hardly less amazed will the Quakers be, to learn that they have not regarded slavery as a *sin*, and have been influenced in their persistent efforts for its abolition only by the considerations of a " *wise expediency !*"

But, says the author of the " View," triumphantly: " that the Church of England held slavery to be perfectly lawful in itself, as well as the Church of Rome, and all the Christian denominations of Europe and America, through the whole period of their history, down to the end of the last century, and far into the present, is as incontrovertible as any fact can be. The Bishops of that church saw no sin in the treaty of Utrecht, to which the religious Queen Anne was a party. They concurred in the Act of Parliament under George III., which regarded the negroes as lawful merchandise. The Puritans of New England sold the Indians as slaves, and were the chief importers of the Africans for the Southern market. Even the Quakers of Pennsylvania had slaves, and William Penn was a slaveholder."

Now here we have a pretty fair specimen of this whole " View of Slavery," and of its style of reasoning. Let us look at it a moment.

1. Observe the petty quibble of "lawful *in itself."* On this the whole hinges.

2. John Wesley, the founder of Methodism, was born in 1703, entered at Christ Church, Oxford, in 1720, took orders in 1725, received a Fellowship in Lincoln College in 1726, and the degree of A. M. in 1727. From 1735 to 1737, he resided as a missionary in Georgia and Carolina, where he had an opportunity to see with his own eyes what slavery was. It is he who so truthfully denominated slavery " the sum of all villanies." The author of the " View" has frequently quoted this phrase to sneer at it, but has entirely omitted the name of John Wesley, while the later Adam Clarke is quoted at large, apparently to illustrate a *modern change* in Methodist opinion. Had John Wesley and his followers been wise enough to remain in the bosom of the English church, and had that church been wise enough to retain them there, it certainly would not have diminished her spiritual life or lowered her Christian character or conscience; and, in my opinion, would have been of inestimable advantage to the Methodists themselves, and to the church at large. John Wesley has as good a right to speak in the name of Christianity, and as an exponent of the genius of the Christian religion, as any

14*

prelate of the English church; but there have not been wanting prelates and doctors of that church who have spoken against slavery with no doubtful utterance, such as Bishop Warburton, Bishop Butler, Bishop Porteus, Bishop Horsley, and Archdeacon Paley. And if the point is, that the English church has not pronounced formally and authoritatively against negro slavery; I answer, on what has the English church pronounced formally and authoritatively for the last two hundred years, except by act of Parliament, or of the privy council?

3. But "the Bishops of that church saw no sin in the treaty of Utrecht, to which the religious Queen Anne was a party. They concurred in the act of Parliament under George III., which regarded the negroes as lawful merchandise." Now what was the treaty of Utrecht? It secured to the English African Company a monopoly in the introduction of negroes into the several ports of Spanish America, for the term of thirty years. And the first article stipulated that this company should bring into the West Indies one hundred and forty-four thousand negroes, within that period, *one-fourth part of the commercial profits being reserved to the King of Spain, and another fourth part to the Queen of England.*

Here it is important to have a fair understanding. Does the author of the "View" approve or disapprove of the African Slave Trade? Does he or does he not see any wrong in it? Let us know distinctly, and without any shuffling. In many parts of his book he seems opposed to the African Slave Trade, to regard it as an inhuman traffic, but to make a broad distinction between the Slave Trade and slaveholding. And then again he seems ready to justify the

African Slave Trade itself. Observe, at all events, that the Bishops of the English church are admitted to be as fully committed to an approbation of the Slave Trade as of slaveholding; and the religious Queen Anne graciously received her share of the profits. Was, then, the Slave Trade wrong? If, though not wrong then, it is wrong now, what makes it wrong now? Is it wrong because it is forbidden, or is it forbidden because it is wrong? Would the author of the " View" have men hung as pirates on the grounds of a *"wise expediency?"* Hung for buying and selling slaves in one latitude, and defended as the best of Christians—yes, the very best of Christians—for doing it in another?

4. But the Puritans were slaveholders and slave-traders, and even William Penn held slaves.—Well, was this to the credit or discredit of the Puritans? If it was to their credit, it is refreshing to find that something can be said to the honour of New England Puritans; but it is a curious thing to allege it as a means of heaping odium on their descendants. If it is to their discredit, then some of their descendants are doing what they can to hold themselves clear from any similar charge, and certainly they should not be found fault with for that. If the Irish author of the " View" were an earnest abolitionist, and was disputing to the New Englanders or the Pennsylvanians their exclusive claim to the credit of the abolition movement, what is said about the Puritans and William Penn, would be none the less ill-natured, but might have the apparent force of an argument. But as the case stands, this stale and ill-natured fling —even if admitted to be true, which it is not—has

not even the merit of possessing the slightest argumentative force.

In fine, as to the position of the English church on this question, it is not here pretended that that position has been " ultra-abolitionist ;" but it is insisted that her heart and her voice have been in favour of emancipation and condemnatory of slavery. That cause must indeed be desperate which is reduced to the forlorn attempt to show that the Christian mind of England is in favour of slavery. The dignitaries of the Church of England, in sympathy with the aristocracy, may have been backward in condemning the system. But a man does not become any more of a Christian, nor is he of course imbued any more deeply with the spirit of Christianity, by being raised to the Episcopal bench. And from the time of St. Paul until now, the aristocracy is the last portion of society where one should seek the true genius and spirit of the Christian religion. If anything is to ruin the church of England, and if anything is to corrupt and enfeeble her American daughter, it is the disposition to sympathize too largely with the aristocracy and too little with the mass of the Christian people.

England is not only anti-slavery, but, notwithstanding all national and political jealousies, she is in favour of the side of freedom in our present struggle. And in this case, as in regard to the question of slavery itself, the opposition to our cause is found among the aristocracy, and the clergy of the established church who affiliate with them.

On the whole, it cannot be doubted that Christianity is an anti-slavery religion, that the enlightened Christian church is, and ever has been, an anti-slavery church, that the prevailing sentiment of Christian Europe is an anti-slavery sentiment, and that those whether on the continent or in Great Britain, who are opposed to us in our present contest and sympathize with the rebellion, are actuated solely by political considerations and prejudices, in spite of their anti-slavery feelings. They favour the Southern oligarchy and oppose the free republic of the North, or rather the great republic of the United States, because they *so far harmonize* with our " Christian Bishop" as to sneer at the principles of the immortal Declaration of Independence, to reject the natural rights of man, and to decry the idea of the people's being capable of self-government; and because they dread the future power, moral, political, and physical, of this rising Western Empire, if it be allowed to wax to its full growth as one great free Commonwealth.

I venture to add the following from a vigorous English writer, as indicating, from an Englishman's point of view, the character and spirit of the persistent efforts made in certain quarters to poison and prejudice English opinion, in relation to our present national struggle and its proper causes :

" It is a melancholy reflection, that on no question in our day has so much want of candor been displayed, or so much dishonest perversion been resorted to, as on this question of the American revolt. The origin of the war, the object of the war, the progress of the war, the spirit in which the war is conducted, in spite of the clearest possible facts, have, one after the other, been disputed, denied, or perverted. When Southern politicians, from Davis to Toombs, and from Stephens to Spratt, tell us that they design to establish a Government, based on the bondage of the laborer—when the bishops of the Episcopal Church declare that the 'abolition of slavery is hateful, infidel, and pestilent,' and the Rev. Dr. Palmer adds that 'the providential trust of the South is to perpetuate the institution of domestic slavery now existing, with the freest scope for its natural development;' when the statesmen, journalists, and divines of the South join in one chorus of admiration for slavery, people among us are yet dishonest enough to aver that the question of slavery neither had nor has anything whatever to do with the rebellion of the South; that that rebellion was simply and entirely a question of tariff!

"Precisely the same spirit is shown in dealing with the events of the war. When Sherman drives Johnston into the interior of Georgia, Johnston succeeds in drawing Sherman from his base. When Grant attacks Lee in front, he is credited with the qualities of a bear. When he outflanks Lee, he is afraid to meet him in the field. When he at last succeeds, by strength, courage, or strategy, in driving him from Fredericksburg to Richmond—why, then we are told that the Federal general might have reached that point long ago. While the opposing armies were on the Rapidan, we had no end of predictions that Grant would never see Richmond. When he at length does see it, we are assured that Grant is a fool for not taking a shorter route. Ever since Butler landed on the James, we have had almost daily assurances that the next mail would bring us news of his having been driven into the river. On the other hand, every repulse of the Federals, however trifling, has been magnified into a rout; while more than one success for the Confederates has been reported and gloried in twice or thrice over.

"If one had read the exclusive news of the Copperhead newspapers only, one would have been sorely puzzled to understand how it is that the North is not overrun; that Washington is not destroyed, and that the Armies of the Potomac and Cumberland exist at all. In the same, if Semmes didn't take the Kearsage, it was only because his ship was out of repair and his enemy was chain-plated. Semmes wasn't beaten; he only committed 'a mistake.' But if the critics are severe on the Federals, they are exceedingly charitable to the slaveholders. Semmes burns unarmed ships; runs away from the Federal cruisers; libels the victor in his first fair encounter, and the critics celebrate his gallantry, and call him a hero. Like kings in the constitutional axiom, the slaveholders can do no wrong. They shoot negro teamsters at Murfreesboro'; they give no quarter to the negro troops at Port Hudson; they burn alive the negro garrison at Port Pillow—and never a word of protest or censure is uttered by the critics. They chain cannon-balls to the legs of Federal officers at Atlanta; they starve Federal prisoners at Belle Isle; they make arrangements to blow up a military prison at Richmond; they slaughter men, women and children in Kansas; they play at nine-pins with the bones of the Federal dead; they commit every conceivable atrocity, and many atrocities that are absolutely inconceivable—and yet no Confederate commentator on the war goes out of his way to condemn them. Such is the way in which contemporary events are chronicled in England!"

CHAPTER VI.

SLAVERY AND ETHICS.

SLAVEHOLDERS and their advocates are accustomed to give proof of their extraordinary piety by their constant devout recognition of *Divine Providence*. This belongs almost as invariably to the staple of their argument as does the *curse of Ham* or the *Epistle to Philemon*. What brought the Negroes from Africa? Not the wickedness of the slave trade, but Divine Providence. What perpetuates their bondage? Not the cupidity of their masters, but Divine Providence. What deprives them of their rights? Not the iniquitous course of men, but the Providence of God. The prohibition of their instruction, the infliction of cruel treatment, the system of concubinage, the compulsory separation of families —these are all dispensations of God's holy Providence. And if the slaves are now to be emancipated, it will be brought about in the Providence of God, in his own good time; and *men must beware of meddling with God's work, or attempting to forestall the Divine decrees.* Says Bishop Hopkins: "If any man can seriously contemplate the awful debasement of the native Africans, and candidly compare it with the present condition of the Southern slaves, and then *denounce as a sin* the means which Divine Providence has chosen to save them from their former

(168)

state of wretched barbarism, ... I can only say
that I am at a loss whether I should be most astonished at the waywardness of his heart, or the blindness of his understanding." " In the Providence of
God, the negro slavery of the South has been the
means of saving millions of those poor creatures
from the horrible state in which they must otherwise have lived and died." Observe, by the way,
that this argument justifies the slave trade even
more directly than it does the " negro slavery of the
South." And further on, he says : " Until it comes"
—the time when the race of Canaan shall be relieved
from the curse,—" it is our duty to submit with pa-
tient faith to our allotted condition ; not rebelliously
warring against the will of the Most High, nor vainly
opposing ourselves to the arrangements of his Providence, nor accusing our brethren in Christ as *sinners* because they keep in slavery the race which
God saw fit to doom to servitude." And again :
" When the time for the total abolition of slavery
comes, it will not be by the insane projects of politicians, through blood and desolation. The Supreme
Ruler of nations, in whose hands are the hearts of
men, will incline the minds of the South, when he
sees it to be right, to institute and carry on the process, in the only safe and effectual way, which has
been pursued by the other States in relation to it.
Since the world began slavery has never been abolished by external force and violence. It has been
done away by *internal action* on the part of those who
are directly concerned." He then cites, in illustration, the two cases of St. Domingo and the British
West Indies. Now this, by the way, seems to me a
most singular perversion. Since the world began

15

was it ever heard that a legislature controlled by
slaveholders freely abolished slavery ? The legislatures of all our free States were, by immense ma-
jorities, under the control of non-slaveholders, when
they abolished slavery. Not a slaveholder was represented in the British Parliament which passed
the emancipation act. If the abolition of slavery
had been left to the "*internal action*" of the West
India Colonial legislatures, it would not have been
abolished to this day,—not to say, never;—nor, if
the doctrines of this " View of Slavery" were adopted
and acted on by slaveholders, would they ever abolish
slavery anywhere; for why should they ? Is it not
a Divine institution—an unspeakable blessing, an
ordination of God's Providence, perfectly just and
right ? How soon would the "Supreme Ruler of
nations," under such instructions as those, and while
" Cotton is king," incline the hearts of Southern
slaveholders to the " total abolition of slavery ?"
Has slavery been abolished in Missouri, in Louisiana,
in Maryland, in West Virginia, in Virginia herself,
—or would it ever have been abolished, by the influence of such doctrines as those contained in this
" View," or by the "*internal action*" of the slaveholders themselves ?

But this by the way. What I have now to comment upon is—this very pious appeal to Divine Providence. The author of the " View" is not alone in
this. It is quite characteristic of slaveholding logic.
The Professor of Agricultural Chemistry in the Uni-
versity of Georgia remarks on the " Providential "
proportion of the untilled lands of the South and
" the unemployed power of human muscles in
Africa."—" I trace, he exclaims, " the growing de-

mand for negro muscles, bones, and brains to the good providence of God." But I will not multiply quotations. It will be found, as I have said, that this appeal to the Providence of God underlies a large part of the argument, and is the basis of some of the most fervid denunciations of this " View of Slavery," and of pro-slavery writers generally. I shall not call it blasphemous;* but shall endeavour, once for all, to expose its fallacy, its utter and insufferable nonsense, considered as a matter of reasoning.

The whole question lies in a small compass. It must be plain, upon the slightest reflection, that the " Providence of God " has nothing whatever to do with determining the moral character of the actions of men. What sin was ever wrought, what

* The one-sided notions which pro-slavery men entertain of Divine Providence are well illustrated by the following fact: In the Episcopal Convention of the Diocese of Pennsylvania, held at Pittsburg, in May, 1864, this resolution was offered:— " Resolved, That in the long delay of success in suppressing this monstrous rebellion, we see wonderfully manifest the hand of God, training by his severest chastisements, this reluctant people to a readiness to do justice and show mercy to a long-oppressed and outraged race;" whereupon, the Rev. Mr. Swope, of Pittsburg, was understood to denounce the resolution as "*blasphemous.*" But wherein did the blasphemy consist? In recognizing the Providence of God? That can hardly be. In professing to fathom God's *designs?* If so, what is Paley's Theology but one mass of blasphemies? In ascribing *such* a design to God, as leading men "to do justice and show mercy?" But what design could be more worthy of his Providence? Or, finally, did it consist in this, that the Rev. Mr. Swope knew that God had no such design as was ascribed to him? But that would be a mere question of fact; and besides there would then be as much "blasphemous" presumption on one side as on the other.

crime was ever perpetrated, what cruelty or villainy
was ever committed, what action, right or wrong,
was ever done by man, what event, of whatever character, ever transpired in human history,—which did
not take place by the Providence of God? Because
God brings good out of evil, does that justify the
evil? If so, not slavery, alone, but all sin, would
find speedy absolution. God's Providence, but not
the evil, is thereby justified. The justification of
God's Providence, and the justification of man's
agency, are two distinct things. A Theodicy is not
a. system of ethics. "Whatever is, is right," is
true in relation to Divine Providence, but not true,
most assuredly, in relation to human actions. The
slave trade, with all its execrable and horrible bar-
barities, took place under Divine Providence. The
slave trade was abolished and declared piracy, under
Divine Providence. All the atrocities of the old
French Revolution were committed under Divine
Providence. The American Revolution was achieved
under Divine Providence. Negro slavery was established in America under Divine Providence. And
wherever, and by whatever means, internal or external,—violent or peaceful,—sudden or gradual,—
it shall ever be abolished, it is to be presumed it will
be *under Divine Providence.* Why, has not the " abolition fanaticism" itself, as well as the institution of
slavery, arisen under *Divine Providence?* And yet
abolitionists are denounced because they would "interfere with the Providence of God." If a man can
get outside of the Providence of God, to interfere
with it, he must go somewhere that I never heard
of. Did the steamship interfere with the Providence
of God? Did the telegraph interfere with the Provi-

dence of God? Does the teacher, with his instructions for the ignorant, interfere with the Providence
of God? Does the physician, with his remedies,
interfere with the Providence of God? But are not
darkness and death, both spiritual and temporal,
sent upon mankind as the result of a Divine *curse?*
Why, then, should it be an interference with the
Providence of God, to preach deliverance to the captive, to seek the freedom of the slave, to endeavour
to enlighten and elevate the long-oppressed and be-
nighted Negro race? What there should be so
peculiar, in just this particular case, in relation to
Divine Providence, passes all comprehension. In the
name of common sense, then, let us hear no more
justifications of slavery and denunciations of abolition, *from the Providence of God.*

Another great gun in the slaveholders' ethical
logic, which they never fail to bring into requisition,
and which the author of the " View" has several
times discharged with evident satisfaction at its expected execution,—is this, that " slavery is not wrong
per se, not wrong *in itself,* and irrespective of the
question of *treatment.*" But if the whole question of
right or wrong lies in the treatment, then slavery
in itself has no character at all. What is slavery *in
itself?* Where was it ever seen? It becomes a pure
abstraction. It exists only in the mind; and it may
readily be admitted that the idea of slavery, as it
exists in a man's mind, is not morally wrong. But
wherever slavery exists as a fact, it exists in the
concrete. Nothing really exists in itself, but God.
If all slavery were abolished except slavery in the
abstract, slavery in itself, the most rabid abolitionist
might well be satisfied. Killing a man is not wrong

15 *

in itself. Taking my neighbour's goods is not wrong *in itself.* Desiring another's property is not wrong *in itself;* for, if it were, the tenth commandment would be violated in every case of trade or barter, since each party desires that which belongs to the other. No external act or course of action is good or bad *in itself,* i. e., without reference to the agent and his motive. The essence of right and wrong pertains to that which is *internal,* the heart, the will, the purpose. "As a man thinketh in his heart, so is he." Yet we condemn murder, though we can see nothing but the indifferent external act; we condemn it, because that act in certain connexions is held to imply the malicious intent. So of theft, and other crimes. So of slavery. Taken in its concrete connexions, we know it must generally be wrong; and, if there are any exceptions, the burden of proof is upon them; they must show that they are exceptions. Slavery, in general, just as certainly implies, on the part of the master, cupidity, selfishness, disregard for his neighbour's rights, as deliberately killing a man with a bludgeon implies malice prepense. Such slavery as that described by Judge Ruffin is no abstraction; it cannot possibly be right.

Another familiar justification of slavery is derived from its beneficial results; it has improved the condition of the blacks; it has been a most effective missionary institution. But here we meet with the plain moral principle, that good results, unless intended, do not justify our actions, for they do not properly belong to us; nor even when intended do they always furnish a complete vindication; for "the end alone does not justify the means." And what man in his senses can honestly believe that

Southern slaveholders, in general, hold their slaves, and that slave traders buy and sell them, from the dominant motive of improving their condition and saving their souls?   Are the Southern masters educating and preparing their slaves for freedom? How much progress have they made in the work during the last thirty years? and if they go on at this rate when will they be ready to emancipate them all? If it be suggested that they may be, at least in part, controlled by good motives, some more, some less,— I answer that as men usually act from complex and mixed motives, it is rare that any man, in any action, is absolutely good or absolutely bad.   The worst things, even slavery, may have something of good in them, without being thereby justified; and some slaveholders may be comparatively good men, though the system of slavery be thoroughly bad.   Even a murderer may have some good qualities, and may have been prompted to the very act of murder, in part, by good motives.

The advocates of slavery, when the cruelties and oppressions incident to the system are charged upon it, rarely fail to carry the war *out of* Africa; saying, " there are cruelties and oppressions and evils in free countries also,"—" let him that is without sin cast the first stone;" " reform your own social system before you meddle with the reformation of others." But it is no justification of one thing,— rather it is an implied condemnation of it,—to say that other things are as bad, or even worse; nor is it so much as a valid *argumentum ad hominem*, while the party addressed does not defend the latter in passing over them to attack the former.   And even though his passing over the one and assailing the

other should be admitted to be an inconsistency in
him, that would not, in the slightest degree, alter or
affect the intrinsic moral character of the things in
question. "This is as bad or worse,"—then *that* is
confessedly bad. Neither the condemnation nor the
punishment of crimes is to remain in abeyance until
perfect men can be found to apply them; otherwise,
the administration of moral judgment and human
justice must utterly and forever cease. Nor is a
man or a community estopped from attempting any
reformation abroad until there are no evils or faults
to be corrected at home. If the reforming party
claimed to be perfect, there might be ground for a
fair retort; but even this would furnish no defence
or proper justification of that which he would reform. Moreover, the existence of evils or wrongs
in spite of the law, is no excuse for a law or a system
and course of legislation *establishing and protecting* injustice and oppression. The cases are not parallel.
Crimes exist in spite of all laws; but that is no good
reason for legalizing them; nor is it even any good
reason for abolishing all legislation. We must be
content,—if content at all,—with what is short of
perfection; while yet perfection must be our constant goal.

When slavery is defended as being right *in itself*,
and all the wrong, if any, is transferred to the *treatment*, and declared, therefore, to be merely incidental,
the intention must be—unless slavery is left a mere
characterless abstraction — to speak of slavery, the
"relation of master and slave," as a thing, a reality,
embodied in the *law*. Aside from all "treatment,"
what real meaning can be attached to "the relation
of master and slave," except as it is defined, sanc-

tioned, and maintained by the *law?* If that law is
wrong, then that "relation of master and slave" is
wrong. Now the Christian moralist may judge of
the rightfulness of laws, and, if a citizen of a free
country, it is his bounden duty thus to judge; for,
so far as he has a moral or political influence, he is
responsible for their character. I know there are
some who dispute this view. No less a man than
one who had been a distinguished officer in the navy,
and afterwards a senator in congress from the State
of New Jersey, and who considered either his personal importance or the weight of his doctrine sufficient to authorize his publishing a formal *Address to
the People of the North* just before the breaking out
of the Southern Rebellion,—made the distinct an-
nouncement, " whatever the law declares to be right,
is right."* This was a short and easy method to
put an end to all discussion about the right or wrong
of slavery. But, according to this, a legislature is
not only supreme but infallible. A legislature can
do no wrong, can enact no injustice. Neither can
legislators, without absurdity, raise the question of
right or wrong in discussing a proposed measure;
if they only enact it, it cannot help being right. One
might as well say, " whatever the law declares to be
true, is true;" — if the law says " black is white,"
then black *is* white. Those who hold this doctrine

* And yet the honourable Senator would perhaps be among the
first to declare that the emancipation of the slaves by law without compensation to the masters would be wrong : for example,
that an amendment of the Constitution of the United States, constitutionally made, so emancipating all the slaves in the country,
would be wrong; or a similar amendment of a State constitution,
say, of Maryland, similarly made, would still be wrong.

would do well to consider what is their idea of right, and whence it is derived. Is their very *idea of right*, "that which is established by law?" Then to say that "what the law establishes is right," is as much as to say, "what the law establishes, the law establishes." On the other hand, is their idea of *right* derived from the judgment of the moral faculty and independent of the positive enactment of law? Then the statement that "whatever the law declares to be right, is right," becomes a mere opinion of fact, and not a doctrine of necessary truth; the opinion may be false in any given case; it is manifestly false in many cases, and, in every case, the question whether it be true or false must be submitted to the decision of the moral faculty.

Says Bishop Hopkins: "The nearest approach on earth to what men call freedom and equality consists in *subjection to good laws. . . . . .* What compels this subjection? *The Government.* What is the Government? It is the systematic organization of *force.* No law is of any efficacy among men unless there is *a power able to execute it.* But the importance of Government is seen in this, that the force which it exercises is regulated by the fixed principles of justice, and intended to operate on every class in the community, so as to protect their rights and privileges;" and, further on, he speaks of "the rule of a just government." Now whether or not he *means* here to affirm the same doctrine with that of the New Jersey Senator, may be uncertain. There are other statements in his book,—as when he repeats the stereotyped denunciations of "the higher law," —which seem to look in that direction. And, if he means that, as a matter of necessity or of universal fact, " the force which the Government exercises is regulated by the fixed principles of justice, and intended to operate on every class of the community, so as to protect their rights and principles," then he adopts that doctrine in terms. But, if he means that this is the proper *idea* of Government, which may or may not be realized in particular cases; then his is a very different doctrine from the other. And he must mean this, if he would not avoid absurdity; for, otherwise, what sense is there in "*good* government," "*just* government," " government being *regulated by fixed principles* of justice?" Surely this must imply that there may be *bad* government, *unjust* goverment, and that the fixed principles of justice exist *antecedent and superior* to the government which they are to regulate.

But though our moral judgments are properly independent of and superior to the laws,—not our *external actions*, but our *moral judgments*,—still, it must be admitted that the laws under which we have been educated react powerfully upon our moral judgments. If we had grown up where the murder of a human being was punished but slightly, or not at all, while to maintain that slavery is wrong and ought to be abolished was a capital offence, we might very probably come to regard the abolitionist as much worse than the murderer. A Frank inquired of an Arab what he considered the greatest of sins. "The greatest sin," said the Arab, "is, to deny the unity of God," "and the next greatest is, to *drink the shameful*" — (i. e., to use wine) — "these can never be forgiven; let these be avoided, and the rest is of little consequence." "But what of murder, adultery, robbery?" &c., inquired the Frank. "God is merciful," was the Arab's reply. What, then, is the Southern law of slavery? I have already referred to the decision of Judge Ruffin, to show that the "relation of master and slave," as defined and maintained by Southern law, is an immoral relation. That decision does not stand alone. I propose to add here other specimens of slave law, taken almost at random from a collection made by Judge Stroud:

The civil law—except where modified by statute, or by usages which have acquired the force of law—is generally referred to in the slaveholding States, as containing the true principles of the institution. It will be proper, therefore, to give an abstract of its leading doctrines; for which purpose, I use *Dr. Taylor's Elements of the Civil Law,* page 429;—"Slaves," says he, "were held *pro nullis; pro mortuis; pro quadrupedibus.* They had no *head* in the State, no name, title or register; they were not capable of being injured; nor could they take by purchase or descent; they had no heirs, and therefore could make no will; exclusive of what was called their *peculium,* whatever they acquired was their master's; they could not plead nor be pleaded for, but were excluded from all civil concerns whatever; they could not claim the indulgence of absence *reipublicæ causa;* they were not entitled to the rights and considerations of matrimony, and, therefore, had no relief in case of adultery; nor were they proper objects of cognation or affinity, but of *quasi-cognation* only; they could be sold, transferred, or pawned as goods or personal estate; for goods they were, and as such they were esteemed; they might be tortured for evidence, punished at the discretion of their lord, or even put to death by his authority." (p. 9.)

The doctrine of *South Carolina* is equally strong. It is concentrated by *Wardlaw, J.,* in this single sentence:—"Every endeavour to extend to a slave positive rights is an attempt to reconcile inherent contradictions; *for, in the very nature of things,* he is subject to DESPOTISM." *Ex parte* BOYLETON, 2 *Strobhart,* 41. He gives this as a quotation from *Kinlock vs. Harvey,* Harper's Rep., 514, with the commendation, "*as is well said.*" According to the law of Louisiana, "a slave is one who is in the power of a master to

whom he belongs. The master may sell him, dispose of his person, his industry, and his labor; he can do nothing, possess nothing, nor acquire anything, but what must belong to his master."
Civil Code, Art. 35. As to the master's power to punish his slave,
a *limitation seems* to be contemplated by the following article:—
The slave is entirely subject to the will of his master, who may
correct and chastise him, *though not with unusual rigour, or so as to
maim or mutilate him, or to expose him to the danger of loss of life,
or to cause his death.* Art. 173. Yet, as will be fully demonstrated
hereafter, no such limitation actually exists, or can by law be
enforced.

With respect to the other slaveholding States, as none of these
have adopted *entire written codes,* enunciations of such a *general* nature as are exhibited in the quotations just made from the law of
Louisiana are not to be expected. Nevertheless, the cardinal
principle of slavery—that the slave is to be regarded as a thing,—
is an article of property,—a chattel personal,—obtains as un-
doubted law in all of these States. (p. 10.)

Having transcribed acts of South Carolina and of
Louisiana, which are too long to be inserted here,
Judge Stroud adds:

Hence it appears that acording to a statute that was enacted
upon the most solemn deliberation by one legislature, and which
has been adopted since by four distinct bodies of the same nature,
ten hours make up the *longest* space out of twenty-four hours,
which can be demanded for labor from *convicted felons,* whose PUN-
ISHMENT was designed to consist chiefly of HARD LABOR. Yet the
slave of South Carolina, under a law professing to *extend humanity*
towards him, may be subjected to unremitting toil for FIFTEEN
HOURS within the same period!!

If we turn to Louisiana, the condition of the slave will be
found, in this particular, without melioration. For, though the
purpose of the act which I have transcribed is declared to be to
ascertain what hours are to be assigned to the slave for *work* and
REST, the only *rest* which it provides is half an hour at breakfast,
and two hours at dinner. At what time a third meal is to be
taken, whether at sunset or at midnight, is left to the master's

16

pleasure. And, judging from our knowledge of the mode in which sugar is made, and cotton is raised and *pressed*, it is not too much to say, that the going down of the sun is by no means the signal of repose to the weary slave. And let it not be forgotten that the slave, within the short time allotted for *rest*, is under the necessity of preparing food for his meals ! ! (p. 15.)

THE MASTER MAY, AT HIS DISCRETION, INFLICT ANY SPECIES OF PUNISHMENT UPON THE PERSON OF HIS SLAVE.

If the power of the master to the extent here implied were sanctioned by *express* law, we should have no claim to the character of a civilized people. The very being of the slave would be in the hands of the master. Such is not the case ; on the contrary, from the laws which I shall cite, it will be fully evident that, *so far as regards the pages of the statute-book*, the *life*, at least, of the slave is safe from the *authorized* violence of the master. The evil is not that laws are wanting, but that they cannot be enforced ; not that they sanction crime, but that they do not punish it. And this arises chiefly, if not *solely*, from the cause which has been more than once mentioned, the exclusion of the testimony, on the *trial* of a *white* person, of all those who are not white.

There was a time when, in all the old States in which slavery is still maintained, the murder of a slave, whether by his master or a third person, was punished by a pecuniary fine only. South Carolina was the last of these States in which a change in this particular was made.

Since then, (Dec. 20, 1821,) the *wilful, malicious,* and *premeditated* killing of a slave, by whomsoever perpetrated, is a *capital* offence in all the slaveholding States. (p. 20.)

The state of the law in Virginia will appear from the following :

On September 1, 1849, whilst the act of 1847 was yet in force, one of the most, if not the most, *wilful, malicious,* and *deliberate* murders was committed by the master of a slave, *by wilful* and excessive *whipping* and *cruel treatment*, which the criminal records of any country have transmitted. The case is reported in 7 *Grattan's Reports*, 679, under the name of *Souther's* case. The opinion of the court gives this narrative :—"The indictment contains fifteen counts, and sets forth a case of the most cruel and excessive whipping and torture. The negro was tied to a tree and whipped with switches. When Souther became fatigued with the labour of whipping, he called upon a negro man of his, and made him cob Sam with a shingle. He also made a negro woman of his help to cob him. And, after cobbing and whipping, he applied fire to the body of his slave, about his back, belly, and private parts. He then caused him to be rubbed down with hot water, in which pods of red pepper had been steeped. The negro was also tied to a log, and to the bed-post with ropes, which choked him, and he was kicked and stamped by Souther. This sort of punishment was continued and repeated until the negro died under its infliction."

The slave's offences, according to the master's allegation, were "getting drunk," and dealing with two persons,—*white men*,—who were present, and witnessed the whole of the horrible transaction, without, as far as it appears in the report, having interfered in any way to save the life of the slave.

The jury found the master guilty of murder in the *second* degree.* The court expressed a clear opinion that it was murder in the *first* degree, under the act of 1847. What would have been held to be the proper verdict, had the existing law, in which "wilful and excessive whipping," &c., are left out, been in force, is very doubtful. (p. 21.)

In Missouri, the statute on crimes, in treating of homicide, makes no mention of *colour* or *condition* of the person slain.

The fourth section defines *justifiable* homicide in the same undiscriminating language, but it is not necessary to extract it.

The fifth section is in these words :—" Homicide shall be deemed *excusable*, when committed by *accident* or *misfortune*, in either of the following cases: *First*, in *lawfully* correcting a *child*, apprentice, *servant* or slave."

The same language is used in regard to the correction of the *child, apprentice, servant* and SLAVE, and the one word *lawfully* is prefixed as well to the slave as to the child or apprentice. But what is *lawful* correction of a *child* or *apprentice* is accurately defined and easily explained; the common law has settled that, and

---

* Punishment, by statute, might be five years imprisonment.

the transgression of the limits is an indictable offence. But there is no such limit in regard to the power of the *master* over the *slave.* *He* may use any instrument, and may inflict any number of blows which he may choose. This is a principle of slave law, it is believed, of universal application. In North Carolina it has been expressly affirmed by the Supreme Court, and its *necessity* asserted and defended in an elaborate opinion of the Chief Justice, on behalf of the whole court. State vs. Mann, 2 Devereux's Rep. 263, 266.

Here follows the already recited opinion of Judge Ruffin. (p. 22.)

Mr. Bryan Edwards, who, it will be recollected, *was the champion of slavery and of the slave trade,* in his *History of the West Indies,* Vol. II., Book IV., Chap. V., after speaking of certain regulations which had been proposed for the melioration of slavery, uses this language :—"But these and all other regulations, which can be devised for the protection and improvement of this unfortunate class of people will be of little avail, unless, as a preliminary measure, they shall be exempted *from the cruel* hardships to which they are frequently liable, *of being sold by creditors,* and made subject, in a course of administration by executors, to the payment of all debts, both of simple contract and specialty." This he stigmatises as a " *grievance remorseless and tyrannical in its principles, and dreadful in its effects;*" the revival "in a country that pretends to Christianity of the odious severity of the Roman law, which declared sentient beings to be *inter res;* a practice injurious to the national character and disgraceful to humanity." "A good negro," continues he, "with his wife and young family rising about him, is seized on by the sheriff's officer, forcibly separated from his wife and children, dragged to public auction, purchased by a stranger, and perhaps sent to terminate his miserable existence in the mines of Mexico ; and all this without any crime or demerit on his part, real or pretended. He is punished because his master is unfortunate."

"It would be in vain for me to attempt to augment the horror which every well-regulated mind must feel from this eloquent description of the cruelty of the law. For humanity's sake, I rejoice to say that the sphere of its operation is by no means co-extensive with the prevalence of slavery. With the exception of the British colonies in the West Indies, and I suppose at Demarara, and perhaps in the small islands belonging to the Dutch, it obtains only in the *Republican States of North America!*" (p. 34.)

How great the change in the disposition of the law-making power in Virginia, since 1776, may be seen from the following

Preamble to the Constitution of Virginia, promulgated on the 29th June, 1776:—"Whereas George the Third, king, &c., heretofore intrusted with the exercise of the kingly office in this government, hath endeavoured to pervert the same into a detestable and insupportable tyranny, by prompting our negroes to rise in arms among us,—*those very negroes whom,* BY AN INHUMAN USE OF HIS NEGATIVE, HE HATH REFUSED US PERMISSION TO EXCLUDE BY LAW." (p. 37.)

SLAVES CANNOT REDEEM THEMSELVES, NOR OBTAIN A CHANGE OF MASTERS, THOUGH CRUEL TREATMENT MAY HAVE RENDERED SUCH CHANGE NECESSARY FOR THEIR PERSONAL SAFETY.

This proposition holds good as to the right of *redemption* in all the slaveholding States; and equally true is it as respects the right to compel a change of masters, except in Louisiana and Kentucky. (p. 38.)

In Turkey the law is still more favourable to the slave. "For he may allege *contrariety of tempers*, whereby they cannot live together, and the judge will decree that the patron shall carry his slave to market and sell him."—Life of Hon. Sir Dudley North, p. 63, of Vol. III. of lives of his three brothers, by Roger North. London edition of 1826. (p. 39.)

As to the rejection of *slave testimony*—

We must have recourse to the *civil law* for its probable origin. "The general rule of that law certainly was that a slave could not be a witness, though there were exceptions to it, founded in reason and policy; for men of that condition might be examined when the welfare of the State, in cases of weight and difficulty, required such a departure from general rules, *or when other evidence was unattainable. Stephen's West India Slavery*, 171, *citing*

16 *

Vœtus' Commentary on the Pandects. This latter exception, it is obvious, destroys the rule if we are to understand by it that a slave might be examined, in the defect of other proof, for the inculpation of any offender against the laws. And such I suppose to be the true meaning, since "slaves might always (among the Romans) induce an investigation, by flying to the statutes of the princes." Cooper's Justinian, 412, (p. 47.)

And such a right it seems probable obtained in *Massachusetts*, as far as we are informed, without inconvenience; on the contrary, I have no doubt, with decisive public advantage. (p. 49.)

Add to the instance of Massachusetts, given by Judge Stroud, the following from the laws of the Visi-Goths :

"If no one guilty of, or an accomplice in, a crime ought to remain unpunished, with how much more reason ought he to be condemned who has wickedly and rashly committed a homicide! Thus, as masters, in their pride often put their slaves to death without any fault of the latter, it is proper altogether to extirpate this license, and to ordain that the present law shall be forever observed by all. No master or mistress shall put to death, without public trial, any of their slaves, male or female, or any person dependent on them. . . . . Indeed, if the slave, with a fatal audacity, resisting his master, has struck, or attempted to strike, him with a weapon, with a stone, or with any other kind of a blow, and if the master, in defending himself, has killed the slave in his passion, the master shall be in no way subject to the punishment of homicide. But it shall be necessary to prove that the event took place thus, *and that by the testimony or oath of the slaves, male or female,* who shall have been present, and by the oath of the author of the deed himself." (For. Jud. lib. XI., tit. XV.

Compare with the above the following specimen of the peculiar character of Southern slave legislation :

Be it enacted, That if any slaves shall suffer in life, limb, or member, or shall be maimed, beaten or abused, contrary to the directions and true intent and meaning of this act, when no *white persons* shall be present, or, being present, shall neglect or refuse to give evidence, or be examined on oath concerning the same: in every such case the owner, or rather person, who shall have care and government of such slave, and in whose possession or power such slave shall be, shall be deemed, taken, reputed and adjudged to be guilty of such offence, and shall be proceeded against accordingly without further proof, *unless* such owner, or other person as aforesaid, can make the contrary appear by good and sufficient evidence, *or shall by* HIS OWN OATH, *clear and exculpate himself:* which oath every court, where such offence shall be tried, is hereby empowered to administer, and to *acquit the offender*, if clear proof of the offence be not made by *two* witnesses at least." 2 Brevard's Dig., 242. (p. 50.)

Thus a law which professes to be for the protection of the life of the slave, turns out to be, in fact, for the security of the murdering master; for, whereas the testimony of *one* white witness might otherwise have sufficed for his conviction, this statute requires *two at least!* In what fitting terms can we characterize such a law?

A slave cannot be a party to a civil suit; but, through a friend, he may sue for his alleged freedom.

" *But in case judgment shall be given for the defendant, the said court is hereby fully empowered to inflict such* CORPORAL PUNISHMENT, *not extending to life or limb, on the word of the plaintiff, as they in their discretion shall think fit.* Provided, that in any action or suit to be brought in pursuance of the direction of this act, THE BURDEN OF THE PROOF *shall lay upon the plaintiff, and it shall always be presumed that every Negro, Indian,* * *Mulatto, and Mestizos, is a slave,*

---

* Bishop Hopkins charges the enslavement of the Indians, especially, to "the Puritans of New England." The charge is not strictly true in their case at all; but it seems to have a just application elsewhere.

It may excite the surprise of some, to discover Indians and their offspring comprised in the doom of perpetual slavery; yet *unless the contrary be made to appear,* (the Indians in amity with this government excepted, in which case the burden of proof shall be on the defendant.) 2 Brevard's Dig., 229–30.

In Georgia, the act of Assembly of May 10, 1770, is almost literally a copy of this of South Carolina. See Prince's Digest, 446; 2 Cobb's Digest, 971.

It is impossible for any humane and reflecting person to examine the provisions of the above law, without the conviction of its injustice and cruelty. The Negro, &c., claims to be free; and yet he can bring no suit to investigate his master's title to restrain him of his liberty, unless some one can be found merciful enough to become his guardian, subject, in any event, to the

---

not only is *incidental* mention made of them as slaves to be met with in the laws of most of the States of our confederacy, but in one, at least, direct legislation may be cited to sanction their enslavement. In Virginia, "by an act passed in the year 1679, it was, for the *better encouragement of soldiers,* declared, that when INDIAN PRISONERS should be taken in a war in which the colony was then engaged, should be *free purchase* to the *soldiers* taking them. In 1682, it was declared, that all servants brought into this country, (Virginia,) by sea or land, not being *Christians,* whether Negroes, Moors, Mulattoes, or INDIANS, (except Turks and Moors in amity with Great Britain,) and all INDIANS which should thereafter be SOLD by neighbouring Indians, or any other trafficking with us, *as slaves,* should be SLAVES, *to all intents and purposes.* (Stroud, p. 5.)

And in the State of New Jersey, it was decided by the Supreme Court, in the year 1797, "That *Indians* might be held as slaves." No law was adduced to show the origination of such a right, but it appeared by several acts of Assembly, one of which was as early as 1713–14, that they were classed with Negroes and Mulattoes, *as slaves.* Chief Justice Kinsey remarked, "They (Indians) have been so long recognized as slaves, in our law, that it would be as great a violation of the rights of property to establish a contrary doctrine at the present day, as it would in the case of Africans, and as useless to investigate the manner in which they ORIGINALLY lost their freedom.—*The State vs. Waggoner,* 1 *Halstead's Reports,* 374–376. (p. 6.)

expense and trouble of conducting his cause, and, in case of failure, to the costs of the suit. His judges and jurors will, in all probability, be slaveholders, and interested therefore, in some measure, *in the question,* which they are to try. The whole community in which he lives may, so few are the exceptions, be said to be hostile to his success. Being a Negro, &c., by the words of the act, the *burden of the proof* rests upon him, and he is *presumed* to be a slave till he makes the contrary appear. This is to be effected through the instrumentality of *white* witnesses, as has been just shown, exclusive of the testimony of those who are *not white,* even though they may be free, and of the fairest character. And, lastly, notwithstanding all these obstacles to the ascertaining the truth of his allegations, the terror is superadded, should he not succeed in convincing the judge and jury of his right of freedom, *of an infliction of corporal punishment to any extent short of capital execution, or the deprivation of a limb! ! !* And in Georgia, "should death happen by accident in giving this legal (moderate) correction, according to the terms of the constitution already quoted, it will be no crime! (p. 52.)

In 1696, the question, *whether the baptism* of a *negro slave,* WITHOUT THE PRIVITY OR CONSENT OF HIS MASTER, emancipated the slave, underwent an elaborate discussion before the judges of the King's Bench. Owing to a misconception of the *form* of the action, a final decision was not given, and the plaintiff being, of course, unsuccessful on that occasion, the doubts which had resulted from the former case were strengthened rather than impaired.

The arguments of the counsel for the defendant are sufficiently curious to deserve transcription. "Being baptized according to the use of the church, he (the slave) is thereby made a Christian, and Christianity is inconsistent with slavery. And this was allowed even in the time when the Popish religion was established, as appears by Littleton; for in those days, if a villain had entered into religion, and was professed as they called it, the lord could not seize him ; and the reason there given is, because he was dead in law, and if the lord might take him out of his cloister, then he could not live according to his religion. The like reason may now be given for baptism being incorporated into the laws of the land ; if the duties which arise thereby cannot be performed in a state of servitude, the baptism must be a manumission. That such duties cannot be performed is plain; for the persons baptized are to be confirmed by the diocesan, when they can give an account of their faith, and are enjoined, by several acts of Parliament, to come to church. But if the lord hath still an absolute property over him, then he might send him far enough from the performance of those duties, viz., into Turkey, or any other country of infidels, where they neither can nor will be suffered to exercise the Christian religion."

In conclusion, the counsel remarks: "It is observed among the *Turks* that they do not make slaves of those of their own religion, though taken in war; and if a *Christian be so taken, yet if he renounce Christianity and turn Mahometan, he doth thereby obtain his freedom.* And if this custom be allowed among infidels, then baptism, in a Christian nation, as this is, should be immediate enfranchisement to them, as they should thereby acquire the privileges and immunities enjoyed by those of the same religion, and be entitled to the laws of England." See 5 Modern Reports, 190, 191, Chamberline vs. Harvey. (p. 67.)

And yet, to remove the "vain apprehension" that negroes, by receiving the sacrament of baptism, are manumitted and set free, solemn acts have been passed to the contrary in Maryland and South Carolina. *Brevard's Dig.* 229.

It is enacted in Georgia, "If any *slave* shall *presume* to strike *any white person*, such slave upon trial and conviction before the justice or justices, according to the directions of this act, shall for the *first* offence suffer such punishment as the said justice or justices shall in his or their discretion think fit, not extending to life or limb; and for the *second* offence suffer DEATH. Prince's Dig. 450. 2 Cobb's Dig. 976. (p. 68.)

And by the negro act of 1740, of South Carolina, it is declared: —"If any slave who shall be out of the house or plantation, where such slave shall live or shall be usually employed, or without some white person in company with such slave, shall refuse to submit to undergo the examination of *any* white person, it shall be lawful for any such white person to pursue, apprehend, and moderately correct such slave; and if such slave shall assault

and strike such white person, such slave may be *lawfully* killed!!"
Brevard's Dig. 231. (p. 69.)

The cruelty of the Criminal Codes of Slave States, in relation to the slaves, may be seen and inferred from the following results of the examination of those of Virginia and Mississippi.

By the code of Virginia there are sixty-seven crimes for which a slave is punished *with death*, and no alternative; while for the same crimes, the punishment of whites varies from one to twenty years' imprisonment; in twenty-three cases, *one year* being considered penalty enough.

By the code of Mississippi there are thirty-eight offences for which a slave *must suffer death;* but for the punishment of which, in the case of white persons, no provision is made by statute in twenty cases, and eight of them are no offences at common law; in four cases more, the punishment of whites is only payment of damages and imprisonment not exceeding six months; in three cases, a discretionary fine and imprisonment for one year; and in four other cases, the whole punishment may be a fine of three hundred dollars! (See pp. 77 to 88.)

"The indulgent treatment of the slaves by which the Spaniards are so honourably distinguished, and the ample and humane code of laws, which they have enacted and also *enforce*, for the protection of the blacks, both bond and free, occasioned many of the Indian slaves (i. e. of East Florida) who were apprehensive of falling into the power of the Americans, (i. e., citizens of the United States,) and also most of the free people of colour, who resided in St. Augustine, to transport themselves to *Havana* as *soon as they heard of the approach of the American authorities.*"— See "Notices of East Florida, with an account of the Seminole nation of Indians, by a recent traveller in the Province." **p. 42.**

From the tenor of many of his remarks, the writer is evidently an inhabitant of one of our slaveholding States. (p. 71.)

"Every slave who shall endeavour to delude or entice any slave to run away and leave this province, every such slave and slaves and his or her accomplices; aiders, and abettors, shall, upon conviction as aforesaid, suffer death." 2 Brevard's Dig. 233, act of 1740. (p. 72.)

After an experiment of eleven years' duration, the legislature relented so far as to declare, "That whereas by, &c., of the act entitled, &c., it is (among other things contained) enacted, 'That every slave, who shall endeavour to delude or entice any slave to run away and leave this province, shall, upon conviction, suffer death,' which is a punishment too great for the nature of the offence, as *such offender might afterwards* alter his intentions, Be it therefore enacted, That such part of the said paragraph as relates only to slaves endeavouring to delude or entice other slaves to run away and leave this province, shall not operate to take effect, unless it shall appear that such slave (so endeavouring to delude or entice other slaves to run away and leave this province) shall have actually prepared provisions, arms, ammunition, horse or horses, or any boat, canoe, or other vessel, *whereby their intention shall be manifested.*" 2 Brev. Dig. 244, act of 1751. It is hardly necessary to remind the intelligent reader that the *principle* upon which the act of 1740 was founded is retained in the amendment of 1751. The *endeavour* on the part of a slave to entice another to run away, is, in both laws, regarded as a *crime worthy of death.* What shall constitute the *evidence* of this *endeavour* is defined in the amendment,—namely, "the preparing provisions, &c., whereby the intention shall be manifested." And this is the only melioration of a law which it is acknowledged in the same breath, imposed a punishment too severe for the offence!! And such is the law still after the lapse of a century. (p. 72.)

Bishop Hopkins boasts of three thousand slaves having been emancipated in one year, forgetting to tell us that about one hundred thousand new recruits to slavery had been added by birth in the same period. The spirit of the system in reference to emancipation may be seen from the following :

In addition to the obstacle to emancipation which is created by the *saving* in favour of creditors, a very extraordinary one is opposed on behalf of the *widows* of deceased slaveholders. For where a widow is entitled by law to one-third of her deceased husband's personal estate, unless he shall have left sufficient other personal estate, after payment of his debts, to satisfy her claim of one-third, his slaves, though declared to be free by his last will, shall nevertheless *not* be free, but shall be held liable for the *third* to which the widow is entitled. (Vir. Rev. Code, 435. Mississippi Rev. Code, 386. 2 Litt. and Swi., Kentucky, 1246.)

But it is in the mode by which emancipation is to be effected that the most formidable difficulties arise. In South Carolina, Georgia, Alabama, and Mississippi, it is only *by authority of the legislature specially granted*, that a valid emancipation can be made. It is not enough that a penalty is imposed upon the benevolence of a master who may permit his slave to work for himself; a slave-owner must continue a slave-owner (unless he disposes of his *chattels* by *sale*) until he can induce the legislature to indulge him in the wish to set his captives free. Prince's Dig. 456 (act of Dec. 5, 1801); James Dig. 398 (act of 1820); Soulmin's Dig. 632. Mississippi Rev. Code, 386.

Formerly, in North Carolina, a slave could not be manumitted *except for meritorious services*, to be adjudged of and allowed by the county court (Hayward's Manual, 525); but by the Revised Statutes of 1836-7, the court on the petition, in writing, of the master, and his entering into a bond with two sufficient securities, in the sum of one thousand dollars, conditioned that the slave so to be emancipated shall honestly and correctly demean himself, while he shall remain within the State, and that he will, within ninety days after granting the prayer of the petitioner to emancipate him, *leave the State, and never afterwards come within the same*, may permit such emancipation. The rights of creditors are expressly saved.

The law of Tennessee on this subject requires the presentation of a petition to the county court, "setting forth the intention and motives for such emancipation;" and these must be consistent, *in the opinion of the court*, with the interest and policy of the State, to authorize its reception. The emancipator must give a

17

bond with sufficient security conditioned that the emancipated slave shall *forthwith* remove from the State. Laws of Tennessee, 277–9. (Act of 1801, ch. 27; and of 1831, ch. 102.)

Mississippi has combined in one act all the obstacles to emancipation which are to be met with in the laws of the other slaveholding States. Thus, the emancipation must be by an *instrument in writing*, a last will or deed, &c., *under seal, attested by at least two credible witnesses, or acknowledged in the court of the county or corporation*, where the emancipator resides; *and proof satisfactory to the General Assembly must be adduced that the slave has done some meritorious act for the benefit of his master, or rendered some distinguished service to the State;* all of which circumstances are but prerequisites, and are of no efficacy until a *special act of Assembly* sanctions the emancipation;—to which may be added, as has been already stated, *a saving of the rights of creditors,* and the protection of *the widow's* third. Mississippi Rev. Code, 385–6. (Act of June 18, 1822.)

In Kentucky, Missouri, Virginia, Maryland, and Arkansas, greater facility is afforded to emancipation. By the last *Constitution* of Virginia, "slaves hereafter emancipated shall FORFEIT *their freedom* by remaining in the Commonwealth more than twelve months after they become *actually free*, and SHALL BE REDUCED TO SLAVERY under such regulations as may be prescribed by law." (pp. 98–99.)

In the Revised Statutes of Louisiana are these enactments:—
"If any white person shall be convicted of being the author, printer, or publisher of any written or printed paper or papers within this State, or shall use any language with the intent to disturb the peace or security of the same, in relation to the slaves of the people of this State, or TO DIMINISH THAT RESPECT *which is commanded to free people of colour for the whites* by law, or *to destroy that line of distinction which the law has established between the several classes of the community,* such person shall be adjudged guilty of high misdemeanor, and shall be *fined* in a sum not less than three hundred dollars, nor exceeding one thousand dollars, and moreover *imprisoned* for a term not less than *six months*, nor exceeding *three years*." Statutes of Louisiana, 1852. (p. 554.)

Whosoever shall write, print, publish, or distribute, anything having a TENDENCY to produce *discontent* among the *free coloured population* of the State, shall, on conviction thereof before any court of competent jurisdiction, be sentenced to IMPRISONMENT AT HARD LABOR FOR LIFE, or SUFFER DEATH, at the discretion of the court." Ibid. (p. 208.)

"Whosoever shall make use of language in any public discourse from the bar, the bench, the stage, the pulpit, or in any place whatsoever, or whoever shall make use of language in private discourses or conversations, or shall make use of signs or actions, *having a tendency to produce discontent* among the *free coloured* population of this State, or excite insubordination among the slaves, or whosoever shall knowingly be instrumental in bringing into this State any paper, pamphlet, or book, having such tendency as aforesaid, shall, on conviction thereof before any court of competent jurisdiction, suffer *imprisonment at hard labor* not less than *three years* nor more than *twenty-one years*, or DEATH, at the discretion of the court." Ibid. (Stroud, p. 104.)

The following laws were enacted in the slave code of the territory of Kansas; and but for the opposition of Republicans, would have been sanctioned by a slaveholding and Democratic Congress, and thus stamped with the authority of the United States Government:

"Section 11. If any person print, write, introduce into, publish, or circulate, or cause to be brought into, printed, written, published or circulated, or shall knowingly aid or assist in bringing into, printing, publishing, or circulating within this territory any book, paper, pamphlet, magazine, handbill or circular containing any statements, arguments, opinions, sentiments, doctrine, advice or innuendo calculated to produce a disorderly, dangerous, or rebellious disaffection among the slaves in this territory, or to induce such slaves to escape from the service of their masters or to resist authority, he shall be guilty of felony, and be punished by imprisonment and hard labour for a term not less than five years.

"Section 12. If any person, by speaking or writing, assert or maintain that persons have not the right to hold slaves in this territory, or shall introduce into this territory, print, publish, write, circulate, or cause to be introduced into this territory, written, printed, published, or circulated in this territory, any book, paper, magazine, pamphlet or circular, containing any denial of the right of persons to hold slaves in this territory, such person shall be deemed guilty of felony, and be punished by imprisonment at hard labor for a term of not less than two years." (p. 108.)

On the 15th September, 1863, Judge Stroud published the following communication over his own signature, which contains a summary of the whole subject:

" From several pamphlets recently published and extensively circulated, it has become evident that a new issue in Pennsylvania party politics has been inaugurated, viz.: Whether negro slavery, as it is maintained in the Southern States now in rebellion against the national government is consistent with the Christian religion ?

" I deem it proper, therefore, in order that every one may be enabled to judge for himself on this important subject, to give a very brief summary of the legal incidents of Southern slavery. Every part and parcel of this summary may be authenticated by the statutes of one or other of those States, and the reported decision of their highest courts of judicature.

" It is a fundamental principle of negro slavery that a slave is a *thing*—a chattel wholly under the dominion of his master, subject to be bought and sold precisely as if he were a horse or a mule. He may be fed and clothed much or little, as his master may prescribe—may be compelled to labor as well on one day as another, and as hard and as long as his master may direct.

" The slave has no legal right whatever; cannot own anything; may be forbidden all society with his fellows; may be kept in the most abject ignorance; is not allowed to be instructed to read; is without any legal provision for acquiring a knowledge of his religious duties; incapable of a lawful marriage; denied all authority over those who are admitted to be his natural offspring; liable to have them at any age torn from him, without the slightest consultation or deference to his judgment or his feelings; and liable himself to be torn from them, and from their mother, with whom he has been permitted and encouraged to cohabit as his wife. He may be thus ruthlessly carried to a returnless distance, not only from his children and their mother, but from all else that he may hold dear.

" The law also expressly sanctions his master in beating him with a horsewhip or cowskin, in chaining him, putting him in irons, compelling him to wear pronged iron collars, confining him in prison, hunting him with dogs, and when *outlawed*, as he may be for running away, he may be killed by any one to whom he may refuse to surrender.

" The whole of this summary I pledge myself to maintain in its literal and full extent, according to the law of one or another of the Southern slaveholding States.

GEO. M. STROUD."

Such are some of the features of negro slavery as maintained by law in the Southern States. If it be said, that, after all, these laws do not *compel* the

17*

master to maltreat his slave, though they may protect him in so doing, that good masters may nevertheless treat their slaves kindly, that cases of outrageous cruelty are probably exceptional, such stories
being greatly exaggerated and often false; and, in
fine, that instances of cruelty and outrage may occur
in any society;—I answer, it is freely admitted that
there may be some masters who, as Chrysostom said
of Abraham, do not treat their servants *as slaves;*
but these laws being made, not by some tyrant over
whose acts the slaveholders have no control, but *by
the slaveholders themselves,* show incontestably the
animus of the system, show what those slaveholders
in general mean to be at liberty to do; and why
should they claim this liberty unless they mean to
exercise it? The overwhelming probability is that,
in general, the practical working of the system is
tenfold worse than its published and acknowledged
theory. Slaveholders are not likely to paint their
system worse than it is. On its own public confession, therefore, we may impeach it before the common judgment of mankind as a monstrous and mea-
sureless wrong; and most assuredly that judgment
will not pronounce an acquittal. " Slavery as maintained in the Southern States" is wrong, morally
wrong.

But is slavery a *sin?* The defenders of slavery
have, of late, made a great point of denying this.
Bishop Hopkins strenuously denies it. Judge Woodward, of the Supreme Court of Pennsylvania, has
said, in a political speech, " If it be a sin, I agree
there is an end to my argument. But what right
has the abolitionist to pronounce it a sin? . . . If a
sin, then it is a violation of some Divine law; for sin

is the transgression of the law. Now I deny that
any such law has ever been revealed."

Here, then, the issue is joined. Will the Judge
deny that *every wrong against man is a sin against God*,
whether expressly forbidden in the Bible or not?
But he will say, it is because God has commanded
us to obey the magistrate and the laws, and, therefore, every violation of the laws *is* a violation of
God's commandment. True, but God has commanded
us to obey the law of reason and conscience, as well
as the laws of the State; every violation of that law,
therefore, is a violation of God's law. "All unright-
eousness is sin."

Will the Judge deny that there is a law—a law of
God—engraven in our reason, as well as that which
is written in the pages of Scripture? The revealed
law of God is not substituted for the moral law
written in man's heart and conscience. Revelation
takes man's moral and rational nature for granted;
*it addresses itself to that nature, and without that na-
ture it could not be so much as understood.* Christianity neither annuls nor contradicts the natural
reason and conscience, but enlightens, elevates, and
enlarges them. This natural law the heathen had,
while destitute of revelation; and it was the law of
God. "Because that which may be known of God
is manifest in them; for God hath showed it unto
them . . . . so that they are without excuse . . . .
knowing the judgment of God, that they which do
such things are worthy of death." " For when the
Gentiles, which have not the law, do by nature the
things contained in the law, these, having not the
law, are a law unto themselves: which show the
work of the law written in their hearts, their con-

science also bearing witness, and their thoughts inwardly accusing or else excusing them." Rom. i. 19, 32, and ii. 14, 15. As for the "natural man," in 1 Cor. ii. 14, "who receiveth not the things of the Spirit," he is not the physical or *ethical*, but the "psychical," the *animal* man. Says the judicious Hooker: "By force of the light of reason, wherewith God illumineth every man that cometh into the world, men being enabled to know truth from falsehood, and good from evil, do thereby learn in many things what the will of God is; which will himself not revealing by any extraordinary means unto them, but they by natural discourse attaining the knowledge thereof, seem the makers of those laws, which indeed are his, and they but only the finders of them out." " The very Law of Nature itself, which no man can deny but God hath instituted, is not of God unless that be of God whereof God is the author as well by the way of natural light as of supernatural revelation." " The will of God which we are to judge our actions by, no sound divine in the world ever denied to be in part made manifest even by light of nature, and not by Scripture alone." " But so it is, the name of the light of nature is made hateful with men; the 'star of reason and learning' [the unanswerable argument of 'French Infidels' and 'German Rationalists' had not then been heard of—would it have silenced Hooker?] and all other such like helps, beginneth no otherwise to be thought of than if it were an unlucky comet; or as if God had so accursed it that it should never shine or give light in things concerning our duty any way towards him, but be esteemed as that star in the Revelation called Wormwood, which being fallen from heaven, maketh rivers and waters in which it falleth so bitter, that men tasting them die thereof. A number there are who think they cannot admire as they ought the power and authority of the word of God, if in things divine they should attribute any force to man's reason. For which cause they never use reason so willingly as to disgrace reason."* Indeed Hooker's great work entire may be considered a defence of the light and law of nature and reason. Moreover, it is not the word, nor even the will, of God, that *constitutes* the law of right or of truth. Right and truth have their roots in the nature of things, in the very being of God, and are not the creatures of his will. God can no more create or annihilate the right by an act of his will or an utterance of his word than he can create or annihilate himself. The right is not right because God wills it, but God wills it because it is right. Otherwise, how could we attribute a moral character to God? He could have no such character at all unless the acts of his will could be compared with some standard independent of them. This absolute and immutable law of right is revealed to us partly in our natural reason and partly by a supernatural instruction. Unless it were, in part at least, revealed to us in our reason, and so revealed that we could rely upon it, how could we appeal to the pure morality of the Scriptures as a confirmation of their divine origin? In order that any such confirmation could be conceived of, must we not have a knowledge of the moral law with which their character is compared, in some way independent of their own dictation?

* Eccles. Pol., Book I. 8, and Book III., 1, 8.

But, at all events, say Bishop Hopkins and Judge Woodward, "slavery is nowhere declared to be a sin in the word of God," and is it well to be wise above that which is written? or, as the Bishop says, "shall we be wiser than the Almighty?"

It is admitted: slavery is not expressly declared in Scripture to be a sin. But no more is the slave-trade, or cannibalism, or private war, or suicide, (for, the original word for "kill," in the sixth commandment, is never applied to killing one's self any more than to killing a sheep,) or gambling, or keeping bawdy houses, or stock-jobbing or gladiatorial shows, or bull-fights, or polygamy, or many other things which would hardly be considered now as "Divine institutions." And if the Judge, as a lawyer, alleges that these, or most of them, are wrong because they are forbidden by the laws of the land; then I observe that some things are admitted to be wrong,—and consequently *sinful*, I suppose,—without being expressly forbidden in Scripture; and, besides, I ask whether these are wrong simply because the law prohibits them, or whether the law prohibits them because they are wrong?

In conclusion, I invite attention to the following discourse of a Mormon Elder:

DISCOURSE OF A MORMON ELDER; CONTAINING A BIBLE VIEW OF POLYGAMY.

My brethren, there is no one thing for which we, the true saints of God, are more reviled by the radical and ranting sects around us, than for our going back to the Divine institution, and restoring the good old patriarchal custom, of having many wives;

—an institution sanctioned, blessed, and even expressly commanded by Almighty God; an institution never disapproved, or repealed, or abolished, by Jesus Christ, or his apostles; a custom which was practised by the holy patriarchs who walked with God, and was preserved as a privilege of his chosen people, sanctioned in their law and never disallowed by their prophets; (while many of the heathen nations, as the Romans, for example, confined each man to one lawful wife;) a custom which began before the flood, and has been continued in the world, without any reproof from Divine revelation, through all ages to the present time, especially among the descendants of the religious Shem, in whose tents God promised to dwell; while it is only some tribes of Japhetic origin, and especially those among whom rationalism, infidelity, atheism, and all ungodliness have become rife, who have adopted and insisted upon the opposite custom.

"But polygamy," they say, "is a sin." If it is a sin, I agree there is an end to my argument. But what right have the monogamists to call polygamy a sin? If a sin, then it is a violation of some Divine law; for sin is the transgression of the law. Now I deny that any such law has ever been revealed. If there be such a law let them show it to us in express terms. If they can find no such law, let them leave off their blasphemous habit of denouncing polygamy as a *sin*—and the very saints of God as *sinners*.

Is it conceivable that God should have walked familiarly with Abraham, should have talked with him face to face, as a man talketh with his friend, should have consulted with him, as it were, in regard to what he himself proposed to do,—as in the case of the Sodomites, whom he was about to punish, not for having many wives, observe, but for crimes which grew out precisely from their leaving the natural use of women—and yet should never have rebuked him for having more than one wife; if polygamy had been a sin—a sin in itself? And are these modern Christian sects purer and holier than Almighty God? Was not Jacob compelled, as it were, "by the Providence of God," to take two wives, when he sought but one; and afterwards led to add more, that he might beget the twelve patriarchs, and thus the promise to Abraham of the multiplication of his seed be fulfilled?—for to fulfil a *promise* is surely as good a justification of any act as to fulfil a *curse*.

Polygamy is not only thus sanctioned by God's presence, communion and blessing; but it is expressly recognized and commanded in his law. In immediate connection with the solemn enactment about Hebrew servants, it is added: "If he take him another wife; her food, her raiment, and her duty of marriage, shall he not diminish." Ex. xxi. 10. Again: "Neither shalt thou take a wife *to her sister*, *to vex her*, to uncover her nakedness, beside the other in her lifetime." Lev. xviii. 18. Here the right of polygamy in general is implied. So in this passage: "If a man take a wife and her mother, it is wickedness." Lev. xx. 14. Also: "if a man have two wives, one beloved and another hated, and they have borne him children, both the beloved and the hated; and if the first-born be hers that was hated," &c Deut. xxi. 15. Of the future king it was written: "Neither shall he multiply wives to himself, that his heart turn not away; neither shall he greatly multiply silver and gold." Deut. xv. 17. The Rabbins restricted the "many wives" to more than three or four; but Solomon, who was wiser than they, extended them to beyond a thousand. But there is one law by which polygamy is, in certain contingencies, expressly commanded: "If brethren dwell together, and one of them die, and have no child, the wife of the dead shall not marry without unto a stranger; her husband's brother shall go in unto her, take her to him to wife, and perform the duty of a husband's brother unto her." Deut. xxv. 5. And then an ignominious punishment is provided for the man who would not obey this precept; and it is plain it made no difference whether he were already married or not. Now here is polygamy required and commanded by the Divine law; and are our modern sectarians wiser than the Almighty?*

This law, neither Christ nor his Apostles expressly abolished. They nowhere expressly prohibited polygamy. Christ was entirely SILENT upon the subject. It is true, an attempt has been made in certain quarters to show that in Christ's comment upon the law of divorce, he indirectly prohibited polygamy, viz., when he declared: "If a man put away his wife, and marry another, he committeth adultery;" for, it is argued, if marrying another *after* divorcing

---

* It has been satisfactorily and unanswerably proved by the Bishop of Vermont, in his late work on Slavery, that slavery is a Divine institution. But we see here that the argument for polygamy is stronger than that for slavery even; for it will hardly be pretended that the holding of slaves is positively enjoined upon any parties as an imperative duty, as we see that polygamy is in this Divine law.

18

the first is adultery, much more would it be, *without* divorcing her. This is sharp, but it will not do. The text probably means that the man is *virtually guilty of adultery, because he exposes his divorced wife to commit it;* for in Christ's formal exposition of the law, in the Sermon on the Mount, he says: " But I say unto you, that whosoever putteth away his wife, saving for the cause of fornication, *causeth her to commit adultery*, and whosoever shall marry her that is divorced committeth adultery." Now this must, in all reason, be received as furnishing the key for the interpretation of the other passages. See a late work of the Rt. Rev. John H. Hopkins, Bishop of the Diocese of Vermont, in which he restrains the meaning of the general law against *man-stealing*, found in one place, by a more specific law against *stealing one of the children of Israel*, found in another place.

As to the injunction of the apostle Paul that " a Bishop should be the husband of one wife," the sects around us very strangely twist it into meaning, that he may be *the husband of no wife at all;* but, at all events, must have but one ! while the true interpretation manifestly is, that he must be the *husband of at least one wife*, and may have as many more as he will. But even if the sectarian interpretation were the true one, it would not follow that polygamy was such a sin as to shut a man out of the communion of the apostolic church, but just the contrary; for if polygamy cut a man off from the communion of the church, there would have been no occasion to tell Timothy not to ordain such a man as bishop or elder, since no such man could be so much as a supposable candidate for that office. Nor would it even follow that polygamy was *any sin at all*, unless a want of "aptness to teach," or having "unbelieving children or children accused of riot or unruly," is a sin; for these are also to be taken into the account in the qualifications of a bishop. And if it were a sin in a bishop to have unbelieving or profligate, or unruly children, it must be equally a sin in all Christians. Now if a man had a son who was guilty of licentious conduct, though it were no fault of this man, it might be very expedient and proper that he should not be ordained to the episcopate; whether, in case of his son's committing debauchery *after* he, the father, was ordained, it might be required that he should resign his office, does not appear. A bishop, therefore, may have been forbidden to have more than one wife, not because it was a sin in itself, but from some special motives of prudence and propriety, pertaining to the office. Thus, even following the monogamist's interpretation, there is nothing in the apostle's injunction which necessarily militates against the right of polygamy.

When the ultra-monogamists appeal from the higher authority of Scripture to the lower authority of the "early church," it must be borne in mind how *early* that church became corrupt, especially in regard to this very subject of marriage and celibacy. Yet for more than three hundred years that church never ventured to declare polygamy to be unlawful. It was at the council of Nice that laymen were, for the first time, forbidden to have more than one wife, and this was after the conversion of Constantine, *when the Roman law began to take precedence of the Divine.* But it is not to be forgotten that this same council, in the very face of St. Paul's injunction that a bishop or elder should be the husband of one wife, was upon the point of decreeing the perpetual celibacy of the clergy; which was warded off only by the zealous opposition of-old father Paphnutius. This principle of the celibacy of the clergy, however,—a corruption which seems to have crept into the church *pari passu* with that of the monogamy of the laity,—was soon after generally established, and has prevailed in far the larger part of the so-called Christian church to the present day; which may serve to show how much the authority of " the church" is worth in the interpretation of Scripture. Yet, it is remarkable that, so late as the beginning of the fifth century, we find no less a man than St. Augustine not venturing to deny the rightfulness of polygamy. "It is plain," says he, "that for a man, with the consent of his wife, to take another by whom he might have children, was right with the ancient fathers: *whether or not it is also right now,* I would not venture to say."* It is true he elsewhere says: "It is not lawful to put away a barren wife and marry another, nor to have more than one wife living,—*in our times, that is to say, and by the Roman custom.*"† Now if this is not inconsistent with his other statement, — and it is well understood that consistency is not one of the peculiar jewels of the early fathers, who seem to have blown hot or cold

---

* Plane uxoris voluntate adhibere aliam, unde communes filii nascantur unius commixtione ac semine, alterius autem jure ac potestate, apud antiquos patres fas erat: utrum et nunc fas sit, non temere dixerim. Aug. De Bono Conj. Cap. 15.

† Possit enim homo dimittere sterilem uxorem, et ducere de qua filios habeat: et tamen non licet; et nostris quidem jam temporibus ac more Romano, nec superinducere ut amplius habeat quam unam vivam. Aug. De Bon. Conj. 7.

as suited the present moment,—it is because he does not say in this last case, "it is not right," but "it is not lawful;"—not *non fas*, but *non licet;*—and he adds expressly, "in our times and by the Roman custom;" showing plainly that he does not declare polygamy to be wrong by the Divine law, but simply "in our times" to be forbidden by the Roman law. And we, latter day Saints, with full safety to our creed, may say as much, "in our times," of the laws of the United States, as "Saint" Augustine said, in his, of the laws of Rome. Indeed it is abundantly evident to any candid reader of history, that the doctrine of monogamy is of heathen origin, and was introduced into the Christian church from the Roman law, introduced gradually with other corruptions, to the entire disregard of the teachings of Scripture, and of the holy, patriarchal institution of polygamy, which had been ordained and approved by God himself. But were the Roman jurists wiser than the Almighty? [See note in Appendix.]

Moreover, the benefits, moral as well as physical, flowing from the system of polygamy are incalculable. It puts an end to whoredom and adultery at once, by removing their occasion. *We* have no bawdy-houses, no actions for *crim. con.*, no starving seamstresses. Think of the tens of thousands of these poor creatures, in London, New York, and other Christian (?) cities, who are literally compelled to give themselves up to prostitution or to starve; and compare them with the well-fed, happy wives of our teeming and patriarchal homes. If any man can candidly make the comparison, and then denounce *polygamy as a sin*, the very means which Divine Providence has chosen to save these women

18*

from that state of wretchedness and degradation, I can only say that I am at a loss whether I should be most astonished at the waywardness of his heart, or the blindness of his understanding.

But the most astounding thing of all, is, that the Divine institution of polygamy, as restored and practised by our little flock of saints here in the wilderness, should be denounced with expressions of holy horror by a people who are actually compelling four millions of human beings to live in a state of universal concubinage. He that causeth another to commit adultery, is guilty of adultery; he that compels another to live in concubinage, is guilty of concubinage; and he that approves of a system which keeps four millions of his fellow men in such a degraded and brutish condition, is guilty of concubinage four millions of times over. Let all such forever shut their mouths in regard to the "sin" of polygamy.

In conclusion, I think it is sufficiently demonstrated that the system of polygamy, as maintained by the Latter Day Saints, is fully authorized by both the Old and the New Testaments.

So far the Elder's discourse. I flatter myself that I should not find it difficult, from my stand-point, to expose its sophistries and refute its arguments. But how Bishop Hopkins could accomplish it, in consistency with his own Bible arguments, I am not able to understand. Indeed, the leading points in the Elder's discourse seem to have been borrowed directly from the Vermont Bishop and the Pennsylvania Judge. And if the learned Judge should attempt to evade the analogy by saying that polygamy is a sin, because, unlike slavery, it is prohibited by the law of the land; I answer that an unconstitutional law is, with us, no law at all; and clearly Congress has no more a constitutional right to meddle with the institution of polygamy than with that of slavery; the former is quite as *domestic* an institution as the latter; and if Congress may constitutionally prohibit polygamy in a territory, Congress may prohibit slavery in a territory. Beyond all cavil this would be true, at least as soon as any one of the United States should legalize polygamy. One State having legalized polygamy, it follows, according to the current Democratic theory, framed for the party by their slaveholding masters and dictators, that polygamy would be inevitably legalized in all the territories of the United States, and Congress would have no constitutional authority to prohibit it; for if one man could go into a territory with his family, another man would have an equal right to go with *his* family. And if it be further insisted that, without any law of Congress, polygamy is forbidden by the common law;—so also is slavery; for the decision of Lord Mansfield is based upon the common law, is a part of the common law, and was antecedent to the American Revolution. Slavery and polygamy are twins. The two " Divine institutions" must stand or fall together.

CHAPTER VII.

IT is well known that, among the slaveholding
States, there are two classes, the breeding States
and the buying States; there are also two sorts of
slave trade, the domestic slave trade and the foreign
slave trade. The breeding States naturally find it for
their interest that the price of slaves should be kept
as high as possible; and consequently they are opposed to foreign competition, i. e., to the African
slave trade; and are in favor of the widest extension
of the system of slavery, as tending to enlarge their
market. The buying and planting States, on the
other hand, while equally in favour of slavery extension, because the enormous profits and the increased
political power come directly into their own hands,
are naturally desirous of procuring the additional
slaves at as cheap a rate as possible; and therefore
have begun to insist upon the re-opening of the African trade. Meantime the domestic trade is fostered
by both parties, and, to the opprobrium of American
civilization, has been continued to this day, with
circumstances of outrage and heart-rending atrocity,
which must be witnessed in order to be understood.

" The story of human beings, reared amid the
softening influences of civilization, who, so soon as

they arrive at the maturity of their physical power, are, like so many cattle, shipped off to a distant region of tropical heat, there to be worked to death—of husbands separated from their wives, children from their parents, brothers and sisters from each other—of exposure on the auction block, and transfer to new masters and strange climates—all this happening not to heathen savages, but to men and women capable of friendship and affection, and sensible to moral suffering,—this story, I say, is familiar to us all."*

"I affirm that there exists in the United States a slave trade, not less odious or demoralizing, nay, I do in my conscience believe, more odious and more demoralizing than that which is carried on between Africa and Brazil. North Carolina and Virginia are to Louisiana and Alabama what Congo is to Rio Janeiro. . . . . God forbid that I should extenuate the horrors of the slave trade in any form! But I do think this is its worst form. Bad enough it is that civilized men should sail to an uncivilized quarter of the world where slavery exists, should there buy wretched barbarians, and should carry them away to labour in a distant land: bad enough! But that a civilized man, a baptized man, a man proud of being a citizen of a free State, a man frequenting a Christian church, should breed slaves for exportation,† and, if the whole horrible truth must be told,

* Cairnes on the Slave Power, p. 72.

† " The citizens of Virginia indignantly deny that they breed and rear slaves for the purpose of selling them. Not only do those who interpose this denial do so, in the vast majority of cases, with a consciousness of truth, but, perhaps, in no single instance can it be truly affirmed, that any individual slave is

should even beget slaves for exportation, should see children, sometimes his own children, gambolling around him from infancy, should watch their growth, should become familiar with their faces, and should then sell them for four or five hundred dollars a head, and send them to lead in a remote country a life which is a lingering death, a life about which the best thing that can be said is that it is sure to be short; this does, I own, excite a horror exceeding even the horror excited by that slave trade which is the curse of the African coast. And mark: I am not speaking of any rare case, of any instance of eccentric depravity. I am speaking of a trade as regular as the trade in pigs between Dublin and Liverpool,

raised for the purpose of being sold. The determination to rear slaves is formed and executed this year, while the act of selling may not take place until twenty years hence. The two things are probably never resolved and consummated as parts of one plan. The fallacy of the denial interposed by the people of Virginia consists in this, that, although no one slave may be raised with a special view to his sale, yet the entire business of raising slaves is carried on with reference to the price of slaves, and solely in consequence of the price of slaves; and this price depends, as they well know, solely upon the domestic slave trade. Of the men who deny for themselves individually the fact of raising slaves for the purpose of selling them, too many make no scruple in insisting upon markets to keep up the price of slaves. The well-known lamentation of a successful candidate for the governorship of Virginia, uttered without rebuke before a Virginia audience, that the closing of the mines of California to slave labour had prevented the price of an able-bodied negro man from rising to five thousand dollars, is only a single example of the freedom and publicity with which the domestic slave trade is advocated in that State." (Weston's Progress of Slavery, pp. 147–8.)

or as the trade in coal between the Tyne and the Thames."*

Take the following from an eye-witness;—for the general fact is, after all, best apprehended from a particular case:

"But the bell rings, and the slaves are ordered on board the cars. They break away from their wives and husbands at the sound of the whip, and start for the 'nigger' car. One of them, whose name was Friday, bounded back and gave his wife the last kiss of affection. Then the husband was pushed on board and the wife was left! Friday's wife had a present tied up in an old cotton handkerchief, which she designed to give her husband as her last token of love for him. But in the more than mortal agony of parting, she had forgotten the present until the cars started, when she ran, screaming, as she tossed the bundle towards the car, 'O here Friday! I meant to give you this!' But instead of reaching the car, it fell to the ground through the space between the cars, and *such a shriek* as that woman gave, when she saw that solitary emblem of the fidelity of her early vow and constant affection for her devoted husband fail to reach him, I never heard uttered by human voice. It thrilled my soul, leaving impressions that will never be effaced till my dying day. Her heart was breaking! She could no longer suppress her grief; and for some distance after the cars started, the air was rent with her bitter lamentations, bursting forth with the most frantic wails ever uttered in despair.

"There were thirty-five passengers in that car,

* Lord Macaulay's Speech on the Sugar Duties.

but no sympathy was expressed for the wretched victims of the billiard-table. Young ladies, daughters of slaveholders, well educated, connected with refined families, were in that car, but they did not seem to pity the poor, despairing slaves. They laughed at them, and ridiculed their expressions of grief. 'Look out here!' said one of the young ladies at a window to a schoolmate opposite, 'just see those niggers! What a rumpus they are making! Just as if niggers cared anything about their babies! See Cuffee kiss Dinah! What a taking on! Likely as not he will have another wife next week!'"*

Now this is a part of the system of slavery "as it is maintained in the Southern States," and, of course, it is held by the "Christian Bishop" to be "fully authorized by both the Old and the New Testaments." Nor does he leave us to infer this from his general statements, but, it will be remembered, he expressly defends this particular feature of the system by a formal argument. And, indeed, so long as slavery is maintained and perpetuated, this trade must go with it as part and parcel of the divine and providential scheme; and the real reasons why the African slave trade is rejected by any, who fully believe in the divine right of slaveholding, are not at all of a humane, moral, or religious nature, but of sheer sordid interest and "a wise" pecuniary "expediency." The "Christian Bishop" sides with these latter, and is opposed to the African slave trade; but it would seem his opposition must be based solely upon the same motives of "a wise expediency;"—and this may serve to show how justly, as a moralist and a

* C. G. Parsons' Inside View of Slavery.

Christian, he deserves the credit which he seems to claim for opposing the "slave trade." I cannot think of a single argument which he has alleged in defence of slavery, that is not equally valid in defence of the "slave trade;"—especially is this true of his grand climax, already cited: "If any man can contemplate the awful debasement of the native Africans, and candidly compare it with the present condition of the Southern slaves, and then *denounce as a sin*, the means which divine Providence has chosen to save them from their former state of wretched barbarism, ... I can only say, that I am at a loss whether I should be most astonished at the waywardness of his heart, or the blindness of his understanding." Of course this is, in terms, applicable directly in justification of the African slave trade. I shall set against it an authority which even the "Christian Bishop," and the politicians who called for his "Views," will consider quite respectable.—I quote from the message of President Buchanan, of December, 1859:

"But we are obliged, as a Christian and moral nation, to consider what would be the effect upon unhappy Africa itself, if we should re-open the slave trade. This would give the trade an impulse and extension which it never had even in its palmiest days. The numerous victims required to supply it would convert the whole slave coast into a perfect pandemonium, for which this country would be held responsible in the eyes both of God and man. Its petty tribes would then be constantly engaged in predatory wars against each other, for the purpose of seizing slaves to supply the American market. All hope of African civilization would thus be ended.

19

"On the other hand, when a market for African slaves shall be no longer furnished in Cuba, and thus all the world be closed against this trade, we may then indulge a reasonable hope for the gradual improvement of Africa. The chief motive of war among the tribes will cease whenever there is no longer any demand for slaves. The resources of that fertile, but miserable country, might be developed by the hand of industry, and afford subjects for legitimate foreign and domestic commerce. In this manner Christianity and civilization may gradually penetrate the existing gloom."

Even Caiaphas prophesied, " being high-priest that year." — And what becomes, now, of all the rhetoric spent upon the moral and religious blessings and benefits accruing to mankind from Negro slavery and the African slave trade? What, now, of these noble gospel and missionary institutions? Look at the great African balance-sheet!

There are two leading arguments, familiarly urged in defence of Negro slavery, which are equally applicable in justification of the slave trade :—either that "the Negro is not a man," or that "the Negroes are an inferior race." The former of these the "Christian Bishop" professedly rejects; the latter he fully adopts. One or other of these arguments is so constantly insisted on as settling the whole question, that they demand some special consideration.

"Negroes are not men;" — this is an old idea; — "slaves are not men," said a Roman lady, (see Juvenal.) Dr. Nott, of Mobile, and Mr. Gliddon, of Philadelphia, published, some years since, an elaborate work, the chief burden of which was to show that the Negro and the white man are not descended from a common origin. How far this Gliddonian infidelity has extended at the South it would be curious to inquire; that it has infected to a considerable extent the Southern mind there can be no doubt. Says one Southern writer:

" The wide-spread delusion that Southern institutions are an evil, and their extension dangerous,— the notion so prevalent at the North that there is a real antagonism, or that the system of the South is hostile to Northern interests; the weakened Union sentiment, and the utter debauchment, the absolute traitorism of a portion of the Northern people, not only to the Union, but to Democratic institutions and to the cause of civilization on this continent; all these, with the minor and most innumerable mischiefs that this mighty world-wide imposture has engendered or drags in its midst, rest upon the dogma, the single assumption, the sole elementary foundation falsehood, *that a Negro is a black man."*

But, " at all events," say the slaveholders, " the Negroes are an *inferior* race ; and may, therefore, justly be kept in slavery ;" — and to this the " Christian Bishop" says, Amen.

" Is it not certain that through his faults, still more than through his figure, the Negro is an inferior being ? He is indolent, inactive, drunken, cruel, incapable of labour, or virtue without compulsion. He is truly formed for his inferior condition ; the little education of which he is susceptible he owes to servitude."— This is the common argument. And, says Governor Adams, of South Carolina, in his message, in 1856, " until Providence decides otherwise, the African must continue to be a hewer of wood and a drawer of water. . . . . . There was a time when a canting philosophy almost inclined our minds to believe that slavery was unjust. Investigations have wholly changed the common opinion on this point. The South now believes that a mysterious Providence has mingled the two races together on this continent with some wise view, and that their mutual relations have been profitable to both. Slavery has elevated the African to a degree of civilization which the black race has never attained in any age or in any country."

It is remarkable that this assumption of inferiority of race should have led to the refusal of almost all means and opportunities of intellectual improvement to the slaves. This, taken in connection with the assumed natural inferiority marked by attendant striking physical characteristics, makes the lot and the prospects of the enslaved Negro sad beyond description.

" 'The only means by which the ancients maintained slavery, were fetters and death; the Americans of the South of the Union have discovered more intellectual securities for the duration of their power. They have employed their despotism and their violence against the human mind. In antiquity, precautions were taken to prevent the slave from breaking his chains; at the present day, measures are adopted to deprive him even of the desire of freedom. The ancients kept the bodies of their slaves in bondage, but they placed no restraint upon the mind, and no check upon education; and they acted consistently with their established principle, since a natural termination of slavery then existed, and one day or other the slave might be set free, and become the equal of his master. But the Americans of the

South, who do not admit that the Negroes can ever be commingled with themselves, have forbidden them to be taught to read and write under severe penalties; and as they will not raise them to their own level, they sink them as nearly possible to that of the brutes.' (De Tocqueville—Democracy in America, Vol. II., pp. 246, 247.) The education of slaves amongst the ancients prepared the way for emancipation. The prohibition of the education of slaves amongst the moderns has naturally suggested the policy of holding them in perpetual bondage; and laws and manners have conspired to interpose obstacles all but insuperable in the way of manumission. Thus the modern slave is cut off from the one great alleviation of his lot—the hope of freedom."*

" The education of slaves was never prohibited in ancient Roman world, and, in point of fact, no small number of them enjoyed the advantage of a simple cultivation. 'The youths of promising genius,' says Gibbon, 'were instructed in the arts and sciences, and almost every profession, liberal and mechanical, might be found in the household of an opulent Senator.' The industrial necessities of Roman society, (and the same was true of society in the middle ages,) in this way, provided for the education of at least a large proportion of the slave population; and education, accompanied as it was by a general elevation of their condition, led, by a natural and almost inevitable tendency, to emancipation."†

" The slave, amongst the ancients, belonged to the same race as his master, and he was often the supe-

* Cairnes, pp. 70, 71.   † Cairnes, p. 68.
19*

rior of the two in education and instruction. Freedom was the only distinction between them; and
when freedom was conferred, they were easily confounded together." . . . . " The greatest difficulty of antiquity [in the way of abolition] was that
of altering the law; amongst the moderns, it is that
of altering the manners; and, as far as we are concerned, the real obstacles begin where those of the
ancients left off. This arises from the circumstance
that, amongst the moderns, the abstract and transient
fact of slavery is fatally united to the physical
and permanent fact of colour. The tradition of
slavery dishonours the race, and the peculiarity of
the race perpetuates the tradition of slavery. No
African has ever voluntarily emigrated to the shores
of the New World; whence it must be inferred, that
all the blacks who are now to be found in that hemi-
sphere are either slaves or freedmen. Thus the Negro
transmits the external mark of his ignominy to all
his descendants. The law may cancel servitude:
God alone can obliterate its brand."*

Says M. Granier de Cassagnac, in his Voyage aux
Antilles (pp. 137-9):

" The slaves sold by the African kings are their
superfluous slaves, who have laboured for them and
been born among them; there are here and there a
few prisoners of war, but these are rare exceptions.
. . . . The slave trade, that pretended commerce in
human flesh, becomes reduced, in the eyes of men
of good sense, to *a simple translocation of workmen, of
incontestable advantage to the latter.* Servitude does
not constitute a condition of violence to those sub-

* De Tocqueville, Democracy in America, Vol. II., pp. 215-17.

jected to it; it is a method of organization of labour which guarantees the maintenance of the labourer during his natural life, in consideration of the sum of efforts of which he is capable. . . . The establishment of liberty in Europe has destroyed the ancient economical organization which resolved the problem of the material assistance of men by obligatory labour, but has not yet found a new and equivalent solution; for at the present time the free labourers consume more than they produce, which is proved by the fact that they receive from society, in addition, alms, vagrant institutions, foundling asylums, and hospitals. . . . ['The free labourers consume more than they produce!' Who produces the balance?]

"Nothing less than the impenetrable crust of absurdity which envelopes the brain of European philanthropists, could prevent them from discerning these truths ! !"*

"But are not the Negroes, after all, really an *infe-*

---

* After such a defining of his position, the testimony of M. Granier de Cassagnac to another point may be received without disparagement. "The whites," writes he, "have failed in their duties of morality and continency as Christians, I admit; but it is unjust to make their fault greater than it is; and if God pardons them, the Negresses will not be the ones to hold malice against them. They consider themselves *very naturally* as the wives of those who feed and lodge them; and when we see the kind of spouses to which they are accustomed in their own country disembark from the slave-ships, we need not carry fatuity very far to believe that the latter can be replaced with them without striking disadvantage. This is, besides, their most sincere and scarcely disguised opinion, and if philanthropists believe them very unhappy in finding themselves exposed to the ardor of their new masters, a short voyage to the Antilles will radically convince them to the contrary." (Voyage aux Antilles, pp. 237, 240.)

rior race?" Suppose they are, does it follow that they should be reduced to slavery? How inferior must a race be in order to authorize their being enslaved? And, when you have settled your rule, who is to judge of its application? There may be other inferior races besides the negroes.* It may be a

---

* The "Christian Bishop" seems much exercised by the treatment which the Indians received from the Puritans of New England and the Quakers of Pennsylvania. But, in his view, the great misfortune, in the case of the aborigines, was, that we failed to reduce them to slavery, (p. 237.) Had they been enslaved like the blacks, he thinks the red race might have been preserved and gradually civilized. Slavery is his panacea. In proof of his position, he has forgotten to refer, as he should have done, to the crucial experiments in Hispaniola, Cuba, and Mexico, where, in the two former cases, *with slavery,* the poor Indians were swiftly and utterly exterminated; and, in the latter case, *without slavery,* the aborigines still remain, by the million, either in pure or mixed breeds, and, with Christian churches and priests, in a state of at least semi-civilization.

When the "Christian Bishop" has expended as much of his sarcastic indignation as he thinks fit upon the Puritans and the Quakers, and as much of his tearful sympathy as he can spare upon their Indian victims, let him turn next to the more modern instances of the Creeks and Choctaws threatened with a sweetly Christian extermination by the tender mercies of the Southern chivalry, and saved only by the interposition of the United States' government, which was compelled to tear them from the homes and graves of their fathers, and ruthlessly thrust them back into the Western wilderness; and of the Seminoles of Florida hunted down like wild beasts through thicket, swamp, and morass, and their bleeding remnant torn from their native haunts and driven to share the abodes allotted to the Cherokees, Choctaws, and Creeks. Let him recount—to the honour of his "dear brethren of the South"—the causes and the course of this Seminole war: that the Indians had attacked and burned no settlements, had committed no acts of violence or barbarity against the whites, but had simply afforded an asylum to runaway negroes; had, in

question whether or not the Celtic race is inferior to the Anglo-Saxon. There may be white slavery, by this rule, as well as black slavery; and this is fully admitted by the "Christian Bishop;" who even claims great credit to the Southern chivalry for their forbearance and self-denial in restricting the exercise of their divine right of enslaving, exclusively to the most degraded race of all. This Southern chivalry seriously claim to be a "superior race" to the free labourers of the North. They themselves are gen-

obedience to an unrepealed divine command, refused to restore to their masters the slaves who had escaped to them for protection;—that, for this, and this only, they were assailed and pursued in an unrelenting war, and men, women, and children, either butchered or expatriated; that the United States' government employed its military force for several years in the work, expending some forty millions of dollars, losing many valuable lives of brave men, and bringing an eternal disgrace upon the American name by seizing the Indian chief Osceola in violation of a solemn promise to which the heroic savage had implicitly trusted. Let him tell us, whether, after all this *national* expenditure of money, men, and honour, in such a cause, we of the North have nothing to do with Southern slavery, and are in no sense responsible for its maintenance and continuance.

It is high time that all the abettors of Southern slavery, and admirers of Southern chivalry, and maligners of New England, whether born in Ireland or in South Carolina, should study the history of the modern Seminole war, instead of expending their righteous indignation upon the "Pilgrim Fathers" and the Quakers, or exhausting their Christian sympathies upon the poor Indians of the distant past. Besides, it would not be amiss for them to inquire, whether it has been their "dear brethren of the Southern church" or the descendants of the stigmatized Puritans and Quakers, who have made the most earnest and successful efforts to civilize and Christianize the Indian aborigines, and particularly those surviving and expatriated tribes of Choctaws, and Creeks, and Seminoles.

tlemen, the others are the "mudsills of society."
The descendants of adventurers and convicts a "superior race" to the descendants of the companions
and co-religionists of Penn, and the sons of the Pilgrim fathers! And having a perfect divine and natural right to make slaves of their inferior Northern
neighbours, — if they could!! But, most amazing
and incredible of all, there are found among Northern men those who are mean and base enough to
admit this outrageous assumption of Southern insolence!!!

I have myself been told to my face, by an eminent
Judge and a distinguished Democratic politician of a
Northern State, upon my suggesting that the South
had no encroachments to complain of, that they had
themselves governed the country ever since the organization of the Union,—"yes, they have governed
the country, and see how well they have governed
it! And don't you know," he added, "that intelligence and virtue will always govern?" Could degrading sycophancy be carried further? Think of
that, freemen of the North. Think of a man coming
and asking for your suffrages, with such an opinion
as that of your *virtue and intelligence* — of the virtue
and intelligence of his neighbours. Are you fit only
to be governed by him and his Southern friends?
"The relations between the North and the South,"
says a Southern organ, " are very analogous to those
which subsisted between Greece and the Roman Empire after the subjugation of Achaia by the consul
Mummius. The dignity and energy of the Roman
character, conspicuous in war and politics, were not
easily toned and adjusted to the arts of industry and
literature. The degenerate and pliant Greeks, on

the contrary, excelled in the handicraft and polite professions. We learn from the vigorous invective of Juvenal, that they were the most useful and capable of servants, whether as pimps or professors of rhetoric. Obsequious, dexterous, and ready, the versatile Greeks monopolized the business of teaching, publishing, and manufacturing in the Roman Empire, allowing their masters ample leisure for the service of the State, in the senate or in the field." " In confirmation of this historical theory," says Goldwin Smith, "it may be remarked that the Romans of the Southern States, like those of the capitol, sprang from an asylum. One who was much concerned in the foundation of Virginia, said of that colony that ' the number of felons and vagabonds transported did bring such evil characters on the place, that some did choose to be hanged ere they would go there, *and were.*' "

And as to the inferiority of the African race, how far it is the result of their condition rather than of nature, the result of immemorial generations of debasement and slavery,* it is impossible to say. That some of the descendants of Ham and even of Canaan, betrayed no remarkable intellectual, military, or po-

* Or even of *fear:*—

"Fear," says Bentham, "leads the labourer to hide his powers, rather than to show them; to remain below, rather than to surpass himself." . . . . "By displaying superior capacity, the slave would only raise the measure of his ordinary duties; by a work of supererogation, he would only prepare punishment for himself! He therefore seeks, by concealing his powers, to reduce to the lowest the standard of requisition. His ambition is the reverse of that of the freeman : he seeks to descend in the scale of industry, rather than to ascend."

litical inferiority, let Nimrod, let the Assyrian and
Babylonian Empires, let Egypt, with her monu-
ments and untold ages of learning and power, let
Tyre and Sidon, with Phenician commerce and letters, let Carthage and Hannibal, bear witness.

And even of the modern Negro races :

" We know now," says Cochin, " that divided into
numerous tribes, some a prey to abominable tyrants,
and to the horrors of a fetichism in which the ser-
pent recalls the ancient symbol of the demon, and
in which human sacrifices are a figure of the instinc-
tive confidence of humanity in an atoning blood;
others subjected to the yoke by the invasion of Mus-
sulman hordes; all the black nations resemble each
other in great kindness and gentleness, remarkable
bodily vigour, a sobriety equal to that of the Indian,
and enough love of labor and commercial intelligence to have cultivated vast regions, and founded
towns of twenty or thirty thousand souls. We know,
too, the sale of slaves to Europeans is the chief origin
and example of the pillages and atrocities which
weigh down the blacks of Africa. We know, lastly,
that, despite the debasement of long centuries of
darkness, blood, superstition, and oppression, several
tribes are handsome, intelligent, and worthy of the
most elevated types of the human family."

Speke and Livingstone show us the African, not
as he is known on the outskirts of his own country,
corrupted and brutalized by his commerce with the
slave traders, " but he is put before us," as an English writer forcibly remarks, " in his true colours,
with all the elements of good and evil that belong
to his native, unsophisticated character. Barbarous
he may be, and liable to gusts of passion that some-

times carry him to deeds of savage violence. Ignorant he may be, and the slave of gross idolatry; but
he is not insensible to kindness; he is not unwilling
to be taught and raised to something that belongs to
a far higher order of humanity. And take him as
he is—untaught, ignorant of the arts of life, and the
sport of savage passion—yet has he learned to be
faithful to his leader, to be true to his word, and
honest in his dealings; and he has learnt so much of
social union, that he is loyal to his chief, and proud
of his tribe and name; and he has many of those
points of character, which, among civilized men, are
called honour and patriotism. Nor is he a mere
fierce and wandering hunter, like the red Indian of
North America. For though he does love to follow
the 'large game,' and to bring back their spoils for
commerce, he also delights in agriculture, and dwells
contentedly among his gardens and fields of corn;
longs to possess new implements and arts of culture,
that he may turn them to profit; delights to improve his stock of domestic animals, to exchange
produce with neighboring tribes, and thus to learn
the arts of peace; he longs, also, for the improved
arts and commerce of the white man, whose fame
has reached him, but whose persons he has never
seen."

We may add, that, from the experiment in Liberia,
we now know, also, that Negroes are capable of
governing themselves, of managing their own political affairs, of developing no mean degree of intelligence and learning, of home industry, of commercial
enterprise, and even of statesmanship. And I have
myself seen a class of Negro boys pass an examination in mental arithmetic, in algebra, in geometry
20

Virgil—would have softened any mob not inspired by slavery, yielded to the ejectment proposed—precisely as the prisoner yields to the officers of the law—and left Charleston, while a person in the crowd was heard to offer himself as "the leader of a tar-and-feather gang, to be called into the service of the city on the occasion." Nor is this all. The Legislature a second time "caught" the fever, and, yielding to its influence, passed another statute, forbidding, under severe penalties, any person within the State from accepting a commission to befriend these coloured mariners; and under penalties severer still, extending even to imprisonment for life, prohibiting any person "on his own behalf, or by virtue of any authority of any State," to come within South Carolina for this purpose; and then, to complete its work, the Legislature took away the writ of *habeas corpus* from all such mariners.

Such is a simple narrative founded on authentic documents.*

Such has been the conduct of South Carolina, and yet Massachusetts neither seceded nor rebelled; and Northern men generally seemed disposed to pocket the insult, and indeed began to be strangely oblivious of its very existence. Yet this same South Carolina, in her declaration, charges the violation of the Constitution in the matter of the rendition of fugitive servants, as one of the causes of her secession;—although she probably never lost half a dozen slaves, and perhaps never a solitary slave, by such violation.

The fact is, that, though the Fugitive Slave Law of 1850 was clearly *not required* by the Constitution, and was held by a large number at the North to be

* See Sumner's speech of 1860.

equality, and the elevation of one's condition, and to make all content with the allotments of Providence, the "Christian Bishop" goes very far towards recommending the same result.

But a high moral motive is suggested in defence of Negro slavery : it is *the education of an inferior race.* This motive calmed the scruples of Louis XIII., and the remorse of Louis XIV.; it was on the lips of the adversaries of Wilberforce and Clarkson, and, three centuries before, in the speeches of the antagonists of Las Casas ;* it was the sole argument of the colonists of Guadaloupe and Jamaica; it is the habitual answer of the tender-hearted ladies of Havana; it is the pretext in the sermons of the preachers of South Carolina; the thesis amplified by the writers of Baltimore; the summary excuse of the planters of New Orleans.

They do not fail to add, that slavery is a means of converting a heathen race to Christianity. The slaves, therefore, are scholars and catechumens, the masters are instructors and preachers, the planta-

* "It is known that Charles V. presided, in 1513, at Barcelona, over a solemn conference, to listen to Quevedo, Bishop of Darien, and Barthélemy de Las Casas, the illustrious and indefatigable protector of the Indians, in the presence of the Admiral of the Indies, Don Diego Columbus. The Bishop of Darien declared that all the inhabitants of the New World whom he had observed, appeared to him a species of men designed for servitude, through the inferiority of their intellect and natural talents, and that it would be impossible to instruct them, or cause them to make any progress towards civilization unless held under the continued authority of a master. Las Casas rose with indignation at the idea that there was any race of men born for servitude, and attacked this opinion as irreligious, inhuman, and false in practice."— Robertson's America, Book III.

tions are boarding-schools and little seminaries, slavery is a method of education and conversion.

After three centuries of this system, freedom is talked of. "Take care!" exclaim the masters, with one voice; "you are about to thrust ignorant and depraved beings into society!" What! the education and conversion of your scholars is not finished? Either the pupils are incorrigible, or the method is bad; it is time to change it, and renounce this pitiful argument. The fears of the masters give the lie to their promises: By the grace of God, servitude is decidedly not a means of civilizing or converting any member of the human family.*

On the whole, if slavery is right,—not *tolerated* for a time and under certain circumstances,—but *justified* as a moral state of human society, authorized and approved by the word of God:—then is the slavery of whites no less justifiable than the slavery of blacks,—it is a mere question of relative force and of fact; if I *can* make you my slave, I have a *right* so to do; if you *are* my slave, you *ought* to be my slave. Only I am bound to feed and clothe you well, and not to overtask or abuse you. It may be my duty, too, so far as it is for my interest, to give you *religious* instruction.† But for the rest, you are a

---

* See Cochin, Results of Emancipation, p. 301.

† The admissions of Queipo upon this point are extremely valuable. He thinks that for the slaves, it suffices for the present to limit the education to religious instruction. He urges the government to facilitate, by every means within its power, instruction so useful; and mark what was the programme of this in his eyes!

"Religious instruction, directed by zealous and learned ecclesiastics, far from influencing the relaxation of discipline, as some

"*mere labourer*," a slave ; you are to serve me and be *content.* Moreover the slave trade must be right also ; and those men must have been guilty, in their day, of making themselves "wiser than the Almighty, and more merciful than Jesus Christ," who laboured, on moral and religious grounds, for the abolition of that infamous traffic ; for, as long as it was established and protected by law, it was fully sanctioned and "authorized by both the Old and the New Testaments." If I may hold slaves, I may buy slaves ; or, at least, if I may buy them of my next neighbour, I certainly may buy them in a market three thousand miles off. The "horrors of the middle passage" have no more to do with condemning the slave trade, as wrong, *per se,* than the undeniable instances of outrageous cruelty in the treatment of slaves have to do with the condemnation of the system of slaveholding, *per se ;* for they may be incidental in one case as well as in the other ; and, moreover, *may be due to the officious intermeddling of abolitionists quite as much in the former case as in the latter.*

If, then, we say that slavery, as it exists, is authorized and justified by the law and word of God and by the Gospel of Christ, and if the slave trade also is thus authorized and justified (which follows of course) ; and if it is deemed by slaveholders to be profitable and desirable to hold slaves and buy slaves and perpetuate slavery ; what boots it for us to add that *we*

perhaps fear, would contribute, on the contrary, to strengthen *the authority of the masters, by accustoming the slaves to submission,* and teaching them to endure the *privations of their transient condition* with the resignation which religion alone can inspire."— Cochin's Results of Slavery, p. 171.

20*

desire the abolition of slavery or of the slave trade?
Why abolish it at another time rather than now?
And why desire its abolition at all? What preparations, with such views, will be made for its ultimate
abolition? *And why should any such preparations be
made?* It is a mere question of loss and gain, of
"wise expediency," of political economy; it has no
moral character, no relation to religious duty. Why
should I meddle with my neighbour's business concerns? Why should I *desire* that he should plant cotton rather than flax, or raise oats rather than barley,
or import lead rather than iron, or cutlery rather
than sugar? Surely, if I *desired* anything in these
cases, it would not be especially as a Christian that I
should desire it; it would not be a desire particularly
appropriate and honourable to a "Christian Bishop,"
but must proceed merely from some selfish or personal
or trivial consideration.

If the "Christian Bishop's" argument proves,—as
I think I have shown it does,—that *white slavery* and
the *slave trade* are fully authorized, in this nineteenth
century, by the word of God;—then his argument
proves too much, and must be a fallacy. And, after
such an argument, it is to no purpose at all that he
adds, as a *salvo* for his own goodness of heart, the
idle, and withal inconsistent *wish* that slavery and the
slave trade might be done away.

Meantime the *argument* is not idle; it has its practical application. For, I shall proceed to show that,
notwithstanding all the interests of their slave-breeding allies, and all the sentimental wishes of their
Northern friends, and all the "indignant reprobation," too, of the Christian world,—the buying and
planting slaveholders, being a large majority of their

craft, and the enterprising progressives withal, were fully bent upon the reopening of the African slave trade, at the earliest possible moment. Indeed, many cargoes of Africans had already been introduced and sold in South Carolina and Georgia; and it is remarkable that though the slave trade had been declared piracy by the laws of the United States, yet, up to the close of Mr. Buchanan's administration, I believe, not a man had been convicted under those laws, or suffered their punishment; and that "public functionary" himself, notwithstanding the very edifying homily against the slave trade introduced into one of his annual messages, would not have ventured to lift a finger to catch a slave-trader, had his Southern masters given him an intimation to mind his own business. It was not till after the commencement of Lincoln's administration that Gordon, in New York, was convicted of being concerned in the slave trade. And one of the most irritating features of the whole business, is, that when this infamous and lawless traffic is charged upon the South, they answer that, on the contrary, it is carried on by Northern men; that the slave ships are furnished by Northern capitalists, fitted out in the Northern ports, manned by Northern seamen, and the profits go into Northern pockets;— that is to say, while the slaveholders encourage, employ and protect these pirates in their nefarious business, protect them against all the efforts of Northern men to bring them to punishment, they turn round and charge upon "the North" the infamy of the whole transaction. And this is of a piece with the shrewd proceeding of the "Christian Bishop" in charging upon the city of New York, upon the free and loyal people of New York, all the crimes and villainies perpetrated there by his own pro-slavery and negro-hating friends.

Some of the evidence that the cotton States had begun to move earnestly in agitation and action for the re-opening of the African slave trade, I add here, as collected by Professor Cairnes, of Galway, in his able work on the Slave Power.

" With a view to the first point—the augmentation of the supply of slave labour—the obvious, and the only adequate expedient, was the re-opening of the African slave trade. . . . . It was, accordingly, determined, that an agitation should forthwith be set on foot for this purpose. The first blast of the trumpet announcing the new policy was sounded by Governor Adams, of South Carolina, in his address to the legislature of that State in 1857. The prohibition of the slave trade was denounced in vehement terms. It was a violation of the Constitution, and it interfered with the essential interests of the South. By the closing of the African slave trade the equilibrium between North and South had been destroyed, and this equilibrium could only be restored in one way— by the re-opening of that trade. Let this once be accomplished—let the South have free access to the only labour market which is suited to her wants— and she has no rival whom she need fear. The keynote having been struck, the burden of the strain was taken up by other speakers, and the usual machinery of agitation was put in motion through the South. The Southern press freely discussed the scheme.* It was brought before the annual conven-

* " The Charleston *Standard*, complaining that the position of the South had hitherto been too much one of defence and apology,

tions for the consideration of Southern affairs, and received the energetic support of the leaders of the extreme Southern party.* At one of these conventions held at Vicksburg, Mississippi, in May, 1859, a

adds, 'to the end of changing our attitude in the contest, and of planting our standard right in the very faces of our adversaries, we propose, as a leading principle of Southern policy, to re-open and legitimate the slave trade.' And it then proceeds, in a series of articles, to argue at length the rightfulness and expediency of this measure, expounding and elaborately enforcing the following propositions, viz. :—'That equality of States is necessary to equality of power in the Senate of the Union ; that equality of population is necessary to equality of power in the House of Representatives ; that we cannot expand our labour into the territories without decreasing it in the States, and what is gained upon the frontier is lost at the centres of the institution ; that pauper white labour will not come into competition with our slaves ; and, if it did, that it would not increase the integrity and strength of slavery ; and that, therefore, to the equality of influence in the Federal Legislature, there is a necessity for the slave trade.' "

* "Mr. Yancey has denied this in a letter to the *Daily News*, and declared that he ' does not know two public men in the South, of any note, who ever' advocated the restoration of the trade, and that 'the people there are and have been almost unanimously opposed to it.' It is unnecessary to re-open a question which has been disposed of, and I therefore refer the reader, who wishes to ascertain the authenticity of Mr. Yancey's statement, to the *Daily News* of the 27th and 28th January, 1862. One or two specimens, however, may be given of the views of Southern politicians on this subject. The Hon. L. W. Spratt, of Georgia, in a speech at Savannah in favour of the African slave trade, thus expressed himself :—' The first reason for its revival is, it will give political power to the South. Imported slaves will increase our representation in the National Legislature. More slaves will give us more States ; and it is, therefore, within the power of the rude untutored savages we bring from Africa to restore to the South the influence she has lost by the suppression of the trade. We want

vote in favour of the re-opening of the trade, was
passed by a large majority; and this was followed up
by the formation of an 'African Labor Supply Asso-
ciation,' of which Mr. De Bow, the editor of the leading Southern review, was president. In Alabama a
'League of United Southerners' issued a manifesto in
which the Federal prohibition of the foreign slave
trade is denounced as an unworthy concession to the
demands of Northern fanaticism, and which insists on
'the necessity of sustaining slavery, not only where

only that kind of population which will extend and secure our
political institutions, and there is no other source but Africa.'
Mr. A. H. Stephens, the present Vice President of the Southern
Confederation, has thus pointedly put the argument for the opening of the trade : — 'We can divide Texas into five slave states,
and get Chihuahua, Sonora, &c., if we have the slave population,
and it is plain that *unless the number of African stock be increased*,
we have not the population, and might as well abandon the race
with our brethren of the North in the colonization of the territories. . . . . Slave States cannot be made without Africans. I am
not telling you to do it, but it is a serious question concerning
our political and domestic policy ; and it is useless to wage war
about abstract rights, or to quarrel and accuse each other of un-
soundness, unless we get more Africans. . . . . Negro slavery is
but in its infancy.' "

And Mr. Jefferson Davis, while declaring his disapprobation
of opening the trade in Mississippi, earnestly disclaimed ' any
coincidence of opinion with those who prate of the inhumanity
and sinfulness of the trade. The interest of Mississippi, not of
the Africans,' he said, ' dictates my conclusion. Her arm is, no
doubt, strengthened by the presence of a *due proportion* of the
servile caste, but it might be paralyzed by such an influx as would
probably follow if the gates of the African slave market were
thrown open.' . . . . ' This conclusion, in relation to Mississippi,
is based upon my view of her *present condition, not upon any general
theory. It is not supposed to be applicable to Texas, to New Mexico,
or to any future acquisition to be made south of the Rio Grande.'* "

its existence is put directly in issue, but where it is
remotely concerned.' In Arkansas and Louisiana the
subject was brought before the State Legislatures.
A motion brought forward in the Senate of the former
State, condemnatory of the agitation for the revival
of the African slave trade, was defeated by a majority
of twenty-two. In the latter a bill embodying the
views of the advocates of the trade was passed suc-
cessfully through the lower House, and only by a narrow majority lost in the Senate. In Georgia the
executive committee of an agricultural society offered
'a premium of twenty-five dollars for the best specimen of a live African imported within the last twelve
months, to be exhibited at the next meeting of the
society.' Nor was the principle of competition confined to the show-yard. Southern notions would have
been shocked if so solemn a work had missed the ben-
ediction of the Church. Accordingly it was proposed
in the *True Southern*, a Mississippi paper, to stimulate
the zeal of the pulpit by founding a prize for the best
sermon in favour of free trade in human flesh. Meanwhile those who were immediately interested in the
question had taken the law into their own hands, and
the trade in slaves with Africa was actually commenced on a large scale. Throughout the years 1859
and 1860 fleets of slaves arrived at Southern ports,
and with little interference from the Federal Government, succeeded in landing their cargoes. The traffic
was carried on with scarcely an attempt at conceal-
ment. Announcements of the arrival of cargoes of
Africans, and advertisements of their sale, appeared
openly in the Southern papers; and depots of newly
imported 'savages' were established in the principal
towns of the South. 'I have had ample evidences of

the fact,' said Mr. Underwood, a gentleman of known respectability, in a letter to the New York *Tribune*, 'that the re-opening of the African slave-trade is already a thing commenced, and the traffic is brisk and rapidly increasing. *In fact, the most vital question of the day is not the opening of the trade, but its suppression.* The arrival of cargoes of negroes, fresh from Africa, in our Southern ports, is an event of frequent occurrence.' " (Cairnes, pp. 121–124.)

"'Take off,' says Mr. Gaulden of Georgia, 'the ruthless restrictions which cut off the supply of slaves from foreign lands, . . . take off the restrictions against the African slave trade, and we should then want no protection, and I would be willing to let you have as much squatter sovereignty as you wish. Give us an equal chance, and I tell you the institution of slavery will take care of itself.' " (Cairnes, p. 137.)

Nor let it be supposed that Virginia, or all the slave-breeding States, would have breasted the rising Southern tide.

" The sympathies which bind slaveholders together have always proved more powerful than the particular interests which would sunder them; and whatever course the necessities of slavery, as a system, have prescribed, that the whole array of slaveholders, with a disregard for private ends which, in a good cause, would be the highest virtue, has never hesitated to pursue."

The advocates of slavery have long and pertinaciously insisted that the philanthropic but fanatical efforts for the suppression of the slave trade have rather resulted in intensifying the horrors than diminishing the amount of the traffic. This is of a piece with the ordinary reasoning of slaveholders and their friends. They are always ready to take advantage of their own or of their clients' wrong. But the allegation is not true. " When we compare what took place a few years ago," said Lord John Russell, June 8, 1860, " when we remember that one hundred and forty thousand slaves were yearly carried away from Africa, while this year the number has not reached thirty thousand, we should neither deny the progress nor abandon the hope of a complete suppression of this traffic."

And Livingstone wrote to Lord Clarendon, March 19, 1856, from the River Zambesi: "A certain Dr. Bryson has written that the measures taken to suppress the slave trade have done nothing but increase its horrors. It has also been gravely affirmed that the Maravi now kill their captives, whereas formerly they kept them to sell to the whites. I can assure your Lordship that such an assertion could not come from a man mixed up, as I am, with slave-traders, in the very country where the traffic is carried on; it is spread by those who have an interest in the slave trade. In the extensive portion of Africa with which I am acquainted wars are now very rare : *they were evidently provoked by the slave trade.* It is rare now to see a *cafilah* of slaves on its way to the sea-shore, and the traffickers know that they risk more than in venturing their money at play. By taking away all possibility of industry, the commerce in slaves is the cause of the complete ruin of East and West Africa."

But, while slaveholders and their allies, including some Christian Bishops, are ready to defend the slave trade, it is comforting to know that there is, at least, one portion of the church where a " Christian Bishop" would not be allowed to maintain the rightfulness of this traffic. I close this chapter with the following extracts from the apostolic letter of Pope Gregory XVI., issued in 1839:

"The law of the Gospel having very soon universally and fundamentally ordained sincere charity towards all, and the Lord Jesus having declared that He would regard as done or refused to Himself all the acts of beneficence and mercy done or refused to the poor and little ones—it naturally followed that Christians not only regarded their slaves as brethren, above all when they were become Christians, but that they were more inclined to give liberty to those who rendered themselves worthy of it. This usually took place particularly on the solemn feasts of Easter, as St. Gregory of Nyssa relates. There were even found some who, inflamed with more ardent charity, *embraced slavery for the redemption of their brethren;* and an apostolic man, our predecessor, Pope Gregory I., of sacred memory, attests that he had known a great many who performed this work of mercy. Wherefore the darkness of Pagan superstition being entirely dissipated in the progress of time, and the manners of the most barbarous nations being softened,—thanks to the benefit of faith working by charity,—things advanced so far, that for many centuries there have been no slaves among the greatest part of the Christian nations. Yet (we say it with profound sorrow) men have been since found, even among Christians, who, shamefully blinded by the desire of sordid gain, have not hesitated to reduce into slavery in distant countries, Indians, Negroes, and other unfortunate races; or to assist in this scandalous crime, by instituting and organizing a traffic in these unfortunate beings, who had been loaded with chains by others.

"Wherefore, desiring to remove such a disgrace from all Christian countries, after having maturely considered the matter with many of our venerable brethren, the Cardinals of the Holy Roman Church, assembled in Council, following the example of our predecessors, by virtue of the apostolic office, we warn and admonish in the Lord all Christians, of whatever condition they may be, and enjoin upon them that, for the future, no one shall venture unjustly to oppress the Indians, Negroes, or other men, whoever they may be; to strip them of their property or reduce them into servitude: or give aid or support to those who commit such excesses, or carry on that infamous traffic, by which the blacks, as if they were not men, but mere impure animals, reduced like them into servitude, without any distinction, contrary to the laws of justice and humanity, are bought, sold, and devoted to endure the hardest labours; and on account of which, dissensions are excited and almost continual wars are fomented among nations by the allurements of gain offered to those who first carry away the Negroes.

"Wherefore, by virtue of the apostolical authority, we condemn all these things aforesaid, as absolutely unworthy of the Christian name; and, by the same authority, we absolutely prohibit and interdict all ecclesiastics and laymen from venturing to maintain that this traffic in blacks is permitted, under any pretext or color whatever."

CHAPTER VIII.

" SINCE the world began," we have been told,
" slavery has never been abolished by external
force and violence. It has only been done away by
internal action on the part of those who are directly concerned. Of this we have two very different examples.
The first was that of St. Domingo, where the slaves,
excited by the pestilent orators of the French Revolution, rose against their masters, and attained their
horrid triumph by the most savage butchery that history has recorded. The other was the abolition movement in England, where the result was regularly effected by the peaceful action of Parliament." (" View,"
&c., pp. 247–8.)

But in the first place, where is the evidence that
the excitement of the slaves in St. Domingo had anything to do with " the pestilent orators of the French
Revolution ?" And as to the " savage butchery,"
when it did come, was it all on one side ? Were there
more whites butchered than there were blacks in that
murderous process of atrocious retaliation ? But, peradventure, the " Christian Bishop," like most aristo-
crats, will think it a far more " horrid" thing for a
civilized white gentleman to be butchered by a black

(244)

savage, than for a savage black to be butchered by a white gentleman.

As his voucher in this case, the author quotes "the eminent Alison, whose 'History of Europe' is one of the most trustworthy productions of modern literature." Now it is notorious that Alison prostituted his office as a historian to the purpose of maintaining certain political dogmas, and that his work abounds with two things—a spirit of aristocratic and absolutist propagandism, and a certain pious twaddle characteristic of that sect. And as for his " trustworthiness," it may be judged of from the fact that he speaks of New England, side by side with Massachusetts and Connecticut, as one of the United States, and declares that " *all* the State judges, from *the highest* to the lowest, are elected by the people, and are liable to be displaced by them ; their tenure of office is sometimes for three, sometimes for four, sometimes for six years, but never for life ;" giving this last as an express proof of the exceedingly radical and corrupt character of our political system, a proposition which, if true, would not have proved his point, but which, at the time he wrote, was false in regard to the judges of the Supreme Courts in a majority of the States. But what may cap the climax of Alison's " trustworthiness" is the unconscious effrontery with which, in his aristocratic ignorance of American affairs, he gravely stated and published before the whole world, in a history which was to be the great work of his life, that " one of the last acts of Washington's life was to carry, *by his casting vote in Congress*, a commercial treaty with Great Britain !"

Yet even such a trustworthy, aristocratic authority fails the Bishop ; for Alison expressly admits that,

21*

when the Constituent Assembly had decreed " the privileges of equality to all persons of color born of a free father and mother," " *the planters openly endeav- ored to resist the decree, and civil war was preparing*," when the negro insurrection broke forth. The truth is the first blood was shed by the whites, and that in resistance to the law of the land. And need we resort to " pestilent orators" to explain what followed ? Un- doubtedly the blacks were savages—a large part of them lately from their wild homes in Africa—and like savages they dealt with their oppressors. But the proper and guilty causes of this horrible tragedy lie far back of pestilent Abolitionists and savage blacks ; they are found in the tearing of these savages from their country and reducing them to slavery. So the " horrors" of the French Revolution itself, about which so much rhetoric is expended, are chargeable not so much upon the immediate actors in the tragedy as upon the tyrannical oppression of the government, the licentious living of the upper classes, and the cor- ruption and hypocrisy in religion, which had preceded and which required this terrible purgation of blood. Such is the general course of history.   The real causes are often remote and concealed ; the apparent causes are merely the present occasions or the last links in the chain. The prime guilt of the St. Do- mingo massacres is not to be charged upon the insur- rection of the savage blacks. You might as well charge upon the rising sun the killing of the tender plants which had been frost-bitten in the preceding night. But whoever may be responsible for the St. Domingo massacres, the fact is that more human be- ings are worked to death in Cuba and on the cotton and sugar plantations of the South—yes, literally *worked to death—every year*, than would equal the number of all the whites who were butchered in St. Domingo. What shall we say to this? Let us remember that wherever we may choose to shed our tears or expend our rhetoric, *God is no respecter of persons*, and the life of the enslaved African, slowly murdered in five years, may be as precious in his sight as that of the chivalrous braggart who is butchered in a moment.

So much for the first case of "internal action." The second is that of the emancipation of eight hundred thousand slaves in the British West Indies, which is represented as also a case "of *internal action by one of the parties concerned.*" This is a very curious description of what was done by an act of the British Parliament, where the slaveholders had not a solitary representative; an act the passage of which was resisted by those slaveholders to the bitter end, and afterwards, in its *execution*, thwarted by them to the best of their ability. Indeed, as I have said, it would be hard to find an instance in the history of the world where slaveholders, having full control of the legislature, have voluntarily relinquished their gripe upon their slaves by a legislative act of emancipation. The emancipation by act of the British Parliament was no more a case of " the *internal action* of one of the parties concerned" than that effected by President Lincoln's proclamation is such a case.

But although the emancipation in the British West Indies is represented as having been "regularly effected by the peaceful action of Parliament," the "Christian Bishop" is far from being satisfied with it after all. The "eminent Alison" is again appealed to, who says: "The precipitate and irretrievable step of emancipation forced on the Legislature in 1834, by benevolent but incautious, and perhaps mistaken, feeling, has already occasioned so great a decline in the produce of the British West Indies, and excited such general expectations of a still greater and increasing deficiency, that the impulse thereby given to the foreign slave trade to fill up the gap, has been unbounded, and, it is to be feared, almost irremediable." And further on, he adds: "The admirable effects of the abolition of the slave trade have been completely frustrated, and the humane but *deluded inhabitants of Great Britain* are burdened with twenty millions, to ruin, in the end, their own planters, consign to barbarism their own Negroes, cut off a principal branch of their naval strength, and double the slave trade in extent, and quadruple it in horrors throughout the world."

As to these crocodile tears over the slave trade, it suffices to refer the reader to the express testimony of Lord John Russell and Dr. Livingstone, already cited. That will show the "trustworthy" character of Alison's statements. And as to another assertion that " the multitude forced on this measure of immediate emancipation" in spite of the counter wishes of Wilberforce and Fox, who are represented to have been in favour of gradual abolition; it is simply a gross misrepresentation. Was Wilberforce opposed to the immediate emancipation of 1834? Rather he was ready to chant his "Nunc dimittis," as upon his death-bed, he received the glorious assurance of its consummation. That Wilberforce and his friends aimed at first, say in 1806, at a gradual emancipation, is undoubtedly true. But who defeated them in this design, and *forced on them* the plan of immediate emancipation ? Not the "fanatical multitude of deluded abolitionists," but the really fanatical and infatuated resistance and obstinacy of the slaveholders themselves, who opposed and thwarted every attempted measure of gradual improvement.

On the 9th of July, 1823, Lord Bathurst Secretary of State for the colonies, addressed a circular to the Governors, commanding them to submit definite *ameliorations* to the legislatures.

After seven years, eight colonies had adopted none of the reforms prescribed. The twelve others had absolutely refused the measures relative to religious instruction and the amelioration of justice; three only had abolished the Sunday markets. All the chartered colonies refused the appointment of protectors, the concession of one day in the week to the slaves, the savings banks, the restrictions on sales, and the modification of punishment. Except at Trinidad and St. Lucia, no important amelioration was accepted, and those which were adopted remained well nigh without effect.*

That the British monarch and the aristocracy, which controlled the Parliament, were natually and instinctively opposed to the abolition of slavery; and that they required some *force* to be brought to bear upon them from some quarter, in order to secure their consent to the measure, need not be denied. But that this force was that of an ignorant rabble, of a "deluded multitude," is a flagrant misrepresentation. It was the force of the Christian sentiment of the great mass of the intelligent people of Great

* See Cochin's Results of Emancipation, pp. 318 and 320, where the proposed ameliorations are given at large.

Britain. This has been well stated by the Duke de Broglie, in the following terms:

"We do too much honour, in fact, to the English government, and we would wrong her too much, in attributing the abolition of slavery on her part either to lofty views of wisdom and foresight or to Machiavellian combinations; on this point the English government has neither gone in advance of the times nor directed events; it has limited itself to maintaining the *statu quo,* so long as it has not been forced from it; it has resisted for fifteen years the abolition of slavery; it has defended all the intermediate positions step by step, and has only yielded, on each occasion, to necessity.

"We would also do too much honour to the philosophy and philanthropy of England in assigning them the chief part in this great enterprise. Philosophers and philanthropists have, doubtlessly, figured gloriously in the number of the combatants, but it is the religious spirit which has borne the heat and burden of the day; and it is to this that reverts, before everything, the honor of success.

"*It is religion that has truly freed the Negroes in the English colonies;* it is this which raised up, in the beginning of the struggle, the Clarksons, the Wilberforces, Granville Sharps, and so many others, and armed them with indomitable courage and unshaken perseverance; it is religion which has progressively formed, first in the nation, then in Parliament itself, that great abolition party, which goes on swelling from day to day, infiltrating itself, as it were, into all parties, calling them all, and the government first of all, to account, and it is this party which, profiting during forty years by every event and

every circumstance, successively carried the abolition of the slave trade in 1807; inspired through its
representatives, in 1815, the declarations of the Congress of Vienna, and, later, those of the Congress
of Verona; dictated in 1823 the motion of Mr. Bux-
ton, the resolutions of Mr. Canning, and the circular
of Lord Bathurst; hurled, in 1831, on the colonies the
Order in the Council of November 2d, thus render-
ing the abolition of slavery inevitable in 1832, and
the maintenance of apprenticeship impossible in
1838."

But the "Christian Bishop" seems controlled almost
exclusively by a "wise expediency" with reference
to certain peculiar views of Political Economy. And,
though he protests his desire for the abolition of
slavery, and speaks half approvingly of the West
India emancipation as having been accomplished by
"internal action," *peacefully*, under the authority of
the British Parliament,—yet he represents this emancipation as an utter failure, and holds up its results
in terrorem before all fanatical abolitionists. 1st, The
production of the islands has been greatly diminished,
as shown by the decrease of exports and imports;
2d, The blacks are lazy, idle, vicious, and becoming
hopelessly degraded. These results were predicted
by the pro-slavery croakers from the start; and they
continue to insist upon the fulfilment of their predictions with as much assurance and solemnity, as
if facts had not already shown their allegations to
be either altogether futile, or utterly false. The first
allegation, if true, proves nothing. Suppose exports
have dwindled, and planters and planters' estates
been ruined; the object was not to increase the exports or the wealth of the islands, but the comfort

and happiness of their inhabitants. The " Christian Bishop" ought to know that the comfort and happiness of the mass of the people is not directly proportional to the increase of national wealth, but, on the contrary, may often be in an inverse ratio. *Distribution and consumption* are quite as important considerations, in any wise and humane Political Economy, as *production*. Suppose the Bishop of Vermont and myself expend upon ourselves and our families some three thousand dollars a year more than would be necessary for our support in some comfortable negro hut, with coarse but wholesome negro fare; and suppose some slave dealer should transfer us and our families from the former condition to the latter, and set us, our wives, our sons, and our daughters, at hard work on his plantation; we should probably produce more merchantable articles than we now do, and our chivalrous and thrifty master would have this surplus, together with the value of the three thousand dollars saved, to add to the gross exports of the country, and would put the proceeds into his pocket. He might grow rich faster than we do—and faster than he would without our services. Whether we, our families, or our country would thereby be benefited, I need not undertake to decide.

The second allegation is simply false. That this is so, and that the first is but partially true, I shall proceed to show by official statements, and by the concurrent testimony of eye-witnesses. I shall show, moreover, that whatever of failure or of incidental evil has been connected with the emancipation, has resulted, not from the freedom or character of the blacks, but, partly from contemporaneous changes in tariff regulations, and, most of all, from the perverse and recalcitrant opposition and interference of the planters themselves.

"The House of Assembly at the time of emancipation possessed the fullest powers to remedy any defect in that great measure. But it abused its powers. Instead of enacting laws calculated to elevate and benefit the people, it pursued the contrary course. By an Ejectment Act it gave to the planters the right to turn out the enfranchised peasantry, without regard to sex or age, at a week's notice, from the houses in which they had been born and bred; to root up their provision grounds, and to cut down the fruit trees which gave them both shelter and food; in order that, through dread of the consequences of refusal, the negroes might be driven to work on the planters' own terms. . . . . Driven from his cabin on the estate by the harsh or unjust treatment of his former master, the free labourer had to build a cottage for himself. Immediately the customs on shingles for the roof to shelter his family from the seasons were more than doubled; while the duty on the staves and hoops for sugar hogsheads, the planters' property, was greatly reduced. And when the houses were built, they were assessed at a rate which, in some parishes, bore so heavily on the occupants, as to lead to the abandonment of their dwellings for shanties of mud and boughs."* . . . . "Some proprietors at emancipation drove their labourers from the estates, and one was mentioned who was living at the time on the north side of the island. He swore that he would not allow a 'nigger'

* Edward Bean Underhill. The West Indies, their social and religious condition. pp. 216–18.

22

to live within three miles of his house. Of course the man was speedily ruined."*

" If the House of Assembly has had any policy at all in its treatment of the labouring classes, it has been a 'policy of alienation.' Only the perpetual interposition of the British government has prevented the enfranchised negro from being reduced to the condition of a serf by the selfish partisan legislation of the Jamaica planters. .... As slaves, the people were never instructed in husbandry, or in the general cultivation of the soil; as free men, the legislature has utterly neglected them, and they have had to learn as they could the commonest processes of agriculture. No attempt has been made to provide a fitting education for them; for the paltry grant of some two thousand five hundred pounds a year cannot in any sense be said to be a provision for their instruction. .... Speaking of this feature of Jamaica legislation, Earl Grey, writing in 1853, says :—' The Statute Book of the island for the last six years presents nearly a blank, as regards laws calculated to improve the condition of the population, and to raise them in the scale of civilization.' .... Happily the present governor, following in the steps of many of his predecessors, deals impartially with every class, strives to prevent as far as possible the mischievous effects of the selfish policy that has been pursued, and exerts himself to rescue the government from the grasp of personal interest and ambition."†

The following is Mr. Underhill's conclusion as to the general results of the experiment in Jamaica:

* Ibid., pp. 268-9.   † Ibid., pp. 222-3.

"Emancipation did not, indeed, bring wealth to the planter; it did not restore fortunes already trembling in the grasp of mortgagees and usurers; it did not bring back the palmy days of foreign commerce to Kingston, nor assist in the maintenance of protective privileges in the markets of Great Britain; it did not give wisdom to planters, nor skill to agriculturists and manufacturers; but it has brought an amount of happiness, of improvement, of material wealth and prospective elevation to the enfranchised slave in which every lover of man must rejoice. Social order everywhere prevails. Breaches of the peace are rare. Crimes, especially in their darker and more sanguinary forms, are few. Persons and property are perfectly safe. The planter sleeps in security, dreads no insurrection, fears not the torch of the incendiary, travels day or night in the loneliest solitudes without anxiety or care. The people are not drunkards, even if they be impure; and this sad feature in the moral life of the people is meeting its check in the growing respect for the marriage tie, and the improved life of the white community in their midst. . . . . The general prospects of the island are improving. Estates are now but rarely abandoned, while in many places portions of old estates are being brought again under cultivation. It is admitted by all parties that sugar cultivation is profitable. At the same time, it is very doubtful whether any large proportion of the emancipated population will ever be induced to return to the estates, or, at least, in sufficient numbers to secure the enlargement of the area of cultivation to the extent of former days. Higher wages will do somewhat to obtain labourers, and they can be afforded, and the return of confidence will bring capital; but the taste and habit of independence will continue to operate, and induce the agricultural classes to cling to the little holdings which they so industriously occupy." *

Captain Darling, the Governor of Jamaica, gives the following testimony to the capacity of the Negro for freedom:—" The proportion of those who are settling themselves industriously on their holdings, and rapidly rising in the social scale, while commanding the respect of all classes of the community, and some of whom are, to a limited extent, themselves the employers of hired labour, paid for either in money or kind, is, I am happy to think, not only steadily increasing, but at the present moment is far more extensive than was anticipated by those who are cognizant of all that took place in this colony in the earlier days of Negro freedom. There can be no doubt, in fact, that an independent, respectable, and, I believe, trustworthy middle class is rapidly forming. If the real object of emancipation was to place the freed man in such a position that he might work out his own advancement in the social scale, and prove his capacity for the full and rational enjoyment of personal independence secured by constitutional liberty, Jamaica will afford more instances, even in proportion to its large population, of such gratifying results, than any other land in which African slavery once existed. Jamaica at this moment presents, as I believe, at once the strongest proof of the complete success of the great measure of emancipation as relates to the capacity of the emancipated race for freedom, and the most unfortunate instance of a descent in the scale of agricultural and commercial importance as a colonial community."

* Ibid., pp. 455-7.

Lord John Russell, on opening the discussion, June 16, 1848, on the conclusions of the report of the committee, was able to sum up the history of the results of emancipation at this epoch in these words:

" The object of the act of 1834 was to give liberty to eight hundred thousand persons, and to secure the independence, prosperity, and happiness of those who were slaves. No one denies, I think, that this has been accomplished. I believe that there is nowhere a happier class of labourers than in the West Indies. This satisfactory condition is the consequence of the act of 1834."

Let us interrogate the history of the ten years following, and we encounter the same facts, verified by the most severe or the most indulgent testimony.

At Guiana, a magnificent province of sixty thousand square miles, traversed by the beautiful river Essequibo, twenty-one miles broad at the mouth, and inhabited by more than one hundred and twenty thousand souls, a colonist, who is, moreover, very much of a pessimist, writes:

" The portion of the native population which in other countries constitutes the laboring class is estimated at seventy thousand souls. They present the singular spectacle, which can be contemplated in no other part of the world, of people scarcely emerged from slavery, yet already possessing property in houses and lands, for which they have paid more than a million pounds sterling."

A French commission, charged, in 1853, by the government of Martinico with visiting the two islands of Barbadoes and Trinidad, writes :

" The aspect of Barbadoes is dazzling in an agricultural and manufacturing point of view. The entire
22*

island is one vast field of sugar-canes, standing evenly
one after the other, planted at an average distance of
six square feet. Not a weed sullies these beautiful
and regular plantations. The sugar-works are extensive and neat, and all the arrangements for manufacture are exquisite." . . . The population of the island
is immense, amounting to one hundred and thirty-six
thousand souls on one hundred and sixty-seven square
miles, on a soil which does not and cannot belong to
it. . . . . " Trinidad has endured harder trials, from
which she has emerged, as we shall see, by replacing
her twenty thousand freed negroes in part by Indians;
but the happiness and tranquillity of its freedmen are
the same."

Here is the picture which a colonist of Jamaica
drew, at the same epoch, of the state of the coloured
community, which almost entirely composes the population of this island, occupied, on a surface of sixty-four
hundred square miles, by three hundred and sixty-
nine thousand blacks and only sixteen thousand
whites :

" It may be supposed that the whites have the pre-
eminence there. . . . . But apart from that pre-
eminence which results from wealth and intelligence
in every community, the whites have no privilege
over their fellow-citizens. . . . The colored man holds
a position in no wise inferior, and we find no reason
to complain that he is on the same footing with ourselves. . . . Our bar is not crowded, but coloured lawyers hold the first places there. Coloured physicians
practice in concurrence with the whites. . . . These
are facts which it is important to establish, for all this
progress has been accomplished since the abolition of
slavery in the island. We have proved by experience

that the coloured man can raise himself to the first
rank of civil society, and hold his place there as well
as any European by origin." *

It may be affirmed that, if the same protective
tariff had secured the sale of colonial sugar at high
prices a few years longer, production would have rapidly revived, and the colonists would have really
had nothing of which to complain.

Nearly a million of men, women, and children have
passed from the condition of cattle to the rank of
rational beings. Numerous marriages have elevated
the family above the mire of nameless promiscuous-
ness. Paternity has replaced illegitimacy. Churches
and schools are opened. Religion, before mute, fac-
tious, or dishonoured, has resumed its dignity and liberty. Men who had nothing have acquired property;
lands which were waste have been occupied; inade-
quate populations have increased; detestable processes
of culture and manufacture have been replaced by
better; a race reputed inferior, vicious, cruel, lasciv-
ious, idle, refractory to civilization, religion, and
instruction, has shown itself honest, gentle, disposed
to family life, accessible to Christianity, eager for
instruction. Those of its members who have returned
to vagrancy, sloth, and corruption are not a reproach
to their race as much as to the servitude which had
left them wallowing in their native ignorance and
depravity; but these are the minority. The majority
labor, and show themselves far superior to the auxil-
iaries which China and India send to the colonists.
In two words, wealth has suffered little, civilization
has gained much; such is the balance-sheet of the
English experiment.†

* Cochin, Res. of Eman., p. 339.   † See Cochin.

Doubtless numerous blacks refuse to labour, flee to the mountains, and regard freedom as the right to do nothing. Cast the blame of this on the nature of the soil and the nature of man. In no country of the world does man labour more than is necessary to satisfy his needs, tastes, and desires; in no country of the world does man labour willingly for others, when he can find it to his advantage to labour for himself. Cast the blame of it, above all, on slavery. Whence comes, then, this abhorrence by the former slaves of their former labour? Freedom is the occasion of it, but servitude the cause. A man visited an abandoned plantation, about which the freed slaves were lazily sleeping. "See what freedom has made of labour," said his companions. "See what servitude has made of labourers," was his reply.

I add the following statements from a very careful and impartial work by William G. Sewell, who visited the British West Indies, in 1859, and critically scrutinized their condition.

"We, in the United States, have heard of abandoned properties in the West Indies, and, without much investigation, have listened to the planters' excuse—the indolence of the Negro, who refuses to work except under compulsion. But I shall be able to show that, in those colonies where estates have been abandoned, the labouring classes, instead of passing from servitude to indolence and idleness, have set up for themselves, and that small proprietors, since emancipation, have increased a hundred fold." . . . . . "It is a fact which speaks volumes, that, within the last fifteen years, in spite of the extraordinary price of land and the low rate of wages, the small proprietors of Barbadoes holding less than five acres have increased from eleven hundred to three thousand five hundred and thirty-seven. *A great majority of these proprietors were formerly slaves, subsequently free labourers, and finally landholders.* This is certainly an evidence of industrious habits, and a remarkable contradiction to the prevailing idea that the negro will work only under compulsion.

" That idea was formed and fostered from the habits of the Negro as a slave; his habits as a freeman, developed under a wholesome stimulus and settled by time, are in striking contrast to his habits as a slave. I am simply stating a truth in regard to the Barbadian Creole, which here, at least, will not be denied. I have conversed on the subject with all classes and conditions of people, and none are more ready to admit than the planters themselves, that the free labourer in Barbadoes is a better, more cheerful, and more industrious workman than the slave ever was under a system of compulsion."

And, again, of an island very differently circumstanced from Barbadoes, the same author writes: " I have taken some pains to trace the Creole labourers of Trinidad from the time of emancipation, after they left the estates and dispersed, to the present day; and the great majority of them can, I think, be followed, step by step, not downward in the path of idleness and poverty, but upward in the scale of civilization to positions of greater independence."*

" If free labour be tested by any other gauge than that of sugar-production, its success in the West Indies is established beyond all cavil and beyond all

* Sewell's Ordeal of Free Labour in the West Indies, pp. 34, 35, 39, 40.

peradventure. If the people merit any consideration whatever—if their independence, their comfort,
their industry, their education, form any part of a
country's prosperity—then the West Indies are a
hundredfold more prosperous now than they were
in the most flourishing times of slavery. If peace
be an element of prosperity—if it be important to
enjoy uninterrupted tranquillity, and be secure from
servile war and insurrection—then the West Indies
have now an advantage that they never possessed
before it was given them by emancipation. If a
largely-extended commerce be an indication of prosperity, then all the West Indies, Jamaica alone excepted, have progressed under a system of free
labour, although that system hitherto has been but
imperfectly developed.

"I have endeavoured to convey a correct idea of the
depreciation of commerce and decline of the sugar-
cultivation in Jamaica; and I have also endeavoured
to show that this depreciation is an exception to the
present general prosperity of the British West Indies
—that it commenced before emancipation was pro-
jected, and can be traced directly to other causes
than the introduction of freedom. Long before Mr.
Canning, in his place in Parliament, became the unwilling organ of the national will, and explained, in
terms not to be mistaken, that the demand of the
British people for the liberation of slaves could be
no longer resisted, West India commerce was in the
most alarming state of depression, owing to the
heavy outlay and expenditure that a system of slave
labour imperatively required. Testimony pointing
directly and overwhelmingly to this conclusion, has
been given by planters themselves—by men put for-

ward as the special champions of the planting interest—and fills a score of Parliamentary blue-books.
Upon their statements, the report of the select committee on the condition of the West India colonies,
printed in 1832, declared that "there was abundant
evidence of an existing distress for ten or twelve
years previous." That report described an impending, if not an actual, ruin, that we look in vain for it
the present day. Jamaica, in 1860, and she only in
the one particular of sugar-cultivation, is the single
British island whose industry and enterprise remain,
as we are told they formerly were, exhausted and
paralyzed.

"Let us appeal once more to figures. The colony of
British Guiana, for four years prior to emancipation,
exported an annual average of 98,000,000 lbs. of sugar,
while, from 1856 to 1860, its annual average export
rose to 100,600,000 lbs. The colony of Trinidad, for
four years prior to emancipation, annually exported
an average of 37,000,000 lbs. of sugar, while, from
1856 to 1860, its annual average exports rose to
62,000,000 lbs. The colony of Barbadoes, for four
years prior to emancipation, annually exported an
average of 32,800,000 lbs. of sugar, while, from 1856
to 1860, its annual average export rose to 78,000,000
lbs. The colony of Antigua, for four years prior to emancipation, exported an annual average of 19,500,000 lbs.
of sugar, while, from 1856 to 1860, its annual average
export rose to 24,400,000 lbs. This is a total exhibit
of 265,000,000 lbs. annually exported now, instead of
187,300,000 lbs. before emancipation, or *an excess of
exports, with free labour, of seventy-seven million, seven
hundred thousand pounds of sugar.*

"In the matter of imports, we find that the colony

of British Guiana, between the years 1820 and 1834, imported annually to the value of $3,700,000; that the annual imports of Trinidad, during the same period, averaged in value $1,690,000; that the import of Barbadoes averaged in value $2,850,000; and those of Antigua $600,000. In the year 1859 the imports of Guiana were valued at $5,660,000; those of Trinidad at $3,000,000; those of Barbadoes at $4,660,000; and those of Antigua at $1,280,000. The total exhibit represents an annual import trade, at the present time, of the value of $14,600,000, against $8,840,000 before emancipation, or *an excess of imports, under a free system, of the value of five million seven hundred and sixty thousand dollars.*

"In the exports I have made mention of sugar only; but if all other articles of commerce be included and a comparison be instituted between the import and export trade of the colonies of Guiana, Trinidad, Barbadoes, and Antigua, under slavery, and their trade under freedom, the annual balance in favour of freedom, will be found to have reached already FIFTEEN MILLIONS OF DOLLARS at the very lowest estimate.

"This large increase in the trade of four out of the five principal West India colonies is sufficient, I think, to demonstrate (were there no other evidence at hand) that free labour, with which four have prospered, cannot alone be responsible for the decline of the fifth. The increase of sugar-production also demonstrates the improved industry of the islands to a very remarkable extent; for it must be remembered that the agricultural force now engaged in cane-cultivation is scarcely more than half what it was in times of slavery, when the energies of the whole population were directed to this single end. One of the most natural and legitimate results of emancipation was to allow every man to do what seemed to him best—to achieve independence if he could—to pursue, in any case, the path of industry most agreeable to his tastes, and most conducive to his happiness. When we look at the vast political and social structure that has been demolished—the new and grander edifice that has been erected—the enemies that have been vanquished —the prejudices that have been uprooted—the education that has been sown broadcast, the ignorance that has been removed—the industry that has been trained and fostered—we cannot pause to criticise defects, for we are amazed at the progress of so great a revolution within the brief space of twenty-five years. Those, who have never lived in a slave country little know how the institution entwines itself round the vitals of society and poisons the sources of political life. The physical condition of the slave is lost in the contemplation of a more overwhelming argument. Looking at the question from a high national standpoint, it is, comparatively speaking, a matter of temporary interest and minor importance whether the bondsman is treated with kindness and humanity, as in America, or with short-sighted brutality, as in Cuba. It is the influence of the system upon the energies and morality of a people that demands the calmest and most earnest consideration of patriots and statesmen. The present is, perhaps, not so much to be condemned, as the future, from which all eyes are studiously averted, is to be dreaded. An act of the British Parliament, and a vote of twenty millions sterling, were sufficient to release 800,000 slaves; but no act of the British Parliament could thus summarily remove the curse that slavery had bequeathed to those islands, and had

23

left to fester in their heart's core. Time only could
do that; time has not done it yet.

"I have endeavoured to show—and I hope success-
fully—that the experiment of free labour in the West
Indies has established its superior economy, as well as
its possibility. Not a single island fails to demonstrate that the Creoles of African descent, in all their
avocations and in all their pursuits, work, under a
free system, for proper remuneration, though their
labour is often ignorantly wasted and misdirected.
That arises from want of education, want of training,
want of good example. I have not sought to justify
the maudlin sympathy that the mere mention of these
people seems to excite in certain quarters, nor have I
advocated their interests to the detriment of any other
interest whatever—I have simply maintained, from
every evidence before me, that the right of one class
to enjoy the wages and fruits of their labour, does not
and cannot injuriously affect the rights of any other
class, or damage, as some foolishly pretend, a country's
prosperity. An ethnological issue, quite foreign to
the subject, has been dragged into the argument. No
one can deny that, up to the present time, the African, in intelligence, in industry, and in force of character, has been, and still is, the inferior of the European, but it is a tremendous mistake to suppose that
his intelligence can ever be quickened, his industry
sharpened, or his character strengthened under
slavery; and it is worse than a mistake to consign
him to slavery for defects that slavery itself engendered, or to condemn him because the cardinal virtues
of civilization did not spring into life upon the instant
the heel of oppression was removed. With the destiny of the West Indies the welfare of the people is

inseparably bound up, and it is as wrong to overlook their faults as to deny that they have progressed under freedom, or to doubt that by the spread of education and under the dominion of an enlightened government, they will become still more elevated in the scale of civilization. Those who are not afraid of the confession will admit that the West Indian Creole has made a good fight.

" The act of emancipation virtually did no more than place liberty within his reach. Actual independence he had to achieve for himself. All untutored and undisciplined as he was, he had to contend against social prejudice, political power, and a gigantic interest before he could enjoy the boon that the act nominally conferred upon him. The planter was bred to the belief that his business could only be conducted with serf labour, and he clung to the fallacy long after serf labour had been legally abolished. Witness the land tenure, which still exists in a mitigated form throughout all the West Indies, and requires the tenant, on peril of summary ejection, to give his services exclusively to his landlord. The instinct of self-interest, the faintest desire for independence, would prompt any one to reject such a bondage. Yet this rejection is the sole accusation brought against the negro, this the only ground upon which he has been condemned.

" I have endeavoured to point out the two paths that lay open to the West Indian creole after the abolition of slavery. The one was to remain an estate serf and make sugar for the planter, the other was to rent or purchase land, and work for estates, if he pleased, but be socially independent of a master's control. I endeavored to follow these two classes of people in

the paths they pursued—the majority, who have
become independent, and the minority, who have
remained estate laborers, and I have shown that the
condition of the former is infinitely above the condition of the latter. Is this anywhere denied? Can
any one say that it was not the lawful right of these
people thus to seek, and, having found, to cherish
their independence? Can any one say that by doing
so they wronged themselves, the planters, or the government under which they lived? Can any one say
they are to blame if, by their successful attempts to
elevate themselves above the necessitous and precarious career of labour for daily hire, the agricultural
field force was weakened and the production of sugar-
cane diminished?

"Yet this is the fairest case that can be made out
for the oligarchies of these West India islands. They
have denounced the negro for his defective industry;
but what, we may ask, have they themselves done—
in what have *they* given proof of their nobler civilization and higher intelligence? Surely a most important
duty devolved upon them. They were the privileged
aristocracy, the landed proprietors, the capitalists, the
rulers of the colonies—as they still are. Their political power was supreme. Yet what have they done,
not for the permanent prosperity of the islands—for
the question need not be asked—but in behalf of their
own special interests? They arraigned the negro for
deserting their estates and ruining their fortunes,
when they themselves were absentees, and were pay-
ing the legitimate profits of their business to agents
and overseers. They offered the independent peasant
no pecuniary inducement, or its equivalent, to prefer
their service, but they attempted to obtain his work

for less remuneration than he could earn in any other employment. They never cared for the comfort or happiness of their tenants, or sought to inspire them with confidence and contentment. They made no effort to elevate labour above the degraded level at which slavery left it, and they never set an example to their inferiors of the industry that is still needed in the higher as well as in the lower classes of West Indian society. Enterprise never prompted them to encourage the introduction of labour-saving arts. Yet these were measures that demanded the action of an enlightened legislature and the consideration of an influential proprietary long before scarcity of labour became a subject of complaint. Instead of averting the evil they dreaded, they hastened its consummation, and injured their cause still more deeply by the false and evasive plea that the idleness of the creole was the cause of a commercial and agricultural depression that they had brought entirely on themselves. Is it any argument against the industry of the labouring classes of America that a large proportion annually become proprietors and withdraw from service for daily hire? Yet this is precisely what the West Indian creole has done; this is the charge on which he has been arraigned, this is the crime for which he has been condemned.*"

" I have not assumed, in aught I have written, that the West Indian creole is yet capable of self-government. I have simply endeavoured to show that, under freedom, sources of industry and prosperity have been opened that, under slavery, would have remained for ever closed. I have endeavoured to show that for the West Indies freedom has been the best policy, though

* Sewell, p. 312, etc.

23*

the moralist may condemn an argument that sets forth another motive for doing right than the sake of right itself. If emancipation did no more than relieve the West Indian slave from the supervision of a task-master, I should have nothing left to say; for I admitted, at the outset, that the condition of the labouring classes was but one among many interests whose ruin, if personal liberty could ruin them, would make us disbelieve in truth itself. But freedom, when allowed fair play, injured the prosperity of none of these West Indian colonies. It saved them from a far deeper and more lasting depression than any they have yet known. It was a boon conferred upon all classes of society; upon planter and upon labourer; upon all interests—upon commerce and agriculture, upon industry and education, upon morality and religion. And if a perfect measure of success remains to be achieved, let not freedom be condemned; for the obstacles to overcome were great, and the workers were few and unwilling. Let it be remembered that a generation, born in the night of slavery, has not yet passed away, and that men who were taught to believe in that idol and its creations still control the destinies of these distant colonies. Reluctantly they learned the lesson forced upon them; slowly their opposition yielded to the dawning of conviction; but, now that the meridian of truth has been reached, we may hope that light will dispel all the shadows of slavery, and confound the logic of its champions when they falsely assert that emancipation has ruined the British Islands.*"

Such is the result of emancipation in the British West Indies, and it is a triumphant success—a suc-

* Sewell, p. 324.

cess which every year only renders more and more complete and unquestionable—a success which settles forever the practicability and safety of immediate emancipation; for the experiment was tried on a scale sufficiently large, and under circumstances sufficiently untoward; yet eight hundred thousand bondmen are made free without bloodshed and without disturbance. What if more planters had been impoverished? What if exports had really dwindled and commerce decayed? What were all that, to be put in the scale against the freedom and happiness of eight hundred thousand human beings? One would have expected a " Christian Bishop" to have thought of the comfort and elevation of myriads of his fellow men, rather than of the falling off of a few millions in the produce of sugar and coffee.

The author of the " View" has devoted a large space to copious extracts from the recent work of Joseph Kay, Esq., setting forth the almost incredible degradation, ignorance, vice, and wretchedness of the labouring classes in Great Britain;—and all this as an offset for the crimes and cruelties and miseries charged upon slavery. He evidently thinks that he has found a treasure; and he turns it over and examines it on all sides with undissembled satisfaction, emphasizing his description with a copious supply of italics.

In reply, I beg to call attention to the following points :

1st. The " Christian Bishop" seems to have forgotten his Political Economy in this case completely; for, while it is admitted that this degraded and wretched condition of the lower classes in England is the result of modern deterioration, in comparison with the good old times of Fortescue and the feudal system, it is notorious also that no nation in Europe has, in the same time, increased as Great Britain has done, in wealth, in production, in exports, in commercial activity. The social and political system under which such a result has been achieved ought, on the principle of this wretchedly one-sided Political Economy, which looks at money and forgets men, to be regarded as a complete success.

2d. This state of the English poorer classes is not held up and defended by Mr. Kay, or by English or American abolitionists, as being perfectly right, authorized and sanctioned by both the Old Testament and the New. Neither is it a necessary result of their freedom, as the condition of the labouring population of Vermont will suffice to demonstrate.

3d. There is fault somewhere; and that fault is in the laws, in the social system, in the right of primogeniture and in the aristocratic castes, as well as in the people themselves. The legislation of England has been too much on that system of Political Economy which looks at money and not at man, and which tends to make the rich richer and the poor poorer.

4th. This condition of the poor, however, even the aristocracy of England do not endeavour to conceal. They do not forbid the fullest investigation and the freest criticism. They make no threats of tar and feathers, or lifelong imprisonment, or a felon's doom, against the most inquisitive and free-spoken observer; if they did, their responsibility for the existing evils would be very different from what it is.

5th. The wretched condition of the English labourer is not the result of the development of manufacturing industry, but quite the contrary. This alone has saved him from still greater wretchedness. It is admitted on all hands that the pauperism of the agricultural districts exceeds that of the manufacturing; and Ireland has no manufactures worth mentioning. It has been the policy of the slaveholders and of their democratic allies in this country, by withholding protection from our manufactures, to reduce our free labouring classes to a common level with the wretched labourers of Great Britain and Europe, being left to compete with them in the great labour market of the world.

6th. It is triumphantly announced that there are in England and Wales *nearly eight millions of persons who can neither read nor write.* But we must remember that in Nineveh there were " more than sixscore thousand persons that could not discern between their right hand and their left," and yet it is not to be inferred that Nineveh was a city of fools. Besides, it would have been more to the purpose to compare the North with the South in this matter; Vermont, say, with Virginia, or Connecticut with South Carolina. It would be found that, even leaving out of the account the four millions of slaves who are *not allowed* to read or write, the proportion of white adults in the Southern States who are totally illiterate is vastly greater than in the Northern. That they have no free schools is even a matter of congratulation among slaveholders; Governor Wise is said to have boasted that in the county which he represented, Accomac, there was neither a newspaper nor a school-house.

7th. We are told that, by receiving charitable or public assistance, the poor lose their sense of *personal independence;* and the *poor-house* is held up before us *in terrorem;* and we are gravely asked if it is not a great advantage of slavery that the slave is provided for in sickness or old age, and there is no danger of his coming to the poor-house. Think of that for an argument! Slavery suggested as a remedy for the loss of personal independence, and a way of escaping the poor-house! As if one should be advised to cut off his head that he might not chance to take the small-pox! What is there less degrading, or more comfortable in the provision made for the sick or decrepit slave, than in that which is made for the inmates of the poor-house? And besides, *all* the poor, in sickness or in age, do not come to that last resort; while, for the slaves, there is one common doom.

8th. A great point is made of the *immorality* of the English lower classes, and especially of their gross licentiousness, and the great number of illegitimate children. But this state of things, though indirectly chargeable in part upon the English aristocratic system, is not directly encouraged and enforced by the law of the land. It is not a parallel case to the legal promiscuous concubinage of four millions of human beings; where, moreover, the number of mulattoes shows that the licentiousness is not confined to the black population. But the "Christian Bishop," in his zeal to make out a strong case, commits one gross blunder. Mr. Kay had said that, in Norfolk and Suffolk, instances of bastardy were "fifty-three per cent. above the average of England and Wales." Looking back to this statement, the Bishop says that "Mr. Kay informs us that the cases of bastardy among the English peasants amount to fifty-three per cent.;" whereas, by Mr. Kay's statement, they need not amount to one per cent. The fact is, that instances of bastardy may occur in the best regulated societies and in the best regulated families, in the families of Christian men—of clergymen even—possibly of Bishops. But the real question is, what is the remedy?

9th. The remedy, more or less distinctly proposed by the Bishop, for this and all other vices of the labouring classes, is, the whipping-post instead of imprisonment, and slavery instead of free labour. I do not say that he makes this formal proposition; but he passes immediately from an exposure of the miseries and vices of the labouring classes in England to a laudation of the beauties and benefits, the Scriptural and Christian claims, of the whipping-post and corporal punishment, as applied to slaves; and to a setting forth of the superiority of the physical and moral condition of the Southern slave over the English labourer. And he proposes no other remedy—apparently in perfect harmony with the view of Chancellor Harper that the proper condition of *labourers*, is, to be *slaves*. Perhaps the Hebrew etymology might be appealed to as confirming this view of the *patriarchal* institution. Think of this, ye "greasy mechanics," ye "clownish boors," ye "mud-sills," of the North; and ponder the destiny that awaits you.

10th. But the true remedy for those evils in England, is,—next to the influence of earnest and popularized Christian instruction,—a reformation of the laws and of the social and politico-economical system of the country. Those evils in England have their roots just where the evils of slavery have theirs, in a lust of dominion and a greed for gain, in class-legislation, aiming at the wealth of the few instead of the welfare of the many, in the system of caste, in aristocracy. Belgium with a population considerably more dense than that of England, and certainly without any *natural* advantages of soil or climate, raises twice as much food as is needed for the consumption of her population, and her peasantry live in simplicity and comfort; while millions in England are starving in filth and wallowing in vice. Yet Belgium is not growing rich like England; she has not the refined, wealthy, and luxurious aristocracy of England, living in princely palaces, with immense *campagnas* around them, from which yeomanry and tenantry have been utterly expelled and exterminated. In Belgium, on the contrary, the lands have been divided up under a legislation which is the offspring of the "infidel, atheistic, and detestable" doctrines of the French Revolution. Surely the evils under which the mass of the people in England are sinking into utter degradation, are not due to the people themselves, nor to any necessity of nature, but to a false and pernicious artificial system of political and social organization.

11th. Labour is honourable, and the labourer is to be respected. Whatever may have been the system of Hebrew servitude, labour was honourable when David was called from the sheepfold to be made the King of God's people. Christianity honours labour. Her Founder was, in human view, a carpenter; her Apostles fishermen and tent-makers; and she has taught that "if any will not work neither shall he eat," and that we should all "work with our hands at some honest employment, that we may have to give to him that needeth." The honour of labour, and the rights of the labourer are among the fundamental doctrines of any democratic creed that de-

serves the name. The great material end of legislation is " the greatest good of the greatest number,"
—an apothegm of Jeremy Bentham, but, in fact, only
a condensation of the fundamental sentiment of the
New Testament. But slavery dishonours labour,
and aristocracy despises it. It is not surprising that
the aristocracy of England should sympathize with
the slaveholding oligarchy of the South; in idea, in
principle they have much in common; though to the
credit of the English aristocracy, it should be admitted, little in character. But that the poor, starving Lancashire operatives, who suffer most from the
cotton famine, should look through all the woes entailed upon them by our war for the Union, and
steadily side with the North, does show a most wonderful power of *ideal instinct.* Green Mountain boys,
and descendants of the colonists of William Penn,
where shall your sympathies be, in view of such a
struggle?

But what will be the consequence, we are triumphantly asked, of the sudden emancipation of four millions of ignorant and helpless slaves? Look at the
British West Indies, and answer; consider their area
in comparison but with one of our large States; consider the immense preponderance there of the black
population, in numbers, over the whites; consider all
the circumstances;—and it will be evident that the
emancipation of 800,000 slaves, there, was a far more
hazardous experiment than the emancipation of four
millions, among us, *ought* to be. That the slaveholders, if *they will,* can make it perilous to the blacks and
disastrous to themselves, there is no doubt. But, in
that case, let the blame rest where it belongs.

But again, it is insisted,—what would the blacks
24

do? What would become of them? What social sta-
tus are they to have? To all such questions, Justice
answers, Give them a fair chance; and Charity answers, Lend them a helping hand even, if needful.
Leave the rest to Providence. The time to trust to
Providence, to appeal without blasphemy to Providence, is, when we have done our duty to the best of
our power, and yet cannot see through the dangers or
difficulties that beset us. And for our encouragement,
let us look again at the West India experiment. That
settles the whole question. We see there that, though
justice was done, *the heavens did not fall.*

As to the constitutionality and rightfulness of the
President's Emancipation Proclamation of January 1,
1863, they rest upon a very simple basis. The Constitution recognizes the property of slaveholders in
their slaves to be only of the nature of a *debt*,—" service or labour due." But it is a well established principle of the law of nations, that a belligerent has a
right to confiscate and annul all debts due to the
enemy; and the Supreme Court of the United States
have decided the inhabitants of the rebellious States
to be in the position of public enemies.

Now, the moment President Lincoln had the legal
right to emancipate the slaves, it was his bounden
duty — his duty as a moral and Christian man — to
emancipate them. But the objection which, in some
quarters, has been made to the Proclamation, that it
appeals to no high moral and religious considerations,
is altogether impertinent. For, it does not follow that,
because the principles of morality and religion required the emancipation of the slaves, therefore, *President Lincoln* would be justified in emancipating them.
He, therefore, as became him, alleges, and alleges only,

the grounds which justified *him* in issuing his Proclamation; and boasts no further of his act; but leaves
the rest to the blessing of God and the judgment of
mankind.

There has been no little doubt and dispute as to the
ulterior practical and legal effect of the President's
Proclamation. Here we may distinguish four contin-
gent cases:

1st. Suppose we completely suppress the rebellion,
and reduce the slaveholding States one after another
to subjection under our military power; then, by the
very terms of the Proclamation, and the nature of the
case, slavery is abolished throughout those States, for
they are brought into our military possession and
within our military lines; and, whatever any civil
court *may* afterwards decide, any civil court *ought* to
decide, that such abolition is an *accomplished and irre-
versible fact.*

2d. Suppose we are defeated; suppose the rebellion
triumphs, and we are obliged to acknowledge the independence of the Southern Confederacy; then, nobody imagines the Proclamation will have any further
practical or legal effect. The Southern Confederacy
will then proceed to build upon their "corner-stone,"
to their heart's content.

3d. Suppose we treat and make a compromise with
one or more of the seceded States, for the sake of their
restoration to the Union; then, of course, they would
come, with or without slavery, according to the terms
of the compromise, and irrespective of the President's
Proclamation; but for the Government voluntarily to
enter into any such compromise as would annul that
Proclamation and reduce again to slavery millions on
whom the right of freedom had been solemnly con-

ferred, would be a proceeding so utterly disgraceful and detestable that it is not to be thought of or imagined possible. Whose interests are most to be regarded; those of four millions of innocent and loyal blacks, natives and lovers of our common country, or those of six millions of infuriated rebels and traitors, who have thrust the dagger at our very national existence, insulted our flag, ravaged our commerce, desolated our fields, stricken down our young men in battle, bringing agony and bereavement to hundreds of thousands of friends, and butchered or starved our soldiers when taken captive; but towards whom the heart of the "Christian Bishop" still yearns as "belonging to the same spiritual fraternity" with himself? If the "Christian Bishop" means by "spiritual fraternity" the Protestant Episcopal Church, he may not, indeed, be very wide of the mark; for the Southern Bishops tell us in their so-called Pastoral: "In our case, we go forward with the leading minds of our new Republic cheering us on by their communion with us." "In the Episcopal Church, and in her congregations, are found a very large proportion of the great slaveholders of the country." And is it possible that the "Christian Bishop" can have more sympathy with those Episcopal rebels, than with the Negro who has fallen among thieves, or with the Presbyterian or Methodist or Romanist soldier boy who is ready to shed his blood in defence of his country? Where are the sympathies of the Episcopal Church in Vermont? In saying this, I would not stir up or advise any spirit of retaliation, or cruelty, or injustice, or even of irreconciliation, or unkindness, towards those who have so grievously wronged us. I only ask whether we should sacrifice to the pecuniary interests and aristocratic pride of such men, four millions of loyal Americans, who either belong to the "same spiritual fraternity" with ourselves, or, if they do not, it is our own or our rebel "brethren's" fault?

4. Suppose the Union restored, and the State governments re-established where they have been destroyed; could not the States reduce the negroes to slavery again if they saw fit, notwithstanding the President's Proclamation? I answer, yes; if the Constitution remains unamended, I suppose they could. But then, the Proclamation would have had its full effect; the negroes would have been free; all former legal claims of their masters would have been arrested and cut off there; and the negroes from being free would be reduced to slavery by a positive enactment, just as free negroes or free white labourers may be now, at any time, if a State so provide in its Constitution or in its Constitution and laws. It is for the true democracy of the country to decide whether or not such a result should be guarded against by a seasonable amendment to the Federal Constitution.

24*

CHAPTER IX.

SLAVERY AND CIVILIZATION.

IT is not a little significant of the character of slavery in its bearing upon civilization, that its Episcopal eulogist should have been led, in his defence of it, formally and at large, to recommend the restoration of the *whipping post* as a mode of punishment, and to defend it as another of the Divine institutions side by side with slavery itself. And this in the nineteenth century! It makes me strongly disposed to think of a *slave overseer* instead of a *Christian Bishop,* and of a domestic tyrant instead of a father. As to its being " prescribed by the law of God," and that sort of argument so often repeated, I have yet to learn that it is any more prescribed by the " law," the " wisdom," or the " authority" of "Almighty God," than are of the laws of war, already cited from Deuteronomy, or the law of the avenger of blood, or any other civil enactments of the Mosaic code. It is fitting, however, that all men should understand, as by a visible sign, the nature of slavery civilization;—it leads to the whipping post, it consecrates the whipping post as a Divine institution, recommends it as a factor of the highest civilization.

Christian civilization should be of a higher type than either the Hebrew, the Greek, or the Roman ;— the Hebrew, with its bloody laws of war, its prac-

(282)

tice of polygamy, its avenger of blood, and its freedom of divorce; the Greek, with its pugilistic games,
its Bacchanal orgies, and aphrodisiac license, its
national piracy, its domestic tyranny and turpitudes,
its contempt of human life, and the horrible cruelties
of its Peloponnesian war; the Roman, with its gigantic selfishness, its thorough moral corruption, its
cruelty to the vanquished, its proscriptions and mutual slaughters, its populace fed at the public expense, and fêted with the blood of gladiatorial shows,
its character so utterly demoralized and debased,
that, at last, nothing but the strong hand of a most
detestable tyranny could save it from complete dis-
integration. But the chief plague spot of all the
ancient civilizations was slavery; and it hung as a
dead weight upon the progress of Christian civilization, though in a mild and modified form, through
all the feudal period.

Slavery ruins the character of the master as well
as of the slave. It accustoms him to acts of *unbridled* passion and *unbridled* lust. It *familiarizes* him
from childhood to personal violence, to stripes and
groans and blood. It habitually appeals to brute
force. It deals with men not as moral beings, but as
dumb beasts. The spirit and character engendered
in such a school are seen in the duelling, the lynch-
ing, and the street-fights, the habitual carrying and
use of deadly weapons, the knife and the pistol,—
which are characteristic of the slaveholding States.
It will not abide by an appeal to reason, even when
it condescends to enter upon the field of argument.
It always holds ready the *ultima ratio* of violence,
not very far in the back-ground. It communicates
this spirit to its defenders everywhere. This was

seen in the riots in England which accompanied the agitation for the abolition of the slave trade; in the threats of personal violence to Wilberforce, and in the assaults of a savage mob upon Clarkson and Roscoe. It has been seen in this country in the interruption of public meetings for the discussion of slavery, in the burning and destruction of public halls dedicated to its discussion, in the dragging of Garrison through the streets of Boston with a halter round his neck, and in the ferocious murder of Lovejoy at Alton.

Should the riot in Boston for the rescue of the slave, Burns, and one or two attempts at rescue in other places, be referred to as an offset; I answer, that these are entirely unlike the others. They were the resistance of legal force by illegal force. They were still brute force against brute force, and that for the rescue of the oppressed; and yet, being illegal, they were always frowned upon by the Northern community. The others were brute force against reason, against ideas, against simple appeals to the understanding; and they were universally approved by the most aristocratic and chivalrous slaveholders.

In the Southern States prices have been set, sometimes in the public newspapers, sometimes by solemn legislative enactment, upon the heads of the advocates of freedom, including Senators and Representatives in Congress, clergymen and merchants, as well as anti-slavery editors and lecturers. Literature has been subjected to an *Index expurgatorius*, and the United States mail to the supervision of a vigilance committee. No Northern man could venture to lisp a word against slavery on Southern ground, nor, if it were known or suspected that he entertained anti-slavery sentiments, could he safely show himself in some of the Southern States. " In South Carolina a stone-cutter, an Irishman by birth, was stripped naked, and then, amidst cries of 'Brand him!' 'Burn him!' 'Spike him to death!' scourged so that blood came at every stroke, while tar was poured upon his lacerated flesh."*   And this is but one among a host of similar atrocities, perpetrated, of course, without any legal process or judicial investigation.

It is thus that slavery prepares the way for any and every crime and infamy. Its behests override every law, whether of God or man. There is no atrocity or savagery, no fraud or perfidy, no baseness or meanness, which slaveholders are not ready to commit with a good conscience, if the maintenance of the system seems to require it. It is in this sense, rather than in any other, that slavery is the " sum of all villainies." It is a characteristic of high civilization to substitute reason for brute force, right for might, words for blows, kindness for cruelty, courtesy for pride, sympathy for selfishness, and the law of love for the spirit of malignity. Slavery reverses all this. Its spirit is directly antagonistic to that of civilization. This spirit has not only been expressed in acts of individual violence, but has been condensed into public law.

" The ideas which the Slave Power entertained on the subject of freedom of the press may be gathered from one enactment, which provided that the advocacy of anti-slavery opinions should be treated as felony, and punished with imprisonment and hard labour; while its notions of lenity are illustrated by

* See Sumner's speech, June 4, 1860.

its mode of dealing with the offence of facilitating the escape of slaves. Against this—of all crimes in the ethics of the Slave Power the most heinous—and against other modes of attacking slave property, the penalty of death was denounced no less than forty-eight different times."*

The effect of slaveholding upon manners and social character has been most truly depicted by Jefferson, who complained that his native Virginia was rapidly becoming " the Barbary of the Union." " There must be," says he, "an unhappy influence on the manners of our people, produced by the existence of slavery among us. The whole commerce between master and slave is a perpetual exercise of the most boister-ous passions, *the most unremitting despotism* on the one part, and degrading submission on the other; our children see this, and learn to imitate it. . . . . The man must be a prodigy who can retain his manners and morals undepraved by such circumstances. And with what execration should the statesman be loaded who, permitting one half the *citizens* thus to trample on the rights of the other, [so it seems Jefferson con-sidered that the negroes were *citizens* and possessed of *rights,*] transforms them into despots, and then into enemies, destroys the morals of the one part and the *amor patriæ* of the other."

With this singularly agrees the judgment of M. Tourgueneff, one of the principal leaders in the work of Russian emancipation : "If slavery," says he, "degrades the slave, it degrades more the master. This is an old adage, and long observations have proved to me that this adage is not a paradox. In fact, how can that man respect his own dignity, his

* Cairnes, pp. 117, 118.

own rights, who has learned not to respect either the rights or the dignity of his fellow-man? What control can the moral and religious sentiments have over a man who sees himself invested with a power so eminently contrary to morals and religion? The continued exercise of an unjust claim, even when it is moderated, finishes by corrupting the character of the man and spoiling his judgment. . . . . The possession of a slave being the result of injustice, the relations of the master with the slave cannot be otherwise than a succession of injustices. Among good masters (and it is agreed to call so those who do not abuse their power as much as they might) these relations are clothed with forms less repugnant than among others; but here the difference stops. Who could remain always pure, when, carried away by his disposition, excited by his temper, drawn by caprice, he can with impunity oppress, insult, humiliate, his fellows? And let it be carefully remarked that intelligence, civilization, do not avail. The enlightened man, the civilized man, is none the less a man; that he should not oppress, it is necessary that it should be impossible for him to oppress. All men cannot, like Louis XIV., throw their stick from the window when they feel a desire to strike."

Said Colonel Mason, a Virginia slaveholder, in the Convention of 1787: "Slavery discourages arts and manufactures. The poor despise labour when performed by slaves. They prevent the emigration of whites, who really enrich and strengthen a country. *They produce the most pernicious effect on manners. Every master of slaves is born a petty tyrant. They bring the judgment of Heaven on a country.*" So it seems, by the way, that a man could believe slaveholding a sin, and yet continue to hold slaves.

As to the relation of slaveholding to true chivalry, John Locke described it as " So opposite to the *generous temper and courage* of our nation, that 'tis hardly to be conceived that an Englishmen, MUCH LESS A GENTLEMAN, should plead for it." And Adam Smith, with whose doctrines of free trade the Southerners are so much enamoured, in his work on the Moral Sentiments, thus speaks: "There is not a negro from the coast of Africa who does not possess a degree of magnanimity which the soul of his sordid master is too often scarce capable of conceiving. Fortune never exerted more cruelly her empire over mankind than when she subjected these nations of heroes to the refuse of jails of Europe, to wretches who possess the virtues neither of the countries which they come from, nor of those which they go to, and whose *levity, brutality, and baseness* so justly expose them to the contempt of the vanquished." One of these philosophical judgments is about two centuries old, the other about one.

"No one who has not been an *integral part of a slaveholding community* can have any idea of its abominations. It is a whited sepulchre, full of dead men's bones and all uncleanness." These are the words of a Southern lady, the accomplished daughter of Judge Grimké, of South Carolina.

In the words of Professor Cairnes, "Such a system can conduct to only one issue, an organized barbarism of the most relentless and formidable kind."

"To establish their scheme of society on such broad and firm foundations that they may set at defiance the public opinion of free nations, and, in the last resort, resist the combined efforts of their physical power, becomes at length the settled purpose and clearly conceived design of the whole body. To this they devote themselves with the zeal of fanatics, with the persistency and secrecy of conspirators."

The following passage from the Richmond *Enquirer*, is sufficiently explicit: "Two opposite and conflicting forms of society cannot, among civilized men, co-exist and endure. The one must give way and cease to exist; the other become universal. If free society be unnatural, immoral, unchristian, it must fall and give way to slave society, a social system old as the world, universal as man."

"This slave power constitutes the most formidable antagonist to civilized progress which has appeared for many centuries, representing a system of society at once retrograde and aggressive, a system which, containing within it no germs from which improvement can spring, gravitates inevitably towards barbarism, while it is impelled by exigencies, inherent in its position and circumstances, to a constant extension of its territorial domain."

This system of barbarism has a twofold foundation—the lust of gain and the lust of power.

"Mankind, in effect, says this theory, has had to choose between maintaining slavery and abandoning the use of cotton, tobacco, and sugar, and the instincts of humanity have succumbed before the more powerful inducements of substantial gain."

That the system has, for the last half century, gone on strengthening itself, instead of growing weaker, is quite manifest from the historical facts.

"At the epoch of the Revolution, as has been already intimated, slavery was regarded by all the
25

eminent men who took part in that movement as
essentially an evil—an evil which might indeed be
palliated as having come down to that generation
from an earlier and less enlightened age, and which,
having intwined itself with the institutions of the
country, required to be delicately dealt with—but
still an evil, indefensible on moral and religious
grounds, and which ought not to be permanently endured. The convention of 1774 unanimously condemned the practice of holding slaves. The convention of 1787, while legislating for the continuance of
slavery, resolved to exclude from the constitution the
word 'slave,' lest, (as Madison said,) it should be
thought that the American nation gave any sanction
to 'the idea that there could be property in men.'
Washington, a native of the South, and a slaveholder,
declared it to be among his first wishes to see slavery
abolished by law, and in his will provided for the
emancipation of his slaves. Jefferson, also a native
of the South, and a slaveholder, framed a plan of abolition, and declared that, in the presence of slavery
'he trembled for his country when he reflected that
God was just;' that in the event of a rising of slaves,
'the Almighty had no attribute which could take
side with slaveowners in such a contest.' The other
leading statesmen of that time, Franklin, Hamilton,
Patrick Henry, the Randolphs, Monroe, whether
from the North or from the South, whether agreeing
or not in their views on the practical mode of dealing
with the institution, alike concurred in reprobating
at least the principle of slavery."

"In Maryland and Virginia, perhaps also in the
Carolinas and Georgia, free institutions would long
since have taken the place of slavery, were it not

that just as the crisis of the system had arrived, the domestic slave trade opened a door of escape from a position which had become untenable. The conjuncture was peculiar, and would, doubtless, by Southern theologians, be called providential."

" The progress of events, far from conducing to the gradual mitigation and ultimate extinction of the system, has tended distinctly in the opposite direction—to the aggravation of its worst evils and the consolidation of its strength."

That but little is to be hoped for the cause of emancipation from the spontaneous action of the slaveholders themselves, is abundantly evident.

" By the abolition of slavery (in America) not merely would the general prosperity of the inhabitants be promoted, but by the rise of rent which would be the consequence of this measure, there would result to slaveholders a special gain—a gain which, it may reasonably be thought, would form a liberal compensation for any temporary inconvenience they might suffer from the change.

" Considerations so obvious, it is argued, must in the end have their effect on the minds of the ruling class in the South, and must lead them before long to abolish a system which is fraught with such baleful effects to the country and to themselves." . . . . . .
" Nevertheless it would, I conceive, be infinitely precarious from this position to infer that slaveholders will ever be induced voluntarily to abolish slavery. The slaveholders of the South are perfectly aware of the superior prosperity of the free States : it is with them a subject of bitter mortification and envy ; but, with the most conclusive evidence before their eyes, they persist in attributing this to every cause but the

right one." . . . . . . " Whatever be the future advantages which may be expected from the change,
it is vain to deny that the transition from slavery to
freedom could not be effected without great inconvenience, loss, and, doubtless, in many cases, ruin, to
the present race of slaveholders. The accumulated
results of two hundred years of tyranny, cruelty and
disregard of the first of human rights are not thus
easily evaded. A sacrifice there would need to be."

"But, in truth, it is idle to argue this question on
purely economic grounds. It is not simply as a pro-
ductive instrument that slavery is valued by its supporters. It is far rather for its social and political
results—as the means of upholding a form of society
in which slaveholders are the sole depositories of social prestige and political power, as the 'corner-stone'
of an edifice of which they are the masters—that the
system is prized. Abolish slavery and you introduce
a new order of things, in which the ascendancy of the
men who now rule at the South would be at an end.
An immigration of new men would set in rapidly from
various quarters. The planters and their adherents
would soon be placed in a helpless minority in their
old dominions. New interests would take root and
grow; new social ideas would germinate; new political combinations would be formed; and the power
and hopes of the party which has long swayed the
politics of the Union, and which now seeks to break
loose from that Union in order to secure a free career
for the accomplishment of bolder designs, would be
gone forever. It is this which constitutes the real
strength of slavery in the Southern States, and which
precludes even the momentary admission by the do-

minant party there of any proposition which has abolition for its object." *

The organization of the so-called Southern Confederacy is a formal attempt to establish and perpetuate
this system of barbarism in the face of the world.
This confederation, which is the opprobrium of the
age, puts itself forward as a model for its imitation,
and calmly awaits the tardy applause of mankind.
"The ideas entertained at the time of the formation
of the old Constitution," says the Vice-President of
the Southern Confederacy, "were, that the enslavement of the African race was in violation of the laws
of nature; that it was wrong in principle, socially,
morally, and politically. *Our new Government is
founded on exactly opposite ideas;* its foundations are
laid, its corner-stone rests upon the great truth that
the Negro is not equal to the white man; that
slavery—subordination to the superior race—is his
natural and normal condition. *Thus our Government is
the first in the history of the world based upon this great
physical, philosophical, and moral truth.* It is upon this
our social fabric is firmly planted, and I cannot permit myself to doubt the ultimate success of the full
recognition of this principle throughout the civilized and enlightened world. . . . . . . This stone which
was rejected by the first builders 'is become the chief
stone of the corner' in our new edifice." [Speech of Mr.
A. H. Stephens, Vice-President of the Southern Confederacy, delivered March, 1861.] Opinion in the
South has long passed beyond the stage at which
slavery needs to be defended by argument. The subject is now never touched but in a strain such as the

* Professor Cairnes on the Slave Power.

25 *

freedom conquered at Marathon and Platæa inspired
in the orators of Athens. It is "the beneficent source
and wholesome foundation of our civilization;" an
institution, "moral and civilizing, useful at once to
blacks and whites." "To suppress slavery would be
to throw back civilization two hundred years." "It
is not a moral evil. It is the Lord's doing, and mar-
vellous in our eyes. . . . . It is by divine appointment."

Such has been the encroaching, aggressive, impudent and insolent bearing of slavery, for many years
past, with its constant brutal appeal to the bludgeon,
the knife and the pistol, that it had become more and
more evidently impossible to live with slaveholders
on terms of freedom, equality and peace. Either one
party must succumb to the other, or the two must
separate. The character of the intercourse between
the two parties, in and about Congress, may be inferred from the following, among innumerable, similar, instances.

"On the 15th of February, 1837, R. M. Whitney
was arraigned before the House of Representatives
for contempt in refusing to attend, when required,
before a committee of investigation into the administration of the Executive office. His excuse was,
that he could not attend without exposing himself
thereby to outrage and violence in the committee-
room; and on his examination at the bar of the
House, Mr. Fairfield, a member of the committee,
afterward a Senator in Congress, and Governor of
Maine, testified to the actual facts. It appears that
Mr. Peyton, a slave-master from Tennessee, and a
member of the committee, regarding a certain answer in writing by Mr. Whitney, to an interrogatory

propounded by him as offensive, broke out in these
words: "Mr. Chairman, I wish you to inform this
witness, that he is not to insult me in his answers;
if he does, God damn him, I will take his life on the
spot!" The witness, rising, claimed the protection
of the committee; on which Mr. Peyton exclaimed,
"God damn you, you shan't speak; you shan't say
one word while you are in this room; if you do, I
will put you to death!" Mr. Wise, another slave-
master from Virginia, Chairman of the Committee,
and since Governor of Virginia, then intervened, saying, "Yes, this damned insolence is insufferable."
Soon after, Mr. Peyton, observing that the witness
was looking at him, cried out: "Damn him, his eyes
are on me; God damn him, he is looking at me; he
shan't do it; damn him, he shan't look at me."

These things, and much more, disclosed by Mr.
Fairfield, in reply to interrogatories in the House,
were confirmed by other witnesses; and Mr. Wise
himself, in a speech, made the admission, that he was
armed with deadly weapons, saying: "I watched
the motion of that right arm, (of the witness,) the
elbow of which could be seen by me, and had it
moved one inch, he had died on the spot. That was
my determination."

All this will be found in the thirteenth volume of
the *Congressional Debates*, with the evidence in detail,
and the discussion thereupon.

Here is another instance of similar character, which
did not occur in a committee-room, but during de-
bate in the Senate chamber. While the compromise
measures were under discussion, in 1850, on the
17th of April, Mr. Foote, a slave-master, from Mississippi, in the course of his remarks, commenced a

personal allusion to Mr. Benton. This was aggravated by the circumstance that only a few days previously he had made this distinguished gentleman the mark for most bitter and vindictive personalities. Mr. Benton rose at once from his seat, and, with an angry countenance, but without weapons of any kind in his hand, or, as it appeared afterwards before the committee, on his person, advanced in the direction of Mr. Foote, when the latter, gliding backward, drew from his pocket a five-chambered revolver, fully loaded, which he cocked. Meanwhile Mr. Benton, at the suggestion of his friends, was already returning to his seat, when he perceived the pistol. Excited greatly by this deadly menace, he exclaimed: "I am not armed. I have no pistols. I disdain to carry arms. Stand out of the way, and let the assassin fire." Mr. Foote remained standing in the position he had taken, with his pistol in his hand, cocked. "Soon after," says the report of the committee appointed to investigate this occurrence, "both Senators resumed their seats, and order was restored." All this will be found at length in the twenty-first volume of the *Congressional Globe.*

Another instance, which belongs to the same class, is given by the Hon. William Jay, a writer of singular accuracy, and of the truest principle, who has done much to illustrate the history of our country. It is this: Mr. Dawson, a slave-master from Louisiana, and a member of the House of Representatives, went up to another member on the floor of the House, and addressed to him these words: "If you attempt to speak, or rise from your seat, sir, by God, I'll cut your throat."

Mr. Giddings, Representative in Congress from

Ohio, adds : " I was afterwards speaking with regard to a certain transaction in which negroes were concerned in Georgia, when Mr. Black, of Georgia, raising his bludgeon, and standing in front of my seat, said to me : 'If you repeat that language again I will knock you down.' It was a solemn moment for me. I had never been knocked down, and having some curiosity on that subject, I repeated my language. Then Mr. Dawson, of Louisiana, the same who had drawn the bowie knife, placed his hand in his pocket and said, with an oath which I will not repeat, that he would shoot me, at the same time cocking the pistol, so that all around me could hear it click."

Is it possible that such scenes could take place in the legislative halls of a civilized country ? The whole country has, most unjustly, been compelled to bear the infamy of this barbarism.

But the barbarism does not end here. The venerable John Quincy Adams, certainly one of the most distinguished statesmen of the country, who had been President of the United States, and was, at the time now referred to, a member of the House of Representatives, insisted perseveringly upon the popular right of petition, which was as pertinaciously refused by the slaveholders' majority in the House. On one occasion, he happened to present a petition, which, unknown to himself, contained a request for the dissolution of the Union. Immediately he was assailed by a most overwhelming storm of abuse, and threatened with instant expulsion from the House, without even an opportunity of speaking in his own defence. And it is remarkable that this onslaught, in professed defence of the sacredness of the Union, was led by the same Henry A. Wise, who engineered Virginia into secession, and has since been a General in the Confederate service. His hypocrisy still survives among many, who talk loudly of their attachment to the Union and the Constitution, while, at heart, they sympathize with rebellion and treason. The *Charleston Mercury*, which always speaks the true voice of slavery—not content with the quiet expulsion of the venerable patriot—said in 1837: " Public opinion at the South would now, we are sure, justify an immediate resort to force by the Southern delegation, *even on the floor of Congress*, were they forthwith to seize and drag from the Hall, any man who dared to insult them, as that eccentric old show-man, John Quincy Adams, has dared to do."

This advice subsequently bore fruit. On the 22d of May, 1856, just after the adjournment of the Senate, while Mr. Charles Sumner, a Senator from Massachusetts, still remained in his seat in the Senate chamber, engaged pen in hand, Preston S. Brooks, a member of the House of Representatives from South Carolina, accompanied with armed assistants, approached his desk unobserved, and abruptly addressed him. Before he had time to utter a single word in reply, he received a stunning blow upon the head from a heavy cane or bludgeon in the hands of Brooks, which made him blind and almost unconscious. Endeavouring, however, to protect himself, in rising from his chair his desk was overthrown; and while in that condition he was beaten upon the head by repeated blows, until he sunk upon the floor of the Senate exhausted, unconscious, and covered with his own blood. The injuries thus inflicted were of so murderous a character that Senator Sumner narrowly escaped with his life; and scarcely recovered from the consequences after several years of lingering suffering. For this act Brooks was not expelled from the House of Representatives; but, considering himself censured by the large vote in favour of his expulsion, he resigned his seat. *He was immediately returned to it by the unanimous vote of his South Carolina constituents;* his course was loudly applauded by the Southern Press, so far as I know without a dissenting voice; and he was presented with innumerable gold-headed canes and other mementoes in commendation and commemoration of his chivalrous exploit. Now, there may be rowdies and assassins anywhere; but what must be the barbarism of a people where such an act could command universal approbation and applause? The only excuse alleged for the act was, that the Senator had used insulting language towards South Carolina or some of her citizens. Whether his language had been insulting or not is a question of taste and opinion. I think it was not. But suppose it had been, was that the way to meet it, in a civilized community? The same Senator, in 1860, made a speech to which I have above referred, which contained no offensive personalities, and the most insulting part of which were the *facts* which it coolly and remorselessly stated. To this speech Senator Chesnut, of South Carolina, replied, alleging as an excuse in behalf of himself and his fellow Senators for not having arrested Mr. Sumner's speech by a renewed personal assault: " *We are not inclined again to send forth the recipient of* PUNISHMENT, *howling through the world, yelping fresh cries of slander and malice.*"

If such is the character of the very élite of the

Southern chivalry, how is it possible for civilized men
to live with them in meek submission without utter
degradation ?

But this is not all. The " Christian Bishop" closes
his whole volume with a final thrust at the horrible
barbarism of Africa. He cites from Captain Canot
"a graphic statement of the atrocities committed by
the native Africans." He fails to observe, however,
one thing which leaks out of the Captain's account,
and which entirely nullifies his *inference* from the
whole, viz. : that it is only slavery and the slave trade
that have tended to raise the Africans from their savage state. " My mercantile adventure," the Captain
says, " was unhappily destined to be the apple of dis-
cord between the two cousins. The establishment of
so important an institution as a slave factory within
the jurisdiction of the younger savage gave umbrage
to the elder." And then he proceeds to depict the
horrible atrocities which grew out of the quarrel of
the kinsmen, thus confirming the statements of President Buchanan and Dr. Livingstone, that the European slave trade has been the principal cause of the
disgusting barbarism of Africa. But off against the
Bishop's picture I propose to set another picture from
another quarter, drawn by at least as faithful and
trustworthy an artist as the slave-trading Captain
Canot.

The following anecdote is told by Mr. Thomas K.
Gladstone, an Englishman who visited Kansas during
the time of the disturbances, in his work entitled
*Kansas; or, Squatter Life and Border Warfare in the
Far West :* " Individual instances of barbarity continued to occur almost daily. In one instance a man
belonging to General Atchison's camp made a bet of

six dollars against a pair of boots that he would go and return with an Abolitionist's scalp within two hours. He went forth on horseback. Before he had gone two miles from Leavenworth on the road to Lawrence, he met a Mr. Hops, driving a buggy. Mr. Hops was a gentleman of high respectability, who had come home with his wife, a few days previously, to join her brother, the Rev. Mr. Nute of Boston, who had for some time been laboring as a minister in Lawrence. The ruffian asked Mr. Hops where he came from. He replied he was last from Lawrence. Enough! The ruffian drew his revolver and shot him through the head! As the body fell from the chaise, he dismounted, took his knife, scalped his victim, and then returned to Leavenworth, where, having won his boots, he paraded the streets with the bleeding scalp of the murdered man stuck upon a pole. This was on the 19th of August. Eight days later, when the widow, who had been left at Lawrence sick, was brought down by the Rev. Mr. Nute, in the hope of recovering the body of her murdered husband, the whole party, consisting of about twenty persons in five wagons, was seized, robbed of all they had, and placed in confinement. One was shot the next day for attempting to escape. The widow and one or two others were allowed to depart by steamer, but penniless. A German incautiously condemning the outrage was shot, and another saved his life only by precipitate flight."

This is but an illustration of the atrocities which were daily committed, and in every direction.

There remains one chapter more to fill up the measure of the evidence of slaveholding barbarism. It is the savage acts of the rebels in the present war.

26

I shall not dwell upon the using of Yankee skulls for drinking-bowls, and Yankee bones for the manufacture of ten-pins and trinkets and presents to sweethearts, and other things of a similar character, befitting only cannibals, which, though sufficientiy authenticated by the investigations of a Congressional committee, may, after all, be acts only of individual savagery. I shall call attention at once to the scenes of Fort Pillow and of the prisons at Richmond. My citations are taken from a report of a joint committee of the Senate and House of Representatives of the United States, made, after careful personal investigation, in May last.

" It will appear from the testimony taken, that the atrocities committed at Fort Pillow were not the result of passions excited by the heat of conflict, but were the results of a policy deliberately decided upon and unhesitatingly announced. . . . The declarations of Forrest and his officers, both before and after the capture of Fort Pillow, as testified to by such of our men as have escaped after being taken by him; the threats contained in the various demands for surrender made at Paducah, Columbus, and other places; the renewal of the massacre the morning after the capture of Fort Pillow; the statements made by the rebel officers to the officers of our gunboats, who received the few survivors at Fort Pillow—all this proves most conclusively the policy which they have determined to adopt;" that is, with respect to our coloured troops and their officers.

 . . . . . .

" Then followed a scene of cruelty and murder, without a parallel in civilized warfare, which needed but the tomahawk and scalping-knife to exceed the

worst atrocities ever committed by savages. The
rebels commenced an indiscriminate slaughter, spar-
ing neither age nor sex, white or black, soldier or
civilian. The officers and men seemed to vie with
each other in the devilish work; men, women, and
even children, wherever found, were deliberately shot
down, beaten and even hacked with sabres; some
of the children, not more than ten years old, were
forced to stand up and face their murderers while
being shot; the sick and the wounded were butchered
without mercy, the rebels were entering the hospital
building and dragging them out to be shot, or killing
them as they lay there unable to offer the least resistance. All over the hillside the work of murder
was going on. Numbers of our men were collected
together in lines or groups and deliberately shot.
Some were shot while in the river, while others on
the bank were shot and their bodies kicked into the
water; many of them still living but unable to make
any exertions to save themselves from drowning.
Some of the rebels stood upon the top of the hill or
but a short a distance down its side, and called to our
soldiers to come up to them, and, as they approached,
shot them down in cold blood; if their guns or pistols
missed fire, forcing them to stand there until they
were again prepared to fire. All around were heard
cries of 'No quarter!' 'No quarter!' 'Kill the
damned Niggers!' 'Shoot them down!' All who
asked for mercy were answered by the most cruel
taunts and sneers. Some were spared for a time,
only to be murdered under circumstances of greater
cruelty. No cruelty which the most fiendish malignity could devise was omitted by these murderers.
One white soldier who was wounded in one leg,

so as to be unable to walk, was made to stand up while his tormentors shot him; others who were wounded and unable to stand, were held up and again shot. One negro who had been ordered by a rebel officer to hold his horse was killed by him when he remounted; another, a mere child, whom an officer had taken up behind him on his horse, was seen by Chalmers, who at once ordered the officer to put him down and shoot him, which was done. The huts and tents, in which many of the wounded had sought shelter, were set on fire, both that night and the next morning, while the wounded were still in them—those only escaping who were able to get themselves out, or who could prevail on others less injured than themselves to help them out; and even some of those thus seeking to escape the flames, were met by these ruffians and brutally shot down, or had their brains beaten out. One man was deliberately fastened down to the floor of a tent, face upwards, by means of nails driven through his clothing and into the boards under him, so that he could not possibly escape, and then the tent set on fire; another was nailed to the side of a building outside of the Fort, and then the building set on fire and burned. The charred remains of five or six bodies were afterwards found, all but one so much disfigured and consumed by the flames that they could not be identified, and the identification of that one is not absolutely certain, although there can hardly be a doubt that it was the body of Lieutenant Akerstrom, Quartermaster of the Thirteenth Tennessee Cavalry, and a native Tennessean; several witnesses who saw the remains, and who were personally acquainted with him while living, have testified that it is their firm belief that it was his body that was thus treated

" These deeds of murder and cruelty ceased when night came on, only to be renewed the next morning, when the demons carefully sought among the dead lying about in all directions for any of the wounded yet alive, and those they found were deliberately shot !"

Such was the Fort Pillow massacre. As to the treatment of our prisoners of war in and about Richmond, the Committee say :

" The evidence proves, beyond all manner of doubt, a determination on the part of the rebel authorities, deliberately and persistently practiced for a long time past, to subject those of our soldiers, who have been so unfortunate as to fall into their hands, to a system of treatment which has resulted in reducing many of those who have survived and been permitted to return to us, to a condition both physically and mentally, which no language we can use can adequately describe. . . . . . They present literally the appearance of living skeletons, many of them being nothing but skin and bone ; some of them are maimed for life, having been frozen while exposed to the inclemency of the winter season, being compelled to lie on the bare ground without tents or blankets. . . . . In respect to the food furnished to our men by the rebel authorities, the testimony proves that the ration of each man was totally insufficient in quantity to preserve the health of a child, even had it been of proper quality, which it was not. It consisted usually at the most of two small pieces of corn bread, made in many instances, as the witnesses state, of corn and cobs ground together, and badly prepared and cooked ;

26*

of, at times, about two ounces of meat, usually of poor quality, and unfit to be eaten, and occasionally a few black worm-eaten beans, or something of that kind. Many of our men were compelled to sell to their guards, and others, for what price they could get, such clothing and blankets as they were permitted to receive of that forwarded for their use by our government, in order to obtain additional food sufficient to sustain life,"— and thus to avoid perishing from hunger, exposing themselves to perishing from cold.

Such is the boasted chivalry of the South, as exhibiting itself at the very centre of their highest civilization—at Richmond. And yet these monsters are men like ourselves. The demon that possesses them is Slavery. Slavery and true civilization are imcompatible. The conflict is, indeed, "irrepressible." If we are hereafter to live in peace with such men, it can only be on condition, *either of the abolition of slavery, or of the abolition of freedom!*

CHAPTER X.

" AS to *rebellion*, I have always been opposed to everything which deserves the name, in the family, in the Church, in the State, or in any other relation of society. The Apostles commanded obedience, not only to the slave, but to the child, to the wife, and to every subject of earthly government." Such is the "Christian Bishop's" profession of loyalty. Its value and significance, under present circumstances, may be inferred from the fact, that he expressly *justified* the secession of the Southern States, in a letter of 1861, which he authorized to be published "in its original form" in 1863, having then found "no reason for changing his opinion;" that he charges professed philanthropists, not Southern slaveholders, with being the cause of the present war; and adds of the "ultra-abolitionists," that "not merely 'confusion and disturbance,' but the sacrifice of half a million of valuable lives, and the ravages of the most awful desolation, and a multitude of torn and bleeding hearts, and the kindling of bitter hatred and deadly animosity between those who were once friends and brethren, have marked the results of their insane determination." Indeed, from the whole tone of the Bishop's book it would seem abundantly evident that the true *rebels*, in this case, are, in his

(307)

view, no other than the abolitionists and the loyal people of the North; and that *they* are responsible before God for all the consequences. Whether this be or be not his own personal position is a matter of no moment. I will neither impugn his loyalty nor be responsible for it. But doctrines which logically lead to such conclusions, one may surely be permitted to note, refute, and condemn.

But, it is said, if there had been no abolitionists,* there would have been no rebellion, the country would now be in profound peace; therefore abolitionists are manifestly responsible for this fratricidal war and all its results. I answer, if there had been no slavery there would have been no abolitionists; therefore the "insane determination" of the slaveholders to continue and perpetuate slavery is responsible for the existence of the abolitionists, and consequently for "this fratricidal war and all its results."

But, again, it is said, the slaveholders had a legal right to hold their slaves, solemnly guaranteed to them by the Constitution, which is the supreme law of the land. Granted,—and the abolitionists also had a legal right freely to express and publish their opinions, solemnly guaranteed to them by the Constitution, in the following authentic words: "Congress shall make

* As to "ultra-abolitionists," if I understand what is meant by the term, President Lincoln was not an "ultra-abolitionist" at the time of his election, nor were the doctrines of the Republican party "ultra-abolitionist." If the contrary is maintained, it would remain to inquire accurately, what is the distinction between "abolitionist" and "ultra-abolitionist?" Perhaps, it would turn out to be just this,—that the "Christian Bishop" is the type of a *bonâ fide* "abolitionist," and all who go *beyond him* are "ultra-abolitionists?"

no law abridging the freedom of speech or of the press."

But, yet again, it is rejoined; the institution of slavery is of so peculiar and delicate a character that it cannot be maintained—the masters cannot be safe with their property or their lives—if it is allowed to be drawn into discussion, and the opinions of abolitionists are permitted freely to circulate. It may be so, I reply. But so much the worse for slavery. It only shows that slavery is such a peculiar institution that it cannot co-exist with the principles of free government; *it is inconsistent with the provisions of the Federal Constitution.* For, if the Constitution had intended to guarantee slavery in such sense as to allow its free discussion to be prohibited, an exception would have been made in its favour, in the clause forbidding the abridgment of the freedom of speech or of the press. No such exception is made. Many, and probably all, of the framers of the Constitution believed slavery to be wrong; and some of them did not hesitate, in the Constitutional Convention itself, to say so. Surely it can be no more a "crime," under the Constitution, for me "to write about slavery, to preach about slavery, to talk about slavery, to think about slavery," than it was for Benjamin Franklin, one of the framers of that Constitution, and, at the same time, President of an anti-slavery society, to present the following memorial to Congress in 1789:

"From a persuasion that equal liberty was originally the portion, and is still the birthright of all men, and influenced by the strong ties of humanity and the principles of their institutions, your memorialists conceive themselves bound to use all justifiable endeavours to loosen the bands of slavery and promote a general enjoyment of the blessings of freedom.

"Under these impressions they earnestly entreat your serious attention to the subject of slavery; that you will be pleased to countenance the restoration of liberty to those unhappy men who alone, in this land of freedom, are degraded into perpetual bondage, and who, amid the general joy of surrounding freedom, are groaning in servile subjection; that you will devise means for removing this inconsistency from the character of the American people, that you will promote mercy and justice towards this oppressed race; that you will step to the very verge of the power vested in you for discouraging every species of traffic* in the persons of our fellow men."

Such were the words of Benjamin Franklin. Did he "tear to shreds the Constitution" he had helped to make? Was he an "ultra-abolitionist?" Alas, "*tempora mutantur!*" And now grave judges tell us that such language is "*criminal*," Christian bishops refer it to an "atheistic and infidel" origin,† and clergymen, in solemn conventions, even venture to pronounce its reproduction "blasphemous."

---

* It is to be observed that the control and regulation of the *inter-State slave trade*, as of all other domestic commerce, are clearly within the constitutional powers of Congress;—though never exercised. Had Congress, in accordance with the petition of Franklin, from the first, stepped to the verge of its powers on this head, slavery would have died long ago.

† When the Convention of 1787 had anxiously deliberated and laboured for several days without success or progress, difficulties seeming but to increase and darkness to thicken around them, and some already preparing to return home in despair, then it was Franklin who rose, and, "Let us seek the guidance and blessing of God," he said; "unaided by the light of a higher

Nothing can be plainer than, as I have said, that if slavery is inconsistent with free speech, it is inconsistent with the Constitution of the United States. Here the case ends, and slavery goes to the bottom. The very allegation that abolitionism is the cause of the war implies and proves that slavery is the cause of the war. It *is* its *material* cause ; but the true and proper cause of the war is the slaveholders themselves rising in rebellion against the Constitution, the Government, the flag, the very existence of their country.*

wisdom than our own, we shall toil and perplex ourselves to no good purpose." Would 'that this truly Christian counsel had been followed. The Convention might then have been led to the adoption of such provisions as would have saved us from this rebellion and from the horrors of civil war.

* But it is said the Abolitionists at least *provoked* the rebellion. Harry is mercilessly beating his dog. His brother Tom, hearing the moans of the creature, expostulates with Harry. Still the beating goes on. At length says Tom : "It is wrong, it is outrageous, it is positively wicked, to beat that dog so." "If you don't hold your insolent tongue," says Harry, "I will knock you down." Tom, somewhat moved, repeats his statement. Thereupon Harry, bludgeon in hand, falls upon him. Tom defends himself as best he may, and a fight ensues. In the midst of it the father appears, and finds his sons with clothes torn, faces disfigured, and rolling in each other's blood. Having learned the history of the case, he thus decides : "Tom, you should have known better than to speak, when Harry told you to hold your tongue, and especially when you knew that, if you spoke, it would certainly lead to this scene of violence. You deserve all you have suffered, and are responsible for all the suffering you have inflicted upon Harry, and ought to be punished for it. Go away, and learn to keep the peace." "Here Harry, my brave boy, let me kiss you. Never mind." A sage and highly Episcopal decision ! Indeed, some one who stood near, and heard it, very innocently inquired whether the father were not a Bishop.

When it is said that the Abolitionists *provoked* the slaveholders,

Now this rebellion is either justifiable or unjustifiable. If justifiable, the country is bound to submit to its demands and die decently. *If unjustifiable, then are the rebels, and they alone, guilty of all the bloodshed and manifold woes entailed upon both South and North by this unnatural and deplorable war.* Other parties may doubtless be guilty of particular acts of atrocity or violence, but not so as to diminish aught from the guilt of the original conspirators and leaders of the rebellion; rather is their guilt thereby only accumulated. Others may be guilty of a part; but they, and they *alone*, are guilty of the whole.

Is, then, the rebellion justifiable?

In the first place, it is no "unhappy strife between two sections of our common country," as, in their *impartial* loyalty, the Philadelphia politicians denominate it. It is a true and proper rebellion. The country is on one side, the rebels are on the other. *The rebels began by firing upon our flag, by insulting and trampling the very emblem of our country's nationality in the dust. They openly separated from the country, and levied war against it.* Their avowed purpose is and has been to destroy our national Union and our national existence. And is this to be softly called by *loyal* men "an unhappy strife between two sections?" What then *is* loyalty, and what is rebellion?

To an unsophisticated moral judgment it would seem plain that, in case of a rebellion, there are but two sides to the question; there is no middle, no

---

it seems to be forgotten that it is at least equally true that the slaveholders *provoked* the Abolitionists. And here, again, the slaveholders are at the *bottom* of the mischief.

neutral ground. He that is not with his country is against her; and the constitutional government for the time being represents his country, is the organ of his country—the only organ his country has; if the government is demolished, demolished by the rebellion, his country is demolished. If a murderer were in the act of striking down his victim, who should be defending himself to the best of his ability; and a bystander should look quietly on without lifting a finger or calling for help, and talk about "the unhappy con. test between the two parties," would he not be an accessory to the crime?

But even rebellion may sometimes be justifiable. Is it the case with this? Had the rebels exhausted all possible constitutional means of righting their wrongs? To call secession and rebellion itself a *constitutional* means is too grossly absurd to deserve a moment's consideration. Had they remonstrated, had they supplicated, had they prostrated themselves before the Government, imploring a redress of their grievances? In the first place, they had no grievances to complain of against the Government. In the second place, if they had had any, *they* remonstrate? *they* supplicate? *they* petition? No! The Government was their "creature." "They knew their rights and dared defend them." Such have been their uniform language and bearing. In fact, to show that had they had any grievances on the part of the Government to complain of, they had not exhausted all constitutional means of redress, it is sufficient to say that, at the very moment of their secession, they, with the help of their political allies, had entire control of the Supreme Court of the United States, and of both Houses of Congress, with a large majority in

27

the Senate, thus effectually checking and controlling the Executive. But no words can better set forth the utter groundlessness and moral indefensibility of the rebellion, than a speech of Alexander H. Stephens, now Vice-President of the rebel Confederacy, delivered before the Georgia secession convention in January, 1861.

"This step (of secession) once taken can never be recalled; and all the baleful and withering consequences that must follow will rest on the convention for all coming time. When we and our posterity shall see our lovely South desolated by the demon of war, *which this act of yours will inevitably invite and call forth*, when our green fields of waving harvest shall be trodden down by the murderous soldiery and fiery car of war sweeping over our land, our temples of justice laid in ashes, all the horrors and desolations of war upon us, *who but this convention will be held responsible for it?* and who but him who shall have given his vote for this unwise and illtimed measure, as I honestly think and believe, *shall be held to strict account for this suicidal act by the present generation, and probably cursed and execrated by posterity for all coming time,* for the wide and desolating ruin that will inevitably follow this act you now propose to perpetrate. Pause, I entreat you. . . . . *What right has the North assailed?* What interest of the South has been invaded? What justice has been denied, and what claim founded in justice and right has been withheld? Can either of you to-day name one governmental act of wrong, deliberately and purposely done by the Government at Washington, of which the South has a right to complain? I challenge the answer. . . . .

"We have always had the control of the General Government, and can yet if we remain in it, and are as united as we have ever been. We have had a majority of the Presidents chosen from the South, as well as the control and management of most of those chosen from the North. We have had sixty years of Southern Presidents to their twenty-four, thus controlling the Executive Department. So of the Judges of the Supreme Court, we have had eighteen from the South, and but eleven from the North; although nearly four-fifths of the judicial business has arisen in the free States, yet a majority of the court has always been from the South. This we have required, so as to guard against any interpretation of the Constitution unfavourable to us. In like manner we have been equally watchful to guard our interests in the legislative branch of Government. In choosing the presiding presidents (*pro tem.*) of the Senate, we have had twenty-four to their eleven. Speakers of the House, we have had twenty-three and they twelve. While the majority of the representatives, from their greater population, have always been from the North, yet we have so generally secured the Speaker, because he, to a greater extent, shapes and controls the legislation of the country. . . . . Attorney-generals, we have had fourteen, while the North have had but five. Foreign ministers, we have had eighty-six, and they but fifty-four. . . . . . We have had the principal embassies, so as to secure the world market for our cotton, tobacco, and sugar, on the best possible terms. We have had a vast majority of the higher offices of both army and navy, while a large proportion of the soldiers and sailors were drawn from the North. Equally so of clerks, auditors, and comptrollers, filling the Executive departments. The records show for the last fifty years that of three thousand thus employed, we have had more than two-thirds of the same, while we have but one-third of the white population of the Republic. . . . . A fraction over three-fourths of the revenue collected for the support of the Government has uniformly been raised from the North. Pause now while you can, gentlemen, and contemplate carefully and candidly these important items. . . . .

"For you to attempt to overthrow such a Government as this, under which we have lived for more than three quarters of a century, in which we have gained our wealth, our standing as a nation, our domestic safety, while the elements of peril are around us, with peace and tranquillity accompanied with unbounded prosperity, and rights unassailed, is the height of *madness, folly,* and *wickedness,* to which I can neither lend my sanction nor my vote."

Nevertheless Georgia seceded, the Southern Confederacy was formed, and Alexander H. Stephens is said to be its Vice President. "Out of thine own mouth will I judge thee, thou wicked servant."

But though the Southern rebellion is unjustifiable, it must have had some pretended grounds: What were they? What did it demand?

Its demands were four; and they were all connected with slavery :*

1st. The unlimited extension of slavery;

* Alexander H. Stephens said, at Savannah, in a public speech, a few days after his election: "Negro slavery was the immediate cause of the late rupture and present revolution. Jefferson, in his forecast, had anticipated this as the rock upon which the old Union would split."

2d. The silencing of abolitionists throughout the United States;

3d. The surrender of the freedom of elections;

4th. No protection of the free blacks against the hunters of alleged fugitive slaves.

1st. As to the unlimited extension of slavery it was demanded, in the first place, with respect to the Territories—the common property of the United States. But it was demanded in the Territories on grounds which are equally applicable to the States themselves. For the grounds were, that all the States are equal, and that if the citizens of one State, Pennsylvania, for example, may migrate with their property into the common Territories, so may the citizens of another State, Virginia, for example, migrate into them with *their* property; but in Virginia slaves are property; therefore slavery cannot be prohibited in the Territories. Now it is manifest that this reasoning is just as applicable to the several States as to the Territories; for if a Pennsylvanian may remove into Virginia and carry all his movable property with him, then, as the rights of States are equal, a Virginian may remove into Pennsylvania and carry his slaves with him. There can be no reasonable doubt that this doctrine was intended ultimately to have this wider application. The first step was to be taken with the Territories, and when that was firmly secured, the other would follow of course. The Dred Scott decision clearly opened the way to this conclusion, and almost forestalled it.* No present assur-

* Some people affect to speak of the Supreme Court of the United States as if it were not only *supreme* but *infallible.* I cheerfully submit to its supremacy, but I deny its infallibility. Its mandates are to be obeyed, but its *dicta,* its *doctrines,* are fair

27*

ances to the contrary, no solemn compromises, could have protected us from the inevitable result. We should simply have been told, at the proper time, that such compromises, like that of Missouri, were *unconstitutional!*

But, in fact, this claim of the slaveholders is utterly untenable, as a *constitutional* claim, even in regard to the Territories. According to the constitution, Congress has the exclusive right of legislation over the Territories. The States have nothing at all to do with it—have no right whatever, as States, to claim or to act in the premises. And the Supreme Court has decided (McCulloch vs. State of Maryland) that "the Government of the Union, though limited in its power, is supreme *within its sphere of action.*" But are not the States equal? That is a theoretical doctrine, and, in a proper sense, is admitted to be true; but, after all, it is *not an article of the Constitution,* and, in point of fact, is liable to some modifications. The States are equal in the Senate, but not in the House; and, if slaves are property,—as is claimed in this case,

subjects of respectful criticism. Now, it is of small moment for me to say, that I agree with Judge Curtis, and hold the Dred Scott decision to have been wrong, iniquitously wrong,—a decision which must eventually be reversed,—yet, had the execution of the mandate of the court in that case been resisted, I should have been ready, as a good citizen, to render all the assistance required in support of the law. It seems to have been the clear opinion of Mr. A. H. Stephens, in his speech before cited, that a Supreme Court may be packed—packed with Southern partizans—packed so as to secure the interests of slavery. And while the *mandates* of the Supreme Court are the supreme law of the land, its *dicta,* its *dogmas,* pronounced at one time, may be reversed at another. Every court would feel at liberty to correct the errors of its predecessors.

—then some States have a *property representation* in Congress, while others are not allowed the privilege. And, let the States be as equal as you please, the business of Congress is, not to act upon States or sections, but upon individuals; not to legislate for States or sections, but for the people, for the public good, for "the general welfare;"—I say, restricting itself always within its own sphere, it is, within that sphere, to legislate for the "general welfare;" for, this is precisely what the Constitution, in terms, requires. Now even if it were consistent with the general welfare, as it would not always be, it is, in many cases, simply impossible for Congress so to frame its laws that each State shall have exactly its proportion of burden or its proportion of benefit. As President Jackson said to the South Carolina nullifiers, no tariff can be so adjusted as to press with precisely proportional weight upon each individual State. The same is true of any system of taxation, even, in some respects, of "direct taxtion." Congress is constitutionally bound to legislate with an honest and impartial view to the general welfare. If, therefore, in the conscientious judgment of Congress, the general welfare requires the introduction of slavery into the Territories, Congress is constitutionally bound to allow its introduction. But if, on the other hand, in the conscientious judgment of Congress, the general welfare — the welfare of the country as a whole, and particularly of the Territories themselves in the long run*—for in their future

* Even Henry Clay, as late as the year 1850, in answer to Jefferson Davis, then a Senator from Mississippi, used the following language on the floor of the United States Senate:

"I am extremely sorry to hear the Senator from Mississippi

welfare, the welfare of the whole country is most deeply involved — requires that slavery should be prohibited in the Territories; — then is Congress constitutionally and solemnly bound to prohibit it. — No State and no power on earth has any right to interfere. This must be so; otherwise Congress had no right to abolish slavery in the District of Columbia. And, inasmuch as, by the Constitution, Congress has the right "to exercise exclusive legislation over that District in all cases whatsoever," if Congress have not the right to abolish slavery there, it must be because its abolition is not a legitimate subject of legislation at all; and, if so, then no State, and no government under heaven, has a right to abolish slavery; and thus we should have at least one indefeasible and inalienable right—the right of slavery.

But there is another aspect of this Southern claim which deserves to be considered.   It not only makes

say that he requires first, the extension of the Missouri Compromise line to the Pacific; and, also, that he is not satisfied with that, but requires, if I understand him correctly, a positive provision for *the admission of slavery* south of that line.   And now, sir, coming from a slave State, as I do, I owe it to myself, I owe it to truth, I owe it to the subject, to say that no earthly power could induce me to vote for a specific measure for the introduction of slavery where it had not before existed, either south or north of that line.   Coming, as I do, from a slave State, it is my solemn, deliberate, and well-matured determination that no power—no earthly power—shall compel me to vote for the positive introduction of slavery, either south or north of that line. Sir, while you reproach, and justly, too, our British ancestors for the introduction of this institution upon the continent of America, I am, for one, unwilling that the posterity of the present inhabitants of California and New Mexico shall reproach *us* for doing just what we reproach Great Britain for doing *to* us."

the law of slavery the supreme law of the land, gives the precedence to the laws of the Slave States over those of the Free States—in the common Territories;—but, if the slave code of one State be more severe or cruel than that of the others, it gives that code the precedence over all. For, suppose that, by the laws of one State, the master has the unrestrained power of life and death over his slaves, and the slaves are allowed no legal marriage; and, by the laws of another State, a master is allowed to chastise his slave only as he might chastise his child or his apprentice, that the testimony of slaves is admitted in evidence, and that families are not allowed to be separated; and, by the laws of a third State, no persons hereafter born are to be held in slavery, &c., &c.;—and suppose that, in a given Territory, there are emigrants, with their slaves, from those various States, and emigrants from Free States. Now, in this case, what is to be the law in relation to slavery in the Territory? There are but two possible courses to take. Either the immigrants from each State must remain under the laws of the State from which they emigrated;—which, among other anomalies, would lead to this, that a man from a Free State would have no right to buy or hold a slave in the Territory, while his neighbour from a Slave State would have the right;—or, some choice must be made; and, in this case, according to the Southern claim, no other choice could be made but the severest and most cruel slave code of all. For, if otherwise, if any other code could be constitutionally adopted, then it might be the mildest of all—a mere system of apprenticeship; or it might be enacted that no persons born in the Territory should be slaves; or the law of freedom—

for that is only one member of the series—might be established at once.

Now, the party which elected President Lincoln, held it as a part of their creed, that, while they religiously abstained from interfering with slavery as established in the several States, and would even accept the Fugitive Slave Law, as it exists,—*in the Territories, slavery was to be prohibited.* The South saw that, if this were allowed, they should eventually lose the control of the General Government, which they had enjoyed almost uninterruptedly from the beginning. Besides, they professed to think that any restriction of slavery must inevitably lead to its final extinction.

"There is not a slaveholder," says Judge Warner of Georgia, "in this house or out of it, but who knows perfectly well that, whenever slavery is confined within certain specified limits, its future existence is doomed; it is only a question of time as to its final destruction. You may take any single slaveholding county in the Southern States, in which the great staples of cotton and sugar are cultivated to any extent, and confine the present slave population within the limits of that county;—such is the rapid natural increase of the slaves, and the rapid exhaustion of the soil in the cultivation of those crops (which add so much to the commercial wealth of the country), that in a few years it would be impossible to support them within the limits of such county. Both master and slave would be starved out; and what would be the practical effect in any one county, the same result would happen to all the slaveholding States. Slavery cannot be confined within certain specified limits without producing the destruction both of master and slave; it requires fresh lands, plenty of wood and water, not only for the comfort and happiness of the slave, but for the benefit of the owner." Therefore, because a restriction of slavery extension was threatened by the party coming into power, the slaveholders rebelled.

2d. Their second demand was that the Abolitionists should be silenced. South Carolina, in her declaration of causes which induced her secession, declares that the "non-slaveholding States have denounced as sinful the institution of slavery," and concludes "all hope of remedy is rendered vain by the fact that public opinion at the North has invested a great political error with the · sanctions of a more erroneous religious belief." It is abundantly clear that nothing would have satisfied the South on this head, so long as Northern men were allowed "to write about slavery, to preach about slavery, to lecture about slavery, to talk about slavery, to think about slavery." To do so must be constituted a crime throughout the length and breadth of the land; and though there were evidently some politicians at the North ready to yield them this point, and to aid them in gaining it, they themselves had too much common sense to believe that the free people of the North could ever be brought to consent to such a degradation. They therefore said: "There is no hope."

3d. Their third demand was, in substance, that the freedom of elections should be surrendered to their dictation. South Carolina, in her declaration, set forth, as one of the chief causes for her secession, "the election of a man to the high office of President of the United States whose opinions and purposes are hostile to slavery." The flagrant insufficiency of this justification of rebellion cannot be more clearly exhibited than it was, at the time, by the same Alexander H. Stephens, from whom we have heard before.

" The first question that presents itself is, Shall the people of the South secede from the Union in consequence of the election of Mr. Lincoln to the Presidency of the United States? My countrymen, *I tell you frankly, candidly, and earnestly, that I do not think that they ought.* In my judgment, the election of no man, constitutionally chosen to that high office, is sufficient cause for any State to separate from the Union. It ought to stand by, and aid still in maintaining the Constitution of the country. To make a point of resistance to the Government, to withdraw from it because a man has been constitutionally elected, *puts us in the wrong.* We are pledged to maintain the Constitution. Many of us have sworn to support it. Can we, therefore, for the mere election of a man to the Presidency, and that, too, in accordance with the prescribed form of the Constitution, make a point of resistance to the Government without becoming the breaker of that sacred instrument ourselves—or withdraw ourselves from it? Would we not be in the wrong? Whatever fate is to befall this country, let it never be laid to the charge of the people of the South, and especially to the people of Georgia, *that we were untrue to our national engagements.* Let the fault and wrong rest upon others. If all our hopes are to be blasted, if the Republic is to go down, let us be found to the last moment standing on the deck, with the Constitution of the United States waving over our heads. Let the fanatics of the North break the Constitution, if such is their fell purpose· Let the responsibility be upon them. I shall speak presently more of their acts; but let not the South—let us not be the ones to commit the aggression We went into the election with this people. The result was different from what we wished; but the election has been constitutionally held. Were we to make a point of resistance to the Government, and go out of the Union on that account, *the record would be made up hereafter against us.*"

But, even if the election of Mr. Lincoln was no justification of the rebellion, some are ready to ask whether, after all, it would not have been wiser for the free people of the North to have refrained from voting for Mr. Lincoln, and to have elected some man to the Presidency who would have been acceptable to the South, and thus to have avoided the rupture of our glorious and prosperous Union, and all the miseries and horrors of this deplorable war? Does this seem plausible? How much, then, is our freedom worth? How much would we sacrifice for it? How much would we suffer to defend and retain it? These are the real questions. We honour our fathers for having braved the privations, sufferings, and perils of a seven-years' war rather than pay an unconstitutional tax of a few pence a pound on tea; and shall we allow another party to dictate to us whom we shall or shall not vote for? Shall we allow ourselves, by threats of rebellion and war, war to the knife, to be frightened from the exercise of our elective franchise? When we are ready to submit to such dictation as this, we cannot stop at any other imposition, however flagrant, and which will be sure to follow; our liberties are gone; we are slaves. To insist upon the right to elect Mr. Lincoln may seem a small thing; but to insist on the right of free suffrage is

28

everything, if we would be a free people. The election of Mr. Lincoln cannot cost us too much, unless our very freedom may cost too much. Better meet bravely the loss or mortgaging of all the wealth we possess, and be slaughtered by the million on the battle-field, than tamely to submit to the degradation of having our rulers set over us at the dictation of Southern slave masters, or of any other party or power on earth.

4th. The final — and often it was made the foremost — demand of those who threatened rebellion, was, that the Free States should repeal all their "*personal liberty* laws," and leave the free blacks without protection to the slave-hunters of the South.

Now, in the first place, the very idea of one State undertaking to dictate to another State what laws it should make or unmake for the protection of its own citizens, was a piece of the grossest, most unconstitutional and insolent impertinence. If the laws of any of the Free States were alleged to be unconstitutional, the appeal to the Supreme Court of the United States was open and unobstructed; and had that court pronounced them so, they would have been peaceably and quietly annulled. This was the proper and regular course to have pursued. No Free State had ever attempted or threatened to hinder or resist the judgment or the process of the Supreme Court. Yet there was kept up, both North and South, a persistent outcry about the unconstitutionality of these "personal liberty bills,"—though they were enacted, ostensibly at least, for the protection of free citizens from kidnappers

Let us look at the conduct of South Carolina in an analogous case. It is commonly insisted by slave-

masters at the South, and their white slaves at the
North, that the Constitution guarantees the property
in slaves;—as though that were the sum and substance of the whole instrument. Now the fact is,
that the Constitution nowhere mentions slaves or
slavery, or recognizes men as property; and if slavery were utterly abolished, the Constitution would
not need to be altered in a single particular. The
Constitution, in one clause, assumes that there may
be "*persons*" other than " free persons;" (Art. I. sec.
2;) and, in another clause, it provides that "No person held to service or labour in one State, under the
laws thereof, escaping into another, shall, in consequence of any law or regulation therein, be discharged from such service or labour, but shall be
delivered up on claim of the party to whom such
service or labour is due,"—a clause which speaks
only of " persons" who '· owe service or labour," and
is just as applicable to apprentices as to slaves. *And
this is all that the American Constitution says about slaves
or slavery.* But in the same section with this last
cited clause, which is held to be such a solemn guaranty of slave property, the Constitution contains
another clause equally solemn, in these words : "The
citizens of each State shall be entitled to all the privileges and immunities of citizens in the several
States."

Yet, in open defiance of this provision of the Constitution, free persons of colour, citizens of Massachusetts, and, according to the institutions of that
Commonwealth, entitled to equal privileges with
other citizens, being in service as mariners, and
touching at the port of Charleston, in South Carolina, have been seized, and with no allegation against

them, except of entering this port in the discharge of their rightful business, have been cast into prison, and there detained during the delay of the vessel. This is by virtue of a statute of South Carolina, passed in 1823, which further declares, that in failure of the captain to pay the expenses, these freemen "shall be seized and taken as absolute slaves," one moiety of the proceeds of their sale to belong to the sheriff. Against all remonstrance—against the official opinion of Mr. Wirt, as Attorney-general of the United States, declaring it unconstitutional—against the solemn judgment of Mr. Justice Johnson, of the Supreme Court of the United States, himself a slave-master and citizen of South Carolina, also pronouncing it unconstitutional—this statute, which is an obvious injury to Northern ship-owners, as it is an outrage to the mariners whom it seizes, has been upheld to this day by South Carolina.

But this is not all. Massachusetts, in order to obtain for her citizens that protection which was denied, and especially to save them from the dread penalty of being sold into slavery, appointed a citizen of South Carolina to act as her agent for this purpose, and to bring suits in the Circuit Court of the United States in order to try the constitutionality of this pretension. Owing to the sensibility of the people in that State, this agent declined to render this simple service. Massachusetts next selected one of her own sons, a venerable citizen, who had already served with honour in the lower House of Congress, and who was of admitted eminence as a lawyer, the Hon. Samuel Hoar, of Concord, to visit Charleston, and to do what the agent first appointed had shrunk from doing. This excellent gentleman, beloved by all who

knew him, gentle in manners as he was firm in character, and with a countenance that was in itself a
letter of recommendation, arrived at Charleston, accompanied only by his daughter. Straightway all
South Carolina was convulsed. According to a story
in Boswell's Johnson, all the inhabitants of St. Kilda,
a remote island of the Hebrides, on the approach of
a stranger, " catch cold ;" but in South Carolina it is
a fever that they " catch." The Governor at the
time made his arrival the subject of a special message to the Legislature, the Legislature all " caught"
the fever, and swiftly adopted resolutions calling
upon " his Excellency the Governor to expel from
its territory the said agent, after due notice to depart," and promising " to sustain the Executive authority in any measures it may adopt for the purposes aforesaid."

Meanwhile the fever raged in Charléston. The agent
of Massachusetts was first accosted in the streets by
a person unknown to him, who, flourishing a bludgeon
in his hand, (the bludgeon always shows itself where
slavery is in question,) cried out : " You had better be
travelling, and the sooner the better for you ; if you
stay here until to-morrow morning, you will feel
something you will not like, I'm thinking." Next
came threats of an attack, during the following night,
on the hotel in which he was lodged ; then a request
from the landlord that he should quit, in order to preserve the hotel itself from the impending danger of
an infuriated mob ; then a committee of slave-masters,
who politely proposed to conduct him to the boat.
Thus arrested in his simple errand of good will, this
venerable public servant, whose appearance alone—
like that of the " grave and pious man" mentioned by

28*

Virgil—would have softened any mob not inspired by
slavery, yielded to the ejectment proposed—precisely
as the prisoner yields to the officers of the law—and
left Charleston, while a person in the crowd was
heard to offer himself as "the leader of a tar-and-feather gang, to be called into the service of the city on
the occasion." Nor is this all. The Legislature a
second time "caught" the fever, and, yielding to its
influence, passed another statute, forbidding, under
severe penalties, any person within the State from
accepting a commission to befriend these coloured
mariners; and under penalties severer still, extending even to imprisonment for life, prohibiting any
person "on his own behalf, or by virtue of any authority of any State," to come within South Carolina
for this purpose; and then, to complete its work, the
Legislature took away the writ of *habeas corpus* from
all such mariners.

Such is a simple narrative founded on authentic
documents.*

Such has been the conduct of South Carolina, and
yet Massachusetts neither seceded nor rebelled; and
Northern men generally seemed disposed to pocket
the insult, and indeed began to be strangely oblivious
of its very existence. Yet this same South Carolina,
in her declaration, charges the violation of the Constitution in the matter of the rendition of fugitive
servants, as one of the causes of her secession;—
although she probably never lost half a dozen slaves,
and perhaps never a solitary slave, by such violation.

The fact is, that, though the Fugitive Slave Law
of 1850 was clearly *not required* by the Constitution,
and was held by a large number at the North to be

* See Sumner's speech of 1860.

positively *unconstitutional*, and so declared by the solemn judgment of the Supreme Court of one of the States,—yet, according to the testimony of Stephen A. Douglas, *no law of the United States was more faithfully or efficiently executed throughout the country.* Indeed it was looked upon, by many Northern as well as Southern men, and by some Presidents of the United States, as being the law of all laws,—the law to be executed at all hazards and at whatever cost.

But how was it with the laws prohibiting the importation of slaves by the African slave trade ? Were not those laws also constitutional — plainly authorized by the Constitution, after the year 1808 ? And yet, in direct violation of these laws, and with the apparent connivance of the Government itself, was not cargo after cargo of these slaves introduced into the Southern States? and did not agricultural societies offer public premiums for the best specimens of native Africans brought directly from their homes? And we of the North took all this as a matter of course. Yet these very men, upon annulling the Constitution of their country, and rebelling against its Government, have the effrontery to allege in justification, that certain constitutional laws had been violated at the North ; and some among us, alas ! without waiting for a decree of the proper tribunal, were ready to cry *peccavimus*, and fall on our knees to ask forgiveness. The truth is, that, notwithstanding all the belligerent passages which our "Christian Bishop" has gleaned from Parker, Emerson, and a few others, —we Northern people are essentially a Union-loving, a law-loving and a law-abiding people ; and the Southern slaveholders have counted upon it ; we are lovers and followers of peace; and the slaveholders have taken advantage of it ; we enter into war reluctantly, and are with difficulty trained to it ; and to this day, on the floor of the Senate, the taunt is familiarly cast into the teeth of Massachusetts, by such men as the Senators from Kentucky, that her people are not ready to *fight*. No insinuation can be more utterly groundless than that Massachusetts, or any Northern State; or the Republican party, or the anti-slavery men anywhere, were making ready to inaugurate a rebellion or a civil war for the abolition of slavery. Whereas, it is notorious that the Southern conspirators, and particularly in South Carolina, had been plotting and preparing their treason and secession for thirty years past.

The reasons alleged by the slaveholders in justification of their rebellion, are mere plausible pretexts caught at for the moment. If they were all true, they would not suffice to justify the rebellion. What must be its character, then, when they are all shown to be untenable or false ?

As I have said, slavery is at the bottom of them all. And if slavery were removed, no occasion of quarrel could be found. It is sometimes thought impossible to restore the old Union, on account of the sectional bitterness engendered by the war. But, if slavery were once abolished, there is no reason whatever that South Carolinians and Virginians may not live as fraternally with Pennsylvanians, New Yorkers, and New Englanders, as these do with each other, or with Ohians and Indianians. *The country was formed by nature to be one, and must be one on some terms or other.*

On the one hand, the question has been much discussed, how the seceded States may be restored to the Union; and, on the other hand, it has been contended that, as secession is a nullity, as the States have never been out of the Union, there is no need of any restoration at all. If the disputants would define exactly what they mean by a "State," they would find very little left to contend about. A "State" may be regarded as a certain extent of territory, or as a certain aggregation of people, or as a certain political organism; or rather, all these elements, and particularly the last, must be combined in the true and proper sense of the word. Now, so far as a "State" refers to a certain extent of territory, undoubtedly the seceded States are still in the Union; every inch of their territory is in the United States, and is under the jurisdiction of the United States.

So far as a "State" refers to the people inhabiting a certain territory, the seceded States are no less in the Union; every man, woman and child in them is, and has always continued, subject to the laws of the United States. Moreover, the people, the *loyal* people of each seceded State are, potentially, sovereign as before, and may recover all the *constitutional* rights and powers of the people of a sovereign State of the Union. But, at present, they have no *organs* by which that sovereignty can be exercised.

As a people cannot exist as a State without a territory, so they cannot act as a State without an organization. So far as a "State" refers to the political organization of the people of a certain territory— the executive, legislative, and judicial branches of their Government,—*the seceded States are no longer in the Union;* their existing organizations of government are, under our Constitution, nullities; their governors, legislatures, and judges are usurpers, are sworn to maintain the so-called Confederate Constitution and not the Constitution of the United States; those States are destitute of any legitimate governments under the Constitution of the United States; the people cannot proceed, constitutionally, to re-establish such governments by the mere spontaneous movement of private individuals and without any legal authorization; if their present pretended governments are nullities, any enactment, commission, or writ of election proceeding from them, is also a nullity; the only way to start, therefore, is by authorization from the Government of the United States; *the Government of the United States is the only legitimate authority that now exists in the seceded States, the only sound portion of their political organization;* from the Government of the United States, therefore, the *vis medicatrix,* which is to restore their political systems, now lying paralyzed, must proceed. In this sense,—of re-establishing their political organizations as States in the Union,—the seceded States need to be restored to the Union; and they can be thus restored only under authority derived from the Government of the United States. Whether this authority is to emanate from a Proclamation of the President or from an act of Congress, may be a very important, but is still a subordinate, question. I shall not stop to discuss it.

In short, then, secession took no State out of the Union either as a territory or as a people; but, as a political organization, it did take every seceded State out of the Union,—that is to say, it left the State no organization in the Union, and the organization it has substituted is out of the Union; is, *de jure,* spurious, illegitimate, unconstitutional, null; and *de facto* hostile and rebellious. Neither the National Constitution nor national self-respect will allow the United States Government to recognize or in any manner to treat with such treasonable organizations. Such a recognition would itself be an acknowledgment of the dissolution of the Union. The rebellious States are all constitutionally and legally in the Union; but, in order to resume their *political functions* as members of the Union, they must be *organized de novo.* In this sense and so far, they must be treated as "Territories." This reorganization must be based upon some enabling act or some legitimating authority proceeding from the Government of the United States. And such enabling act or legitimating authority cannot, without absurdity, be forbidden to prescribe such conditions, restrictions, and modes of procedure in the process of reorganization, as the rebellion itself has demonstrated to be absolutely necessary to the national existence, the national Union, and national peace. And what *loyal people* will object to such conditions as those?

The Constitution has established a *government*, A SUPREME, *federal government;* but it has omitted to make any special provision for the case either of the secession or of the restoration of States. Of course therefore, any process of restoration, and that above proposed among the rest, must be *extra-constitutional.* But the assertion that such a process is *un-*constitutional, that it is violative of the Constitution, must rest ultimately upon the monstrous doctrine that, *under the Constitution, any State may claim the right not only to secede with impunity, but, having seceded, to return to the Union at pleasure.* It is not denied, however, that a reorganization of a State government effected by the spontaneous action of the loyal people, if so it be possible to effect it, might be legitimated by the subsequent recognition of the Federal Government. But, on the other hand, if the present *rebel officials* in any seceded State should take the oath required by the Constitution of the United States, might *they* be recognized as the constitutional government of such a State? To this I answer, No; because by previously taking and acting upon an oath to support the "Confederate" government, which was levying war against the United States, they have all aided and abetted the rebellion, and are guilty of treason—guilty by solemn official acts. And what can be more unreasonable or unconstitutional than that a body of confederate ringleaders in treason and rebellion should coolly wash their hands, and claim to be forthwith recognized as the constitutional government of a sovereign State in the Union?

But still the question is urged, What right has the Federal Government, under the *Constitution*, to require the abandonment of slavery as a condition of recognizing a State reorganization? Where does the Constitution delegate such a power? I answer, that when men have appealed to the arbitrament of arms, they cannot claim for themselves the rights of peace; rebels cannot, without effrontery, claim the constitutional privileges of dutiful citizens. And who but their sympathizing friends will have the effrontery to make the claim for them? If it be said that even rebels are not to be wronged, and that the claim is made in the name of *justice,* let the rebels and their advocates thank Heaven that the Federal Government is not disposed to deal with them as the strictness of justice requires, but only as necessity and mercy demand. In this case the rights of war, the stern necessities of self-preservation, modify and control the rights of peace. As I have already said, the case is *extra-constitutional*. Besides, I beg to invite the attention of those who so persistently urge a strict construction of the Constitution in favour of slave-holding rebels and traitors, to some other constitutional questions which they may do well to settle before they so confidently draw their pro-slavery conclusion.

The Constitution nowhere confers upon the Federal Government the power to purchase foreign territory. Shall we, therefore, condemn, as a flagrant violation of the Constitution, Jefferson's purchase of Louisiana, or the later purchase of California and New Mexico and Arizona? The Constitution nowhere confers on the Federal Government the power to suspend the writ of *habeas corpus;* yet the Constitution itself takes for granted that the government, as such, possesses that power; and restricts and regulates its exercise. The Constitution does not expressly confer on the Federal Government even the power to suppress insurrections and put down rebellion; but it takes for granted that the government, as such, possesses that power; and points out the process and means by which it may be carried into effect; but even then, the Constitution provides only for calling forth the *militia*, and nowhere expressly delegates to the Federal Government the power to use the *army and navy* for the suppression of insurrection or rebellion;—manifestly presuming, as a matter of course, that no government having an army and navy at its disposal, could, without absur-

29

dity, be supposed incompetent to use them for such a purpose. So thought President Jackson, or he would not have signed the "Force Bill." The Constitution nowhere confers, and yet it expressly restricts, the power of the Federal Government, to prohibit the migration or importation of such persons as any of the then existing States should think proper to admit. The Constitution expressly provides that "the right of the people to keep and bear arms shall not be infringed;" and it *nowhere authorizes the Federal Government to require rebels to lay down their arms, any more than it authorizes that Government to require them to liberate their slaves.* But whatever is plainly and imperatively demanded, not only for the general welfare, but for the national existence, the maintenance of the Union, and the public safety, the Constitution cannot be reasonably interpreted to forbid. It established a government, and endued that government with authority "to make all laws necessary and proper for carrying into execution its appropriate powers;"— including, of course, whatever may be necessary and proper for its self-preservation; for, else, how could those powers be carried into execution? The Constitution is not a *felo de se.*

There are but two modes of terminating the present struggle. The first is, that the North should be victorious. The consequence would be, the Union restored with universal Emancipation. The ultimate result, — peace secure, progressive civilization, the triumph of free government, a glorious and happy republic, which would be the pride of the world and the terror of oppressors. The second is, that the South should be victorious. The consequence would be, either the law of slavery established throughout the whole country at once, or the Union for a time disintegrated only to be subsequently re-established with universal slavery. The ultimate result, — interminable wars, foreign and domestic, governmental despotism, and finally utter barbarism; leaving the once free and happy America to be a by-word and a hissing among the nations of the earth to the end of time.

Any *compromise* with slavery is, in the first place, a triumph to treason, and, in the second place, would end in substantially the same process as that last described. Slavery is an element of so corrupting and insidious a character, that the country cannot be safe while it exists in its bosom. If it remained but in a single corner, it would make itself the supreme law of the land. *Our only election lies between the universal law of freedom and the universal law of slavery.* And the question reaches further than to the blacks; either *we* must be *slaves* side by side with the blacks, or the *blacks* must be *free* side by side with their masters. My countrymen, which will you choose?

APPENDIX.

NOTE.—In reporting the Mormon Elder's discourse, the following passage was overlooked at page 209:

"It is abundantly evident, also, that the so-much-boasted modern *elevation of woman*, the chivalrous regard for her which characterizes Christian Europe and America, is not derived from the Bible, or from the teachings or spirit of Christianity, but from a heathen origin, from the Romans, or, more probably, from the customs of the northern barbarians. In proof of this, see the masterly interpretation of the Tenth Commandment by the Bishop of Vermont, where he demonstrates that, by the law of God, *the wife* is reckoned as a man's *property*, along with his man servant and maid-servant, his ox and his ass.

The citations from St. Augustine, on pages 144 and 145, are here appended at large:

Aug. in Epist. Joan. ad Parth. III. 2040.

Radix omnium malorum avaritia. (Tim. vi. 10.) *Initium omnis peccati Superbia.* (Eccli. x. 15.)

Sic ergo debet esse Christianus, ut non glorietur super alios homines. Dedit enim tibi Deus esse super bestias, id est, meliorem esse quam bestias. Hoc naturale habes; semper melior eris quam bestia. Si vis melior esse quam alius homo, invidebis ei quando tibi esse videbis aequalem. Debes velle omnes homines aequales tibi esse... Audi apostolum dicentem de visceribus charitatis: *Vellem omnes homines esse sicut meip-*

29*   341 *sum.* Quomodo volebat omnes esse aequales? Ideo erat omnibus superior, quia charitate optabat omnes aequales. Excessit ergo homo modum; avarior voluit esse ut super homines esset, qui supra pecora factus est: et ipsa est superbia.

Aug. Serm. XXI. V. 145.

Servum tuum manumittendum manu ducis in ecclesiam. Fit silentium, libellus tuus recitatur, aut fit desiderii tui prosecutio. Dicis te servum manumittere, quod tibi in omnibus servaverit fidem. Hoc diligas, hoc honoras, hoc donas premio libertatis: quidquid potes facis, facis liberum, quia non potes facere sempiternum. Deus tuus clamat ad te et in servo tuo convincit te: dicit tibi in corde tuo, Duxisti servum tuum de domo tua ad domum meam: vis eum de domo mea liberum revocare in domum tuam: tu quare male servis in domo mea? Das illi quod potes; permitto tibi quod possum: tu facis liberum servantem tibi fidem; ego te facio sempiternum, si servaveris mihi fidem. Quid adhuc argumentaris contra me in animo tuo? Redde domino tuo, quod laudas in servo tuo.

Aug. Serm. CCCLVI. V. 1576.

Hoc agitur, hoc sine dilatione peragendum est, ut illi servuli dividantur, manumittantur, et sic det Ecclesiae, ut eorum excipiat alimentum.

Aug. de Serm. Dom. in Monte. III. 1260.

Si quis vult judicio tecum contendere et tunicam tuam tollere. Omnia ergo illa intelligantur, de quibus judicio nobiscum contendi potest, ita ut a nostro jure in jus illius transeant, qui contendit vel pro quo contendit; sicuti est vestis, domus, fundus, jumentum, et generaliter omnis pecunia. Quod utrum etiam de servis accipiendum sit magna quaestio est. Non enim Christianum oportet sic possidere servum quomodo equum aut argentum: quanquam fieri possit ut majore pretio valeat equus quam servus, et multo magis aliquid aureum vel argenteum. Sed ille servus, si rectius et honestius et ad Deum colendum accommodatius abs te domino educatur, aut regitur, quam ab illo potest qui eum cupit conferre; nescio utrum quisnam dicere audeat, ut vestimentum eum debere contemni. Hominem namque homo tanquam seipsum diligere debet.

Aug. De Civ. Dei. VII. 243.

Hinc itaque etiam pax domestica oritur, id est, ordinata imperandi obediendique concordia cohabitantium. Imperant enim qui consulunt: sicut vir uxori, parentes filiis, domini servis. Obediunt antem quibus consulitur: sicut mulieres maritis, filii parentibus, servi dominis. Sed in domo justi viventis ex fide, et adhuc ab illa coelesti civitate peregrinantis, etiam qui imperant serviunt eis quibus videntur imperare. Neque enim dominandi cupiditate imperant, sed officio consulendi; nec principandi superbia, sed providendi misericordia.

Hoc naturalis ordo praescribit; ita Deus hominem condidit. Nam *Dominetur*, inquit, *piscium maris, et volatilium coeli, et omnium repentium quae repunt super terram.* (Gen. i. 26.) Rationalem factum ad imaginem suam noluit nisi irrationabilibus dominari : non hominem homini, sed hominem pecori.

Ibid, 244.

Quocirca etiamsi habuerunt servos justi patres nostri, sic quidem administrabant domesticam pacem, ut secundum haec temporalia bona, filiorum sortem a servorum conditione distinguerent; ad Deum autem colendum, in quo aeterna bona speranda sunt, omnibus domus suae membris pari dilectione consulerent.

THE END.